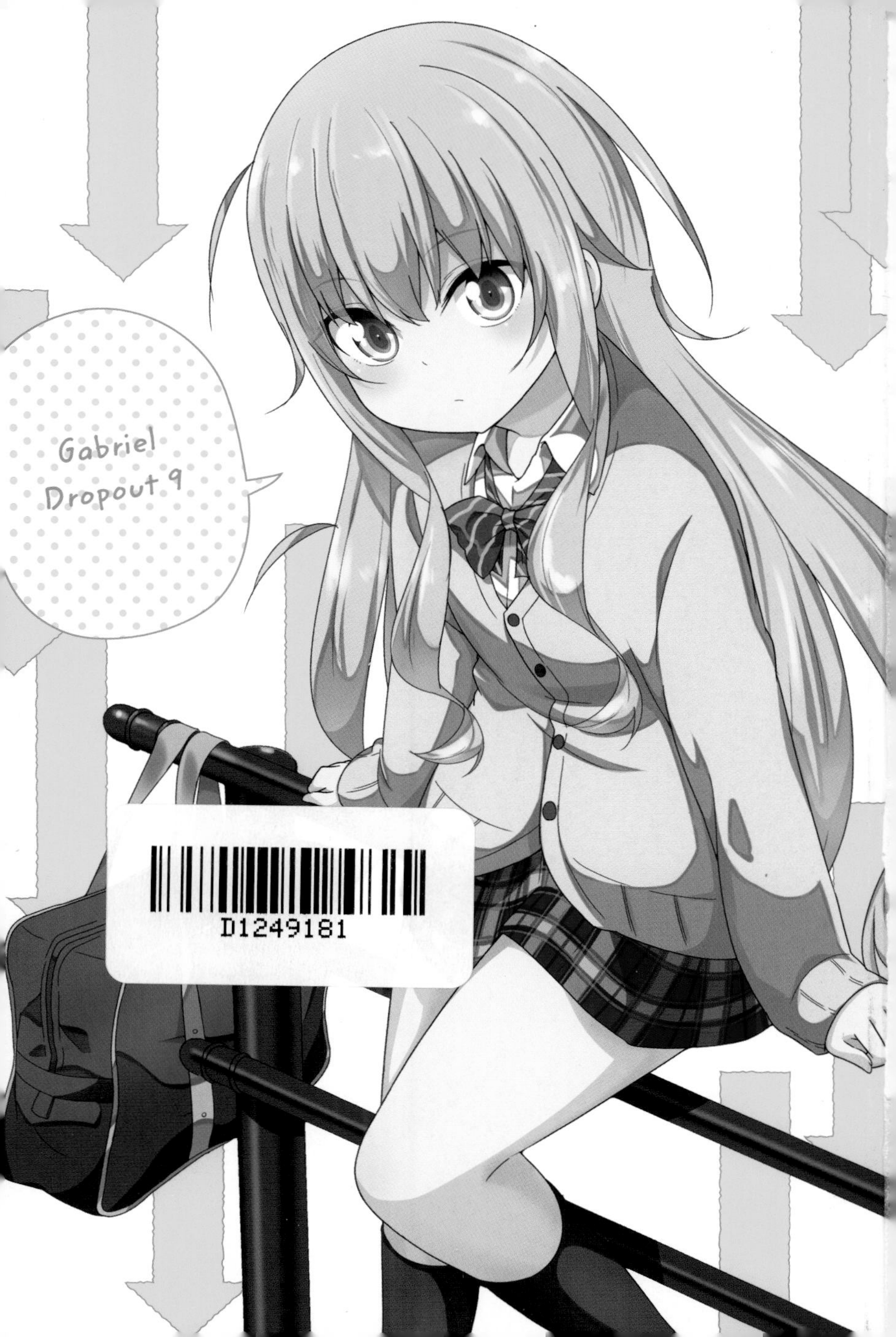
Gabriel
Dropout 9

Contents

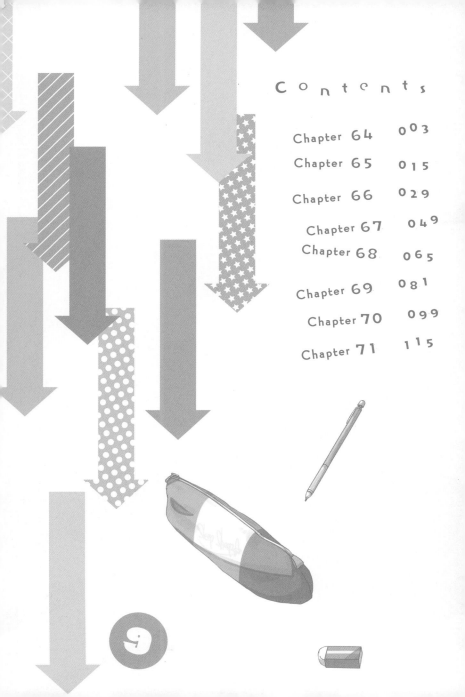

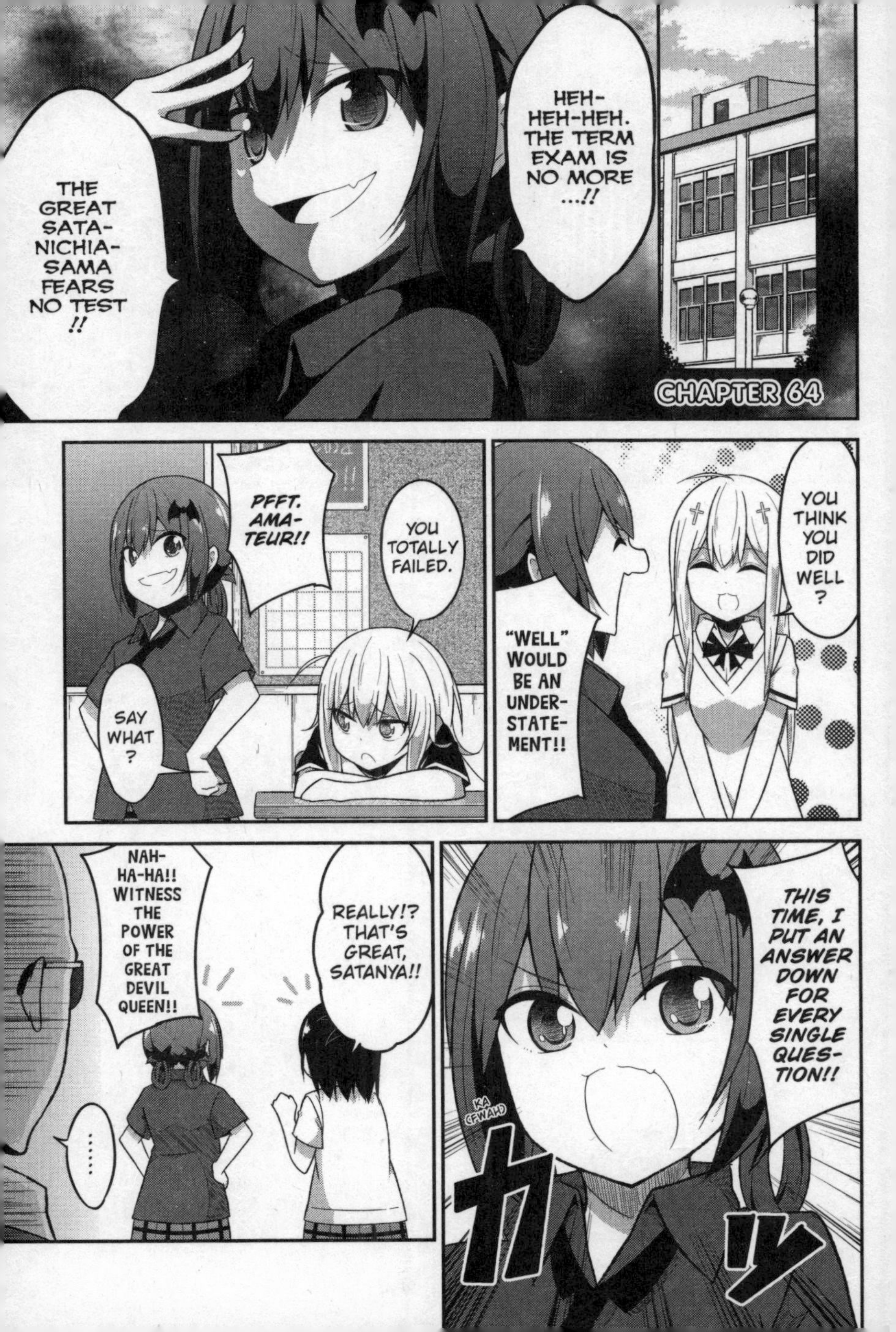
CHAPTER 64
HEH-HEH-HEH. THE TERM EXAM IS NO MORE ...!!
THE GREAT SATANICHIA-SAMA FEARS NO TEST !!
YOU THINK YOU DID WELL?
"WELL" WOULD BE AN UNDERSTATEMENT!!
PFFT. AMATEUR!!
YOU TOTALLY FAILED.
SAY WHAT?
THIS TIME, I PUT AN ANSWER DOWN FOR EVERY SINGLE QUESTION!!
KA (FWAH)
REALLY!? THAT'S GREAT, SATANYA!!
NAH-HA-HA!! WITNESS THE POWER OF THE GREAT DEVIL QUEEN!!
......

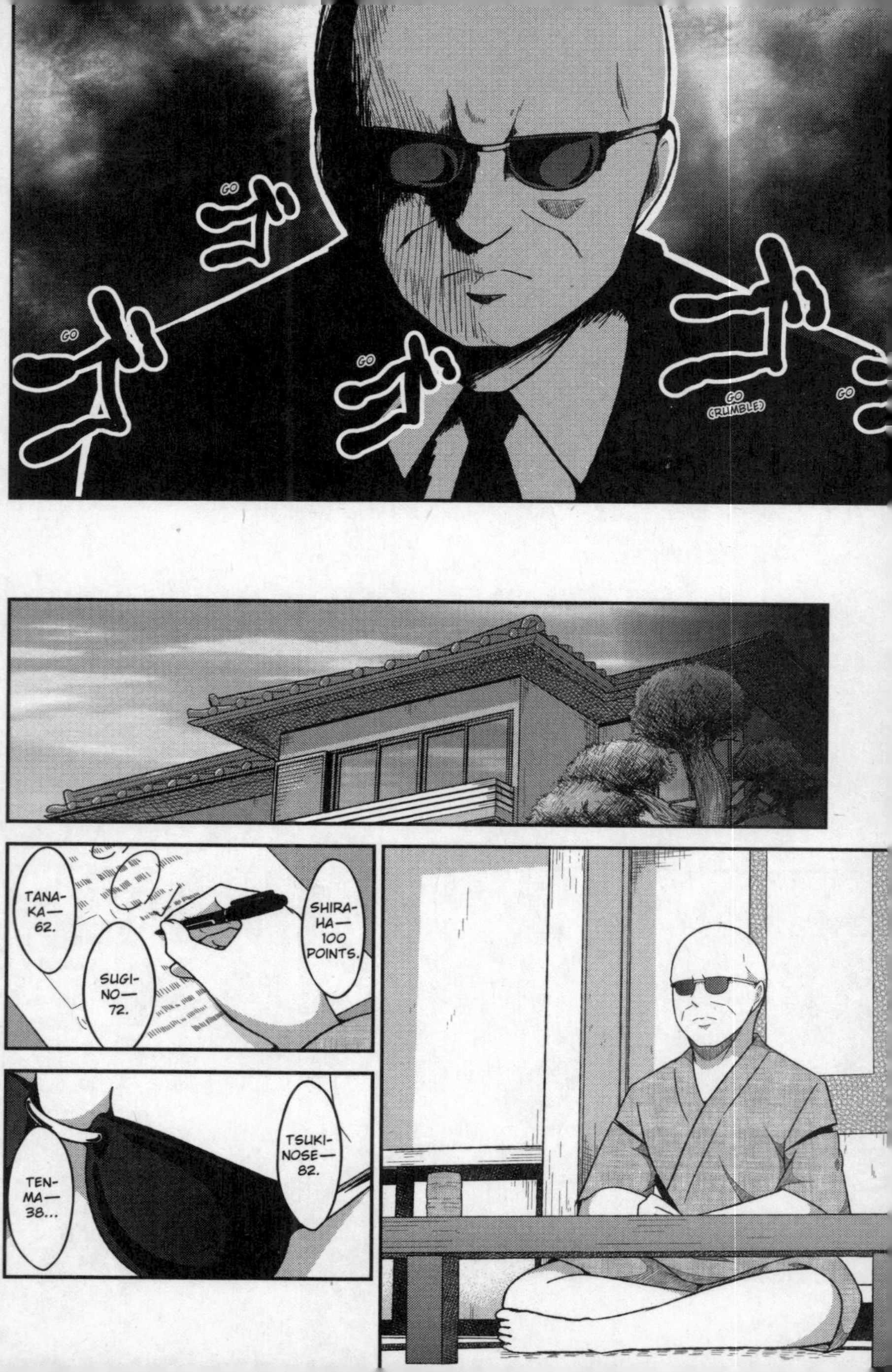
GO
GO
GO
(RUMBLE)
GO
GO
GO
SHIRAHA—100 POINTS.
TANAKA—62.
SUGINO—72.
TSUKINOSE—82.
TENMA—38...

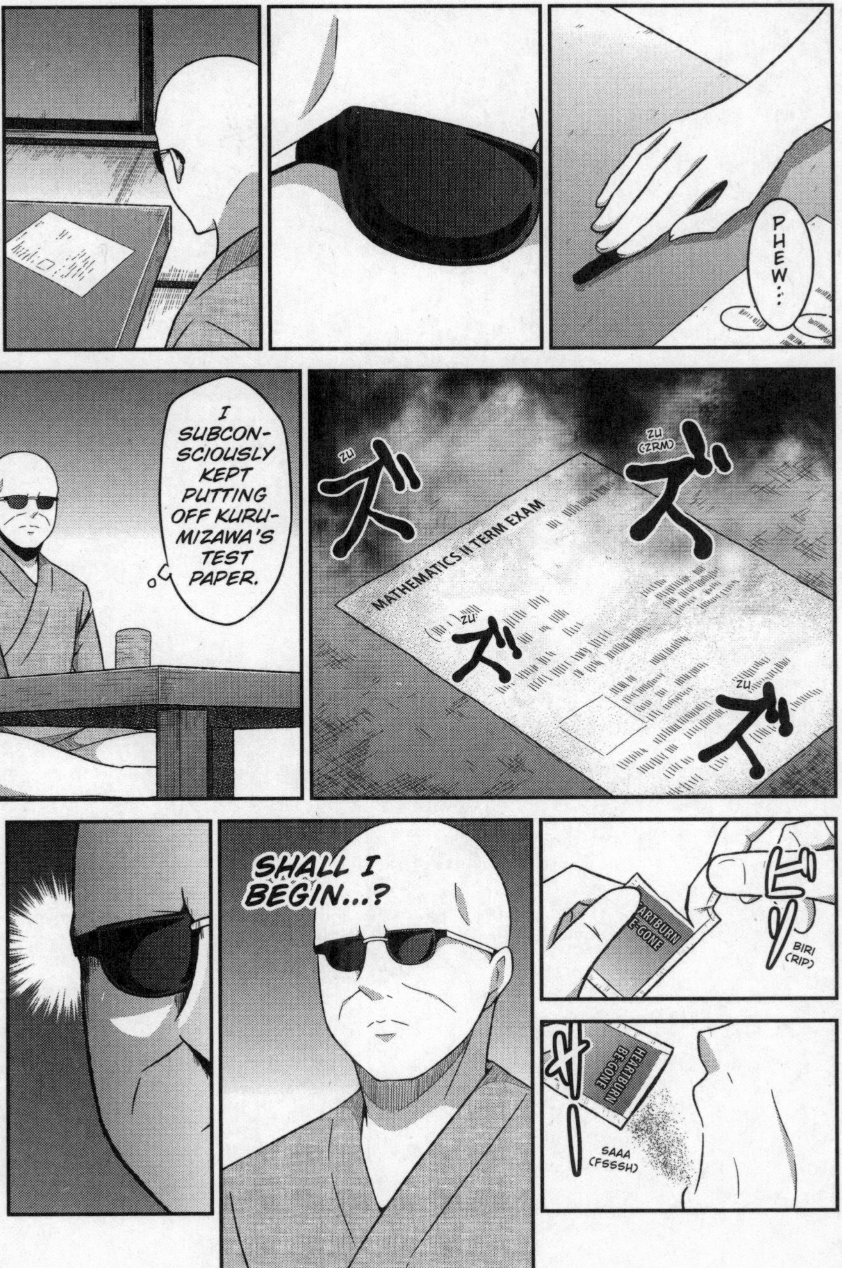

PHEW...
ズ
ZU (ZRM)
ズ
ZU
MATHEMATICS II TERM EXAM
ズ
ZU
ズ
ZU
I SUBCONSCIOUSLY KEPT PUTTING OFF KURUMIZAWA'S TEST PAPER.
HEARTBURN BE-GONE
BIRI (RIP)
HEARTBURN BE-GONE
SAAA (FSSSH)
SHALL I BEGIN...?

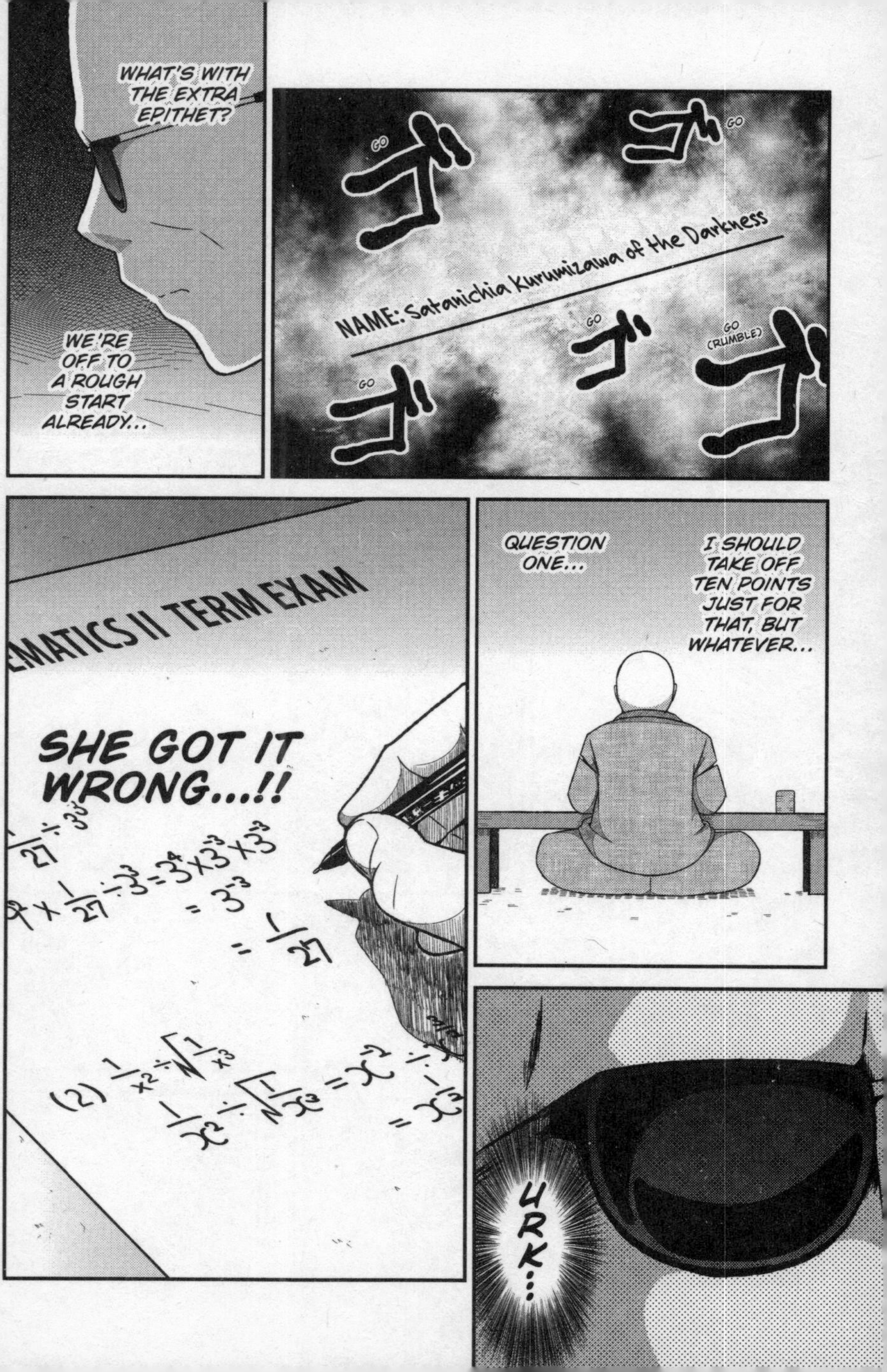

GO
ゴ
GO
ゴ
NAME: Satanichia Kurumizawa of the Darkness
GO (RUMBLE)
ゴ
GO
ゴ
GO
ゴ
WHAT'S WITH THE EXTRA EPITHET?
WE'RE OFF TO A ROUGH START ALREADY...
I SHOULD TAKE OFF TEN POINTS JUST FOR THAT, BUT WHATEVER...
QUESTION ONE...
URK...
EMATICS II TERM EXAM
SHE GOT IT WRONG...!!

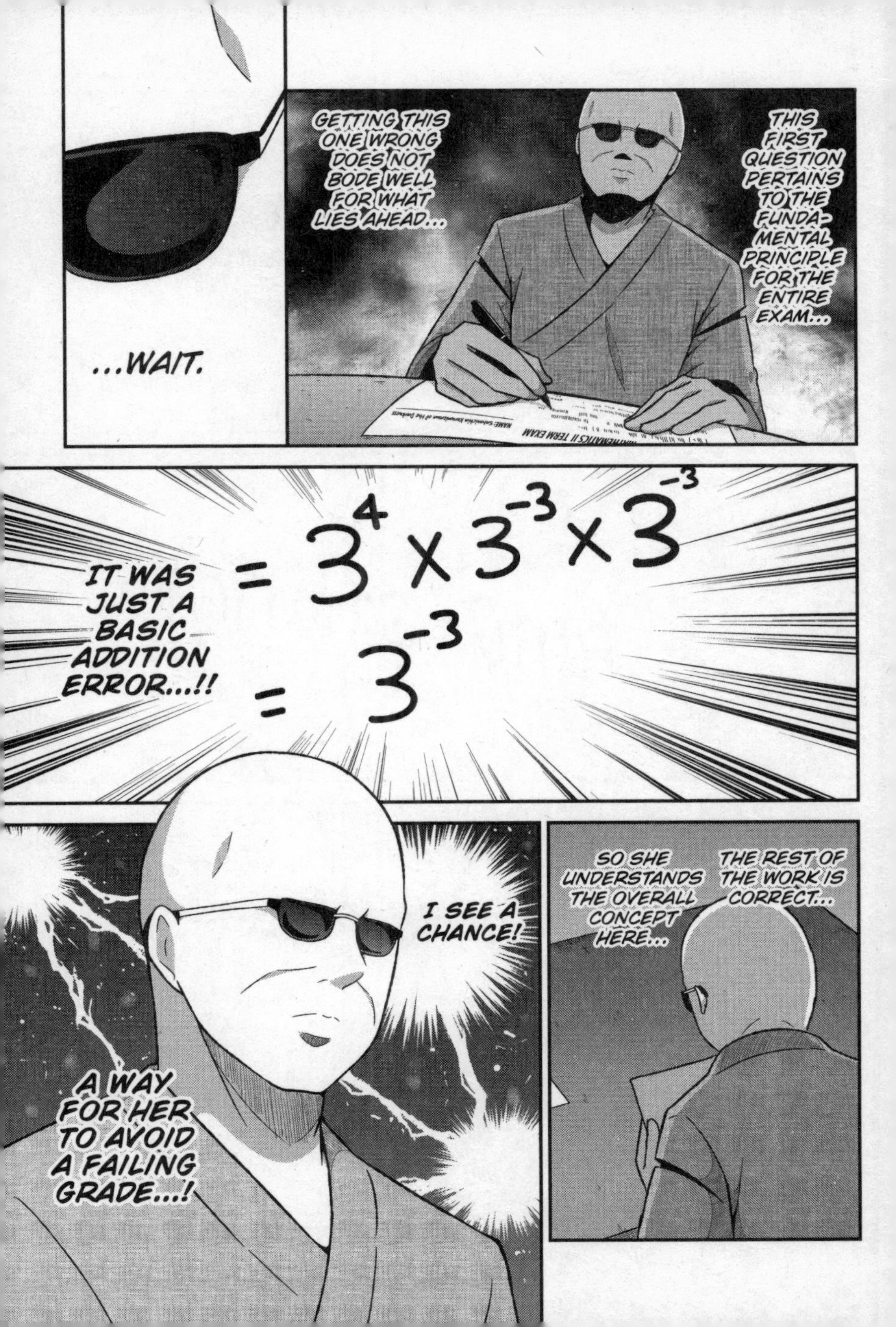
THIS FIRST QUESTION PERTAINS TO THE FUNDAMENTAL PRINCIPLE FOR THE ENTIRE EXAM...
GETTING THIS ONE WRONG DOES NOT BODE WELL FOR WHAT LIES AHEAD...
...WAIT.
= 3^4 x 3^-3 x 3^-3
= 3^-3
IT WAS JUST A BASIC ADDITION ERROR...!!
THE REST OF THE WORK IS CORRECT...
SO SHE UNDERSTANDS THE OVERALL CONCEPT HERE...
I SEE A CHANCE!
A WAY FOR HER TO AVOID A FAILING GRADE...!

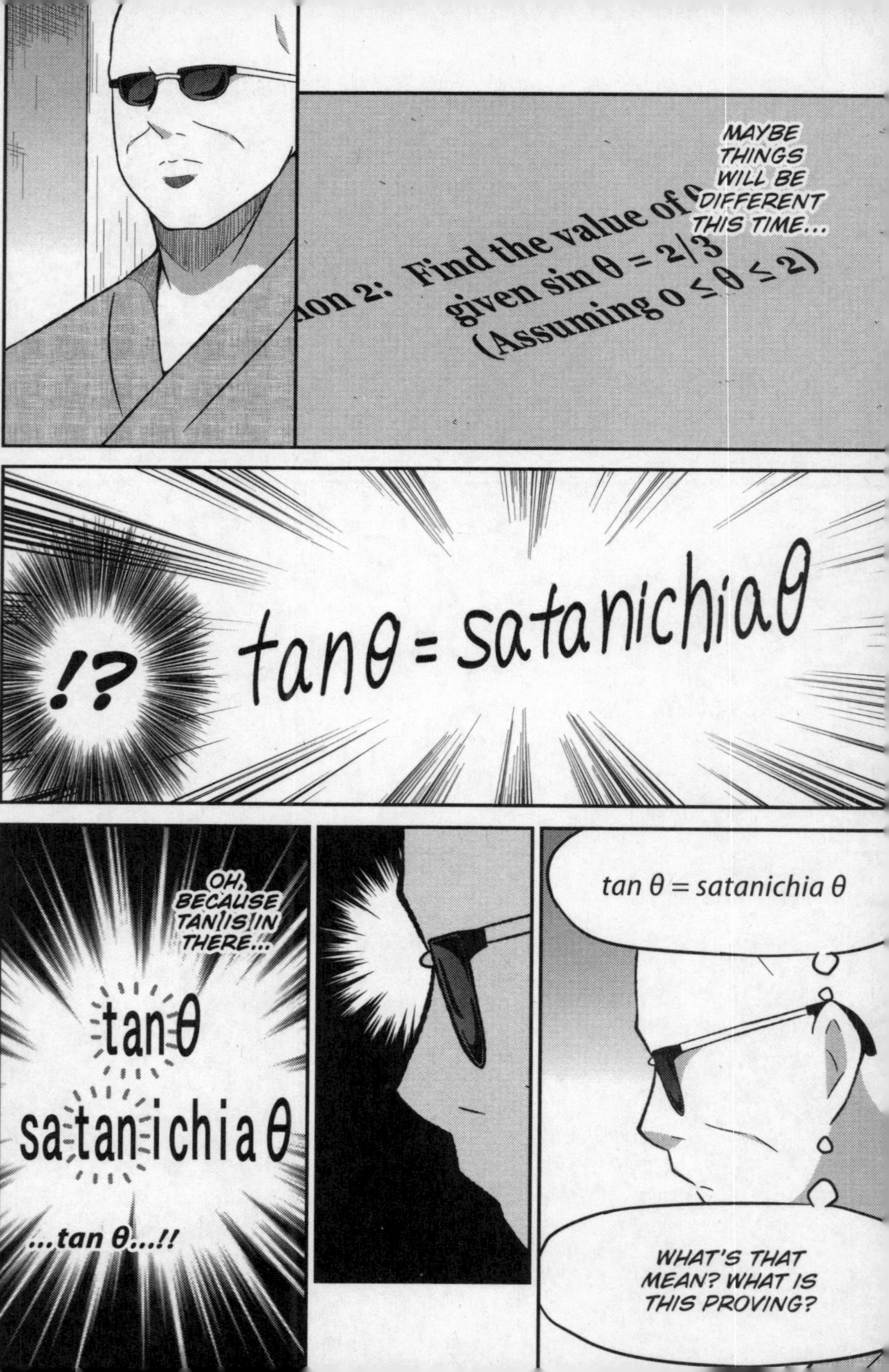
MAYBE THINGS WILL BE DIFFERENT THIS TIME...
ion 2: Find the value of
given sin θ = 2/3
(Assuming 0 ≤ θ ≤ 2)
tanθ = satanichiaθ
!?
tan θ = satanichia θ
WHAT'S THAT MEAN? WHAT IS THIS PROVING?
OH, BECAUSE TAN IS IN THERE...
tan θ
sa tan i chi a θ
...tan θ...!!

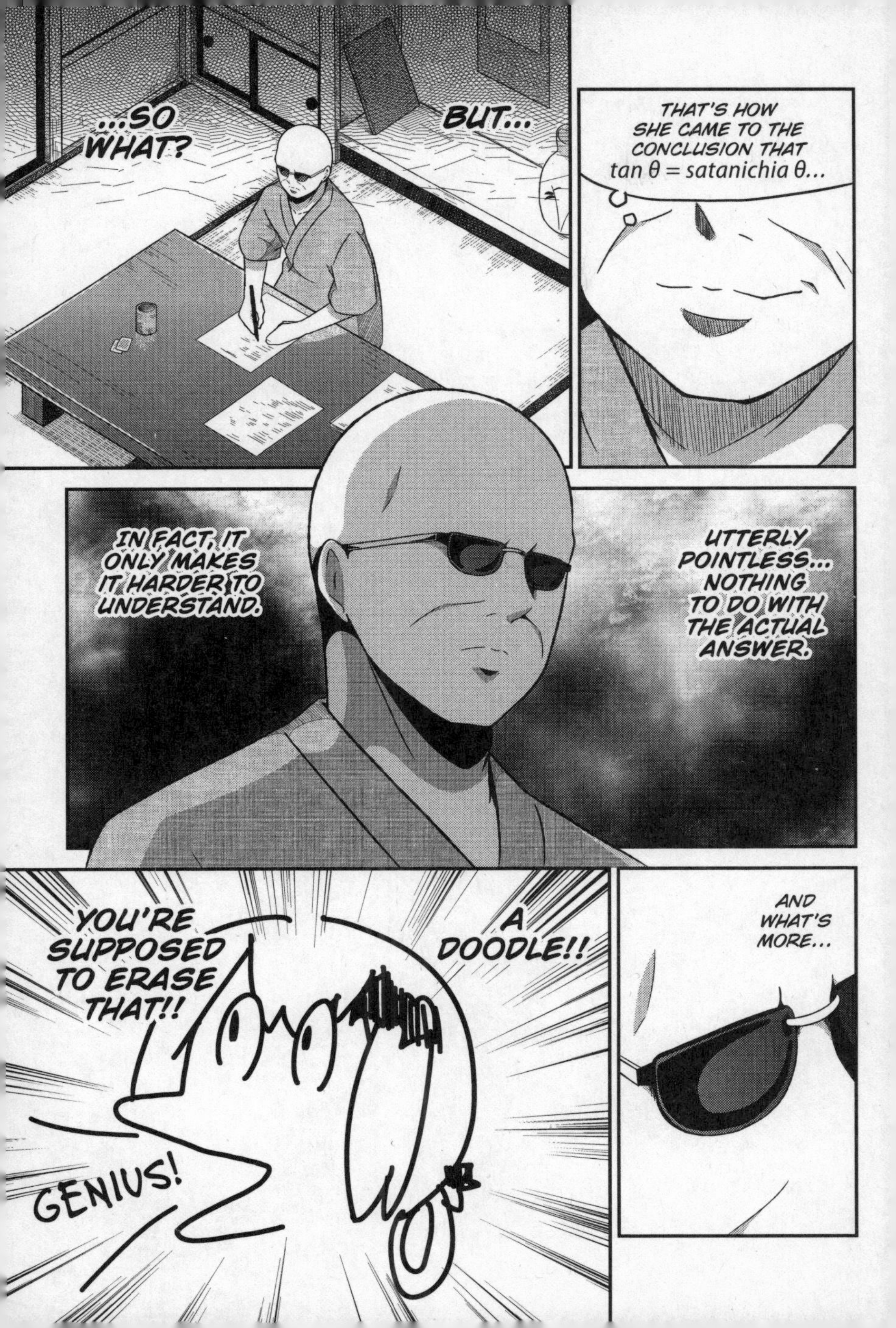
THAT'S HOW SHE CAME TO THE CONCLUSION THAT tan θ = satanichia θ...
BUT...
...SO WHAT?
UTTERLY POINTLESS... NOTHING TO DO WITH THE ACTUAL ANSWER.
IN FACT, IT ONLY MAKES IT HARDER TO UNDERSTAND.
AND WHAT'S MORE...
A DOODLE!!
YOU'RE SUPPOSED TO ERASE THAT!!
GENIUS!

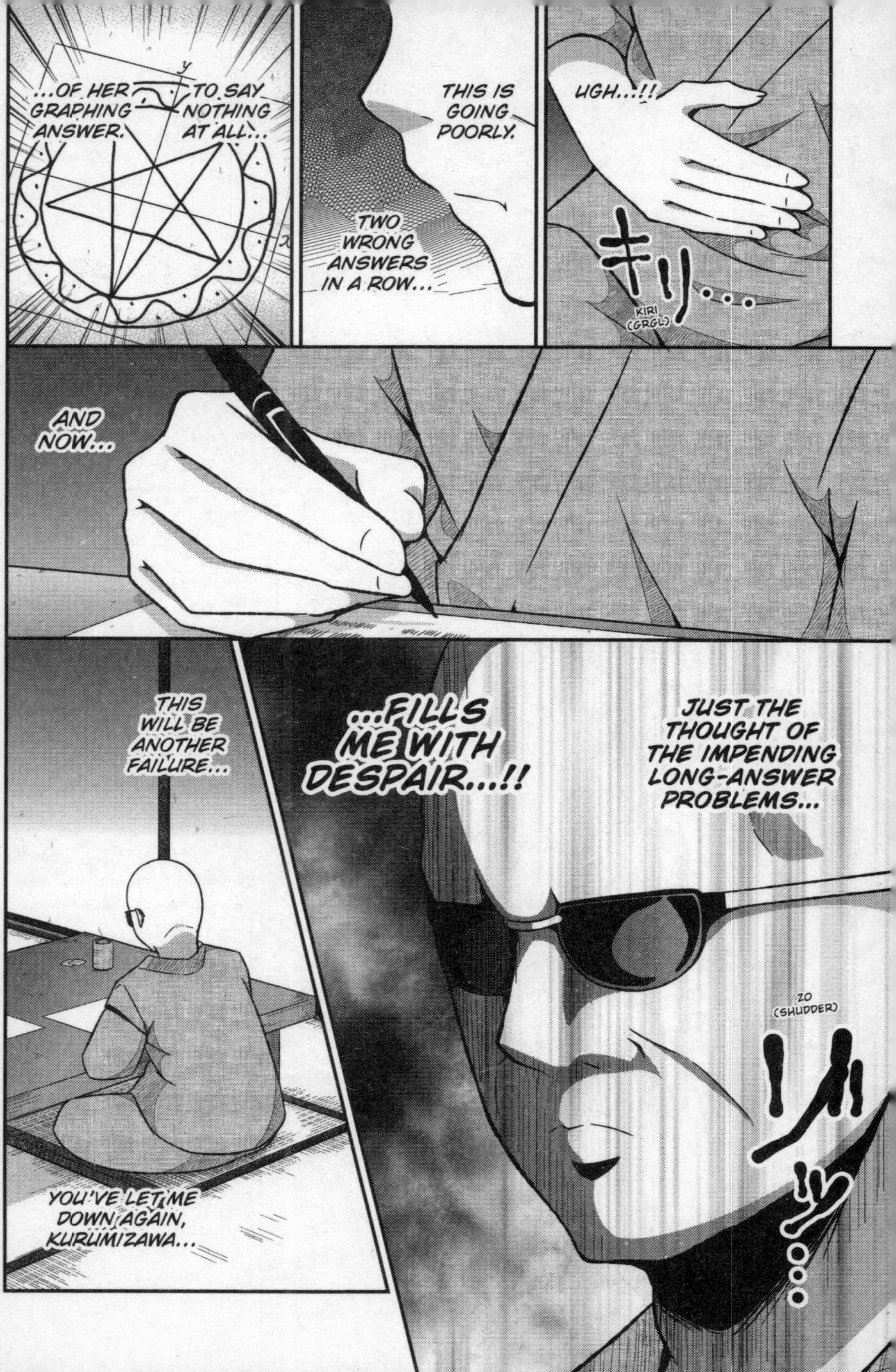
UGH...!!
キリ・・・
KIRI (GRGL)
THIS IS GOING POORLY.
TWO WRONG ANSWERS IN A ROW...
TO SAY NOTHING AT ALL...
...OF HER GRAPHING ANSWER.
AND NOW...
JUST THE THOUGHT OF THE IMPENDING LONG-ANSWER PROBLEMS...
...FILLS ME WITH DESPAIR...!!
ZO (SHUDDER)
ゾッ・・・
THIS WILL BE ANOTHER FAILURE...
YOU'VE LET ME DOWN AGAIN, KURUMIZAWA...

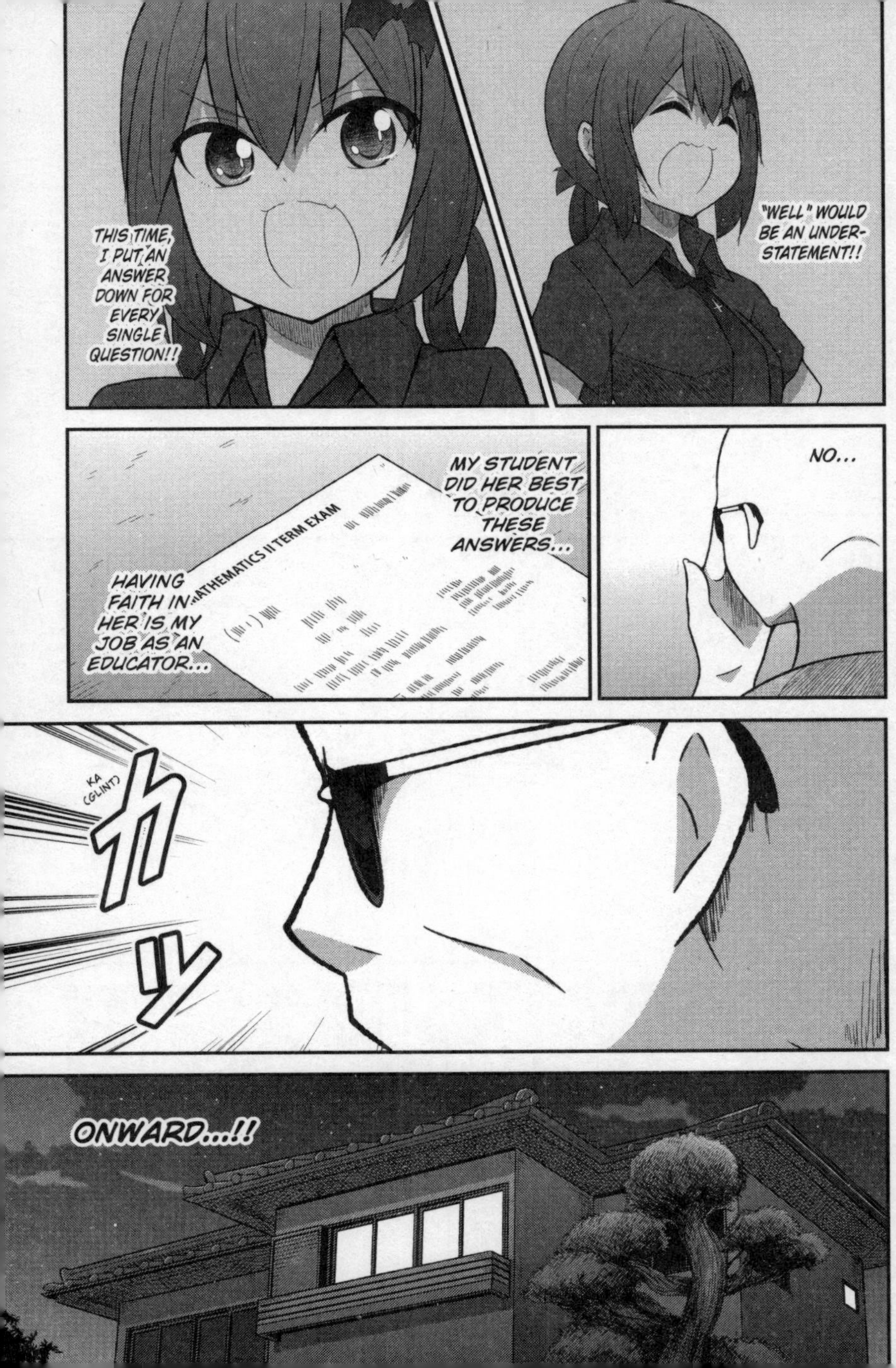
"WELL" WOULD BE AN UNDER-STATEMENT!!
THIS TIME, I PUT AN ANSWER DOWN FOR EVERY SINGLE QUESTION!!
NO...
MY STUDENT DID HER BEST TO PRODUCE THESE ANSWERS...
ATHEMATICS II TERM EXAM
HAVING FAITH IN HER IS MY JOB AS AN EDUCATOR...
KA (GLINT)
カッ
ONWARD...!!

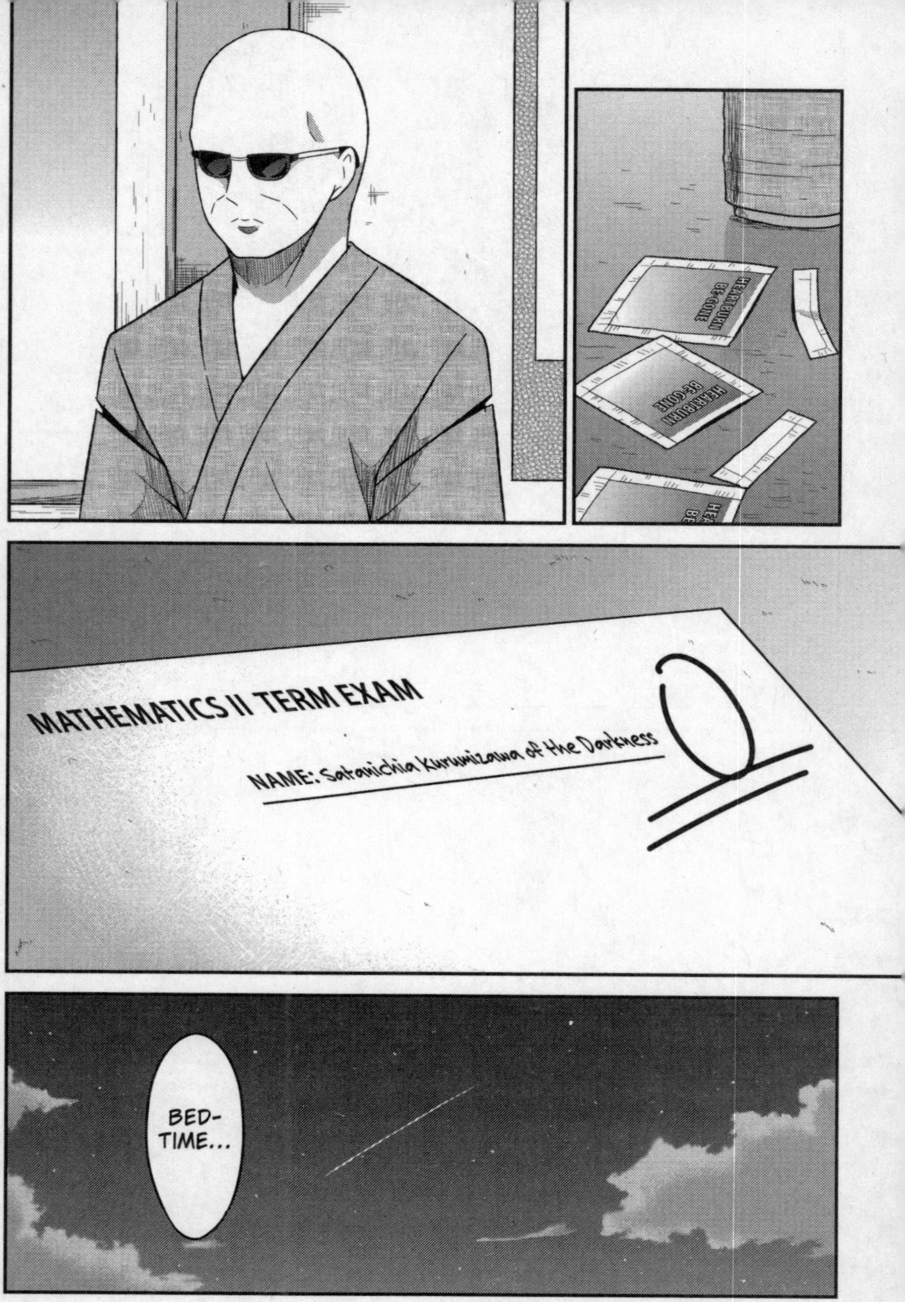
HEARTBURN BE-GONE
HEARTBURN BE-GONE
MATHEMATICS II TERM EXAM
NAME: Satanichia Kurumizawa of the Darkness
0
BED-TIME...

GENIUS!
GENIUS!
GENIUS!
GENIUS!
UGHH...
NIGHT-
MARE

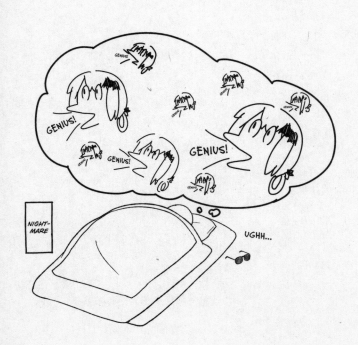

Gabriel DropOut

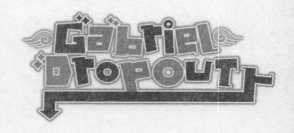

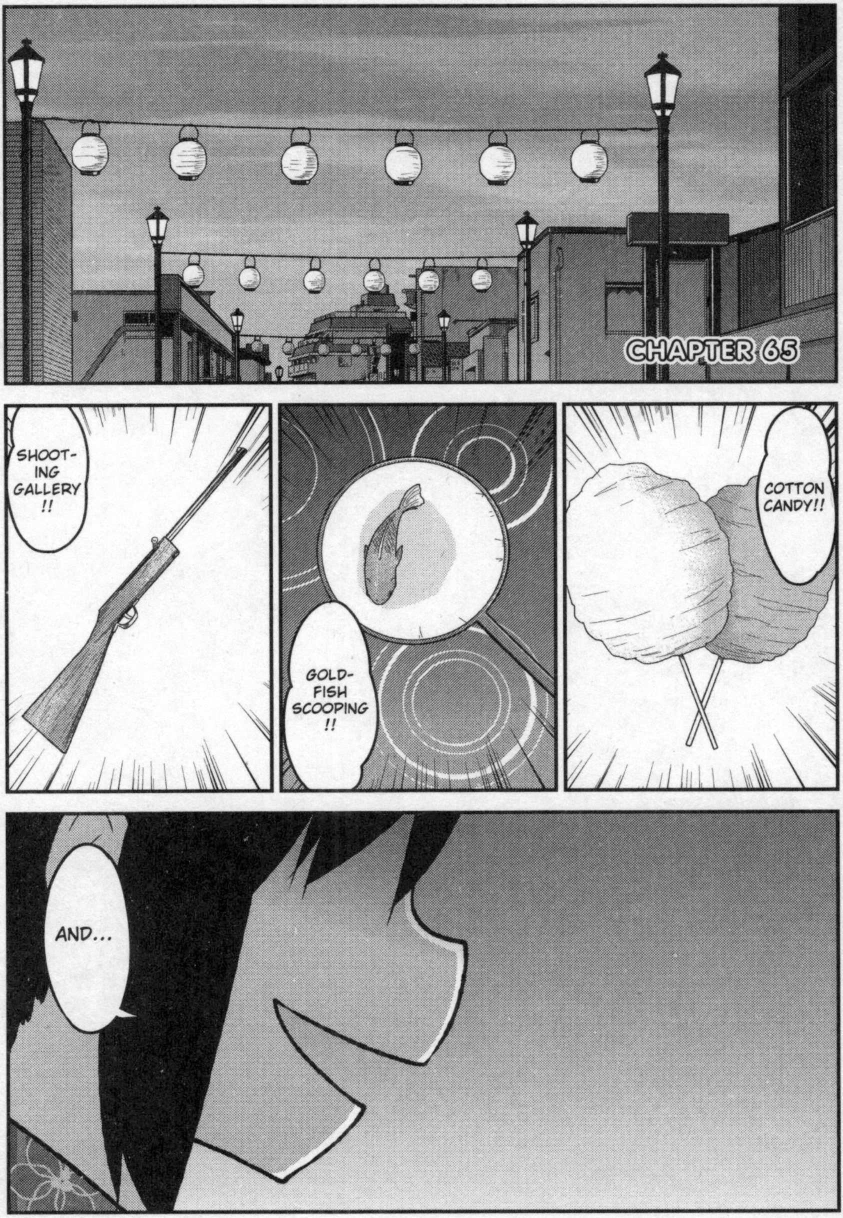
CHAPTER 65
COTTON CANDY!!
GOLD-FISH SCOOPING!!
SHOOT-ING GALLERY!!
AND...

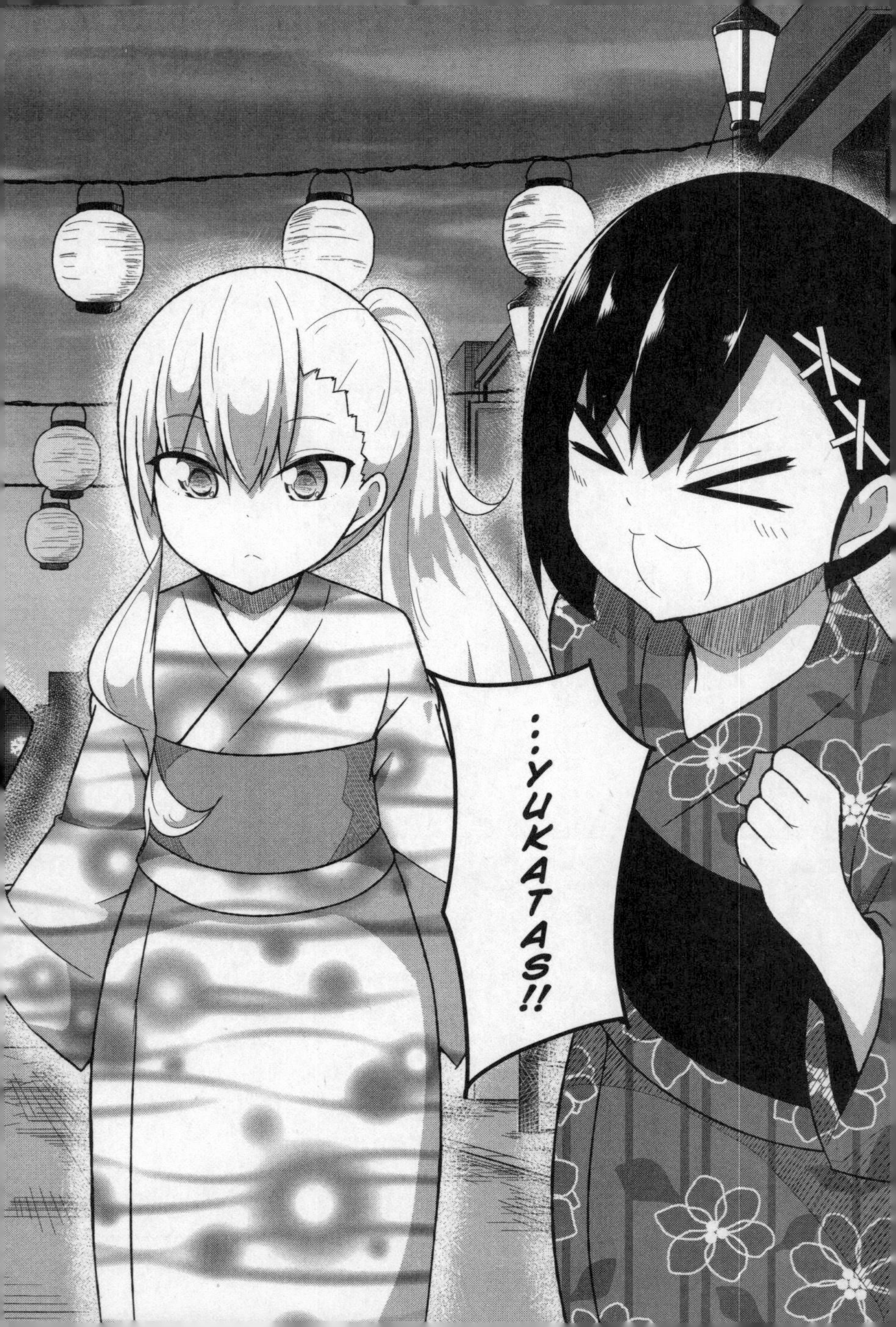
...YUKATAS!!

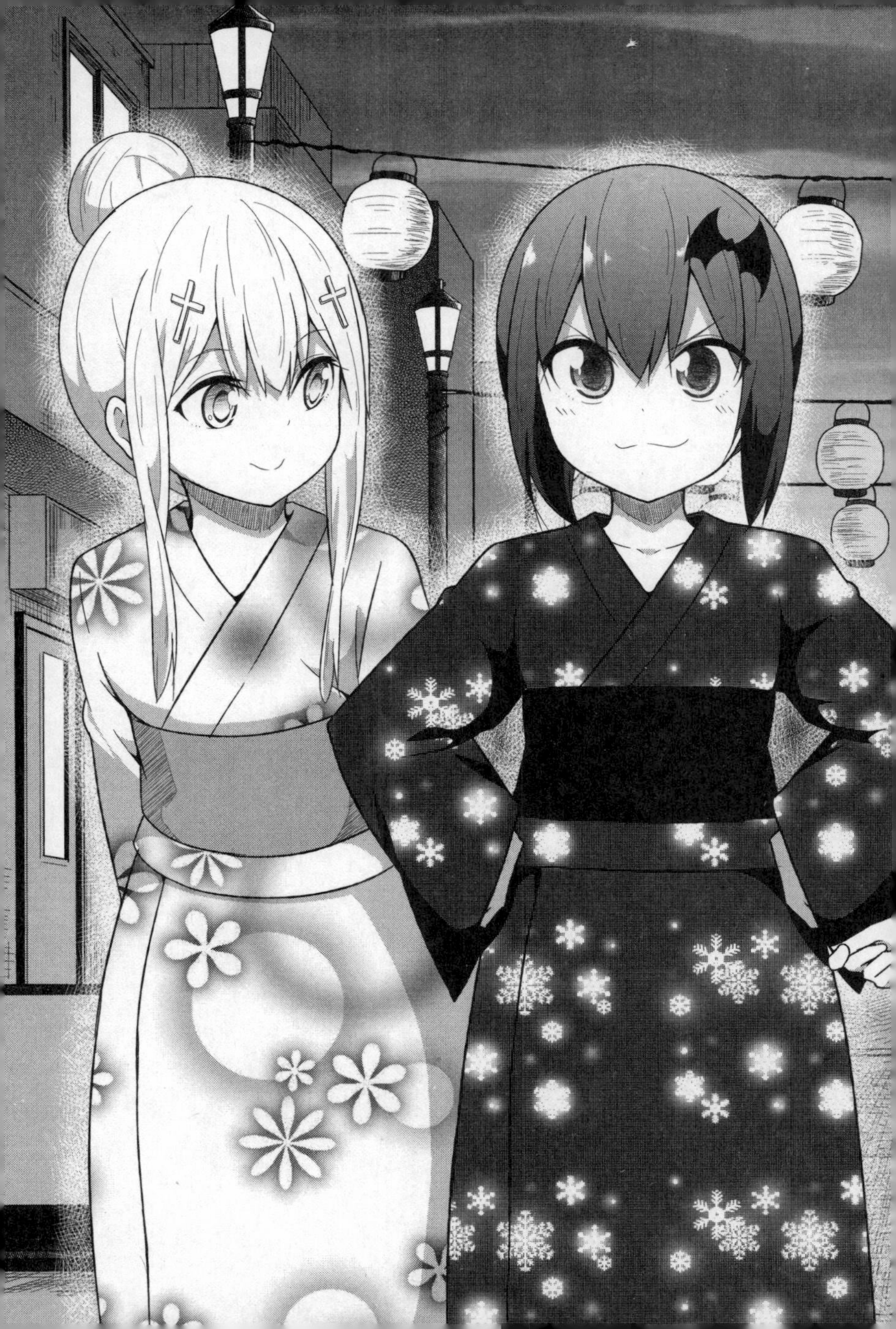

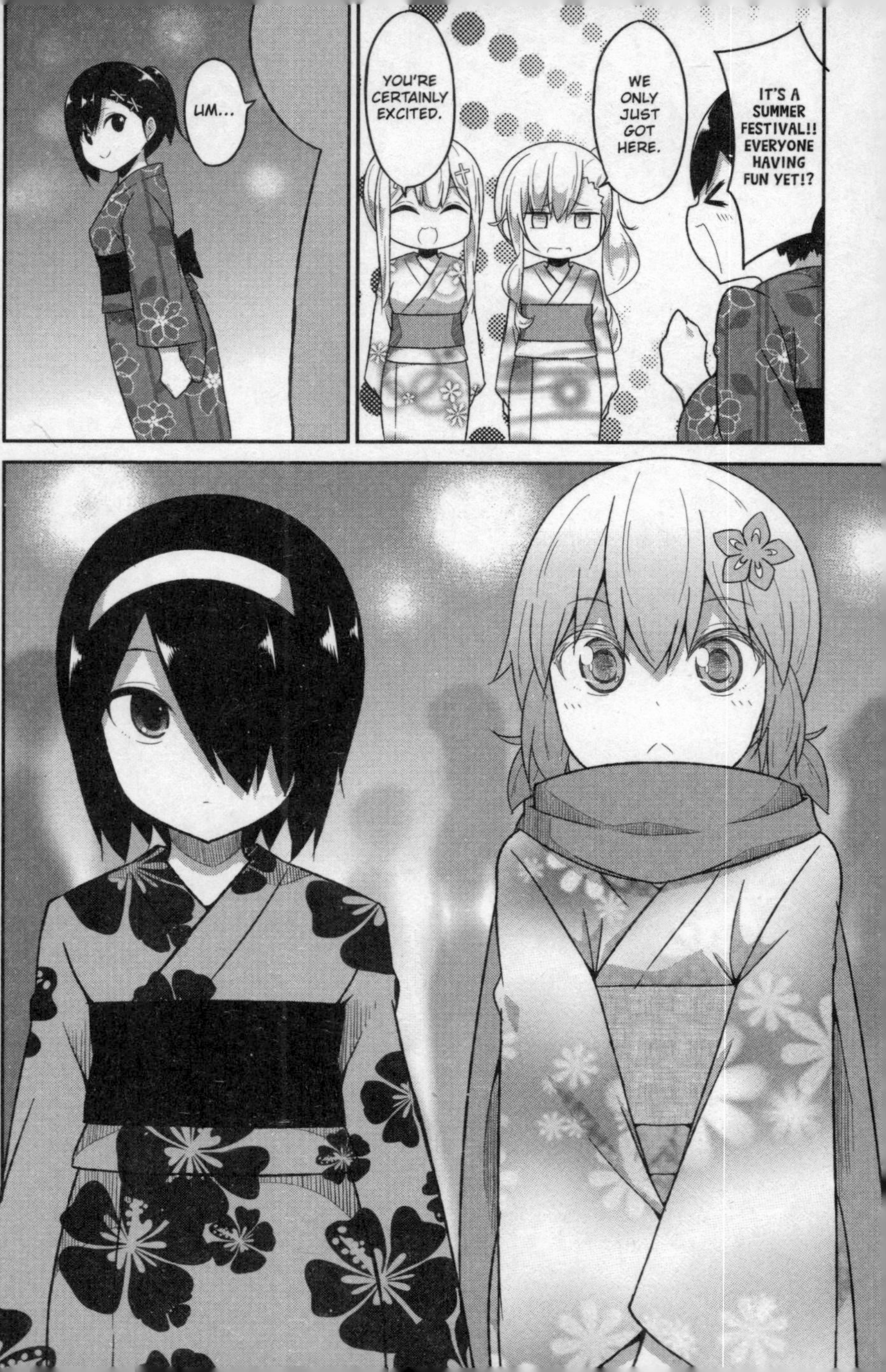
IT'S A SUMMER FESTIVAL!! EVERYONE HAVING FUN YET!?
WE ONLY JUST GOT HERE.
YOU'RE CERTAINLY EXCITED.
UM...

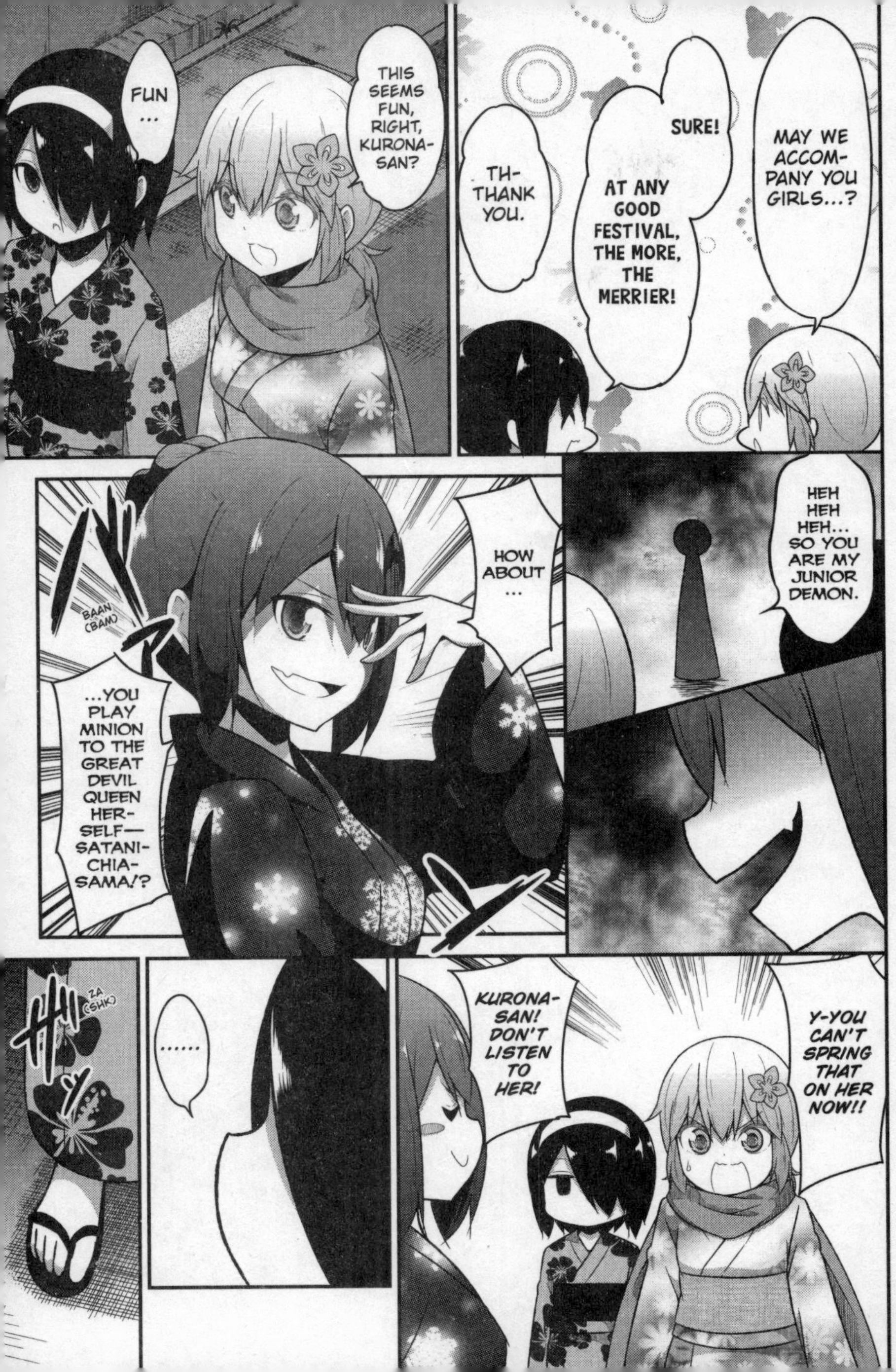
MAY WE ACCOMPANY YOU GIRLS...?
SURE!
AT ANY GOOD FESTIVAL, THE MORE, THE MERRIER!
TH-THANK YOU.
THIS SEEMS FUN, RIGHT, KURONA-SAN?
FUN ...
HEH HEH HEH... SO YOU ARE MY JUNIOR DEMON.
HOW ABOUT ...
BAAN (BAM)
...YOU PLAY MINION TO THE GREAT DEVIL QUEEN HERSELF—SATANICHIA-SAMA!?
Y-YOU CAN'T SPRING THAT ON HER NOW!!
KURONA-SAN! DON'T LISTEN TO HER!
....
ZA (SHK)

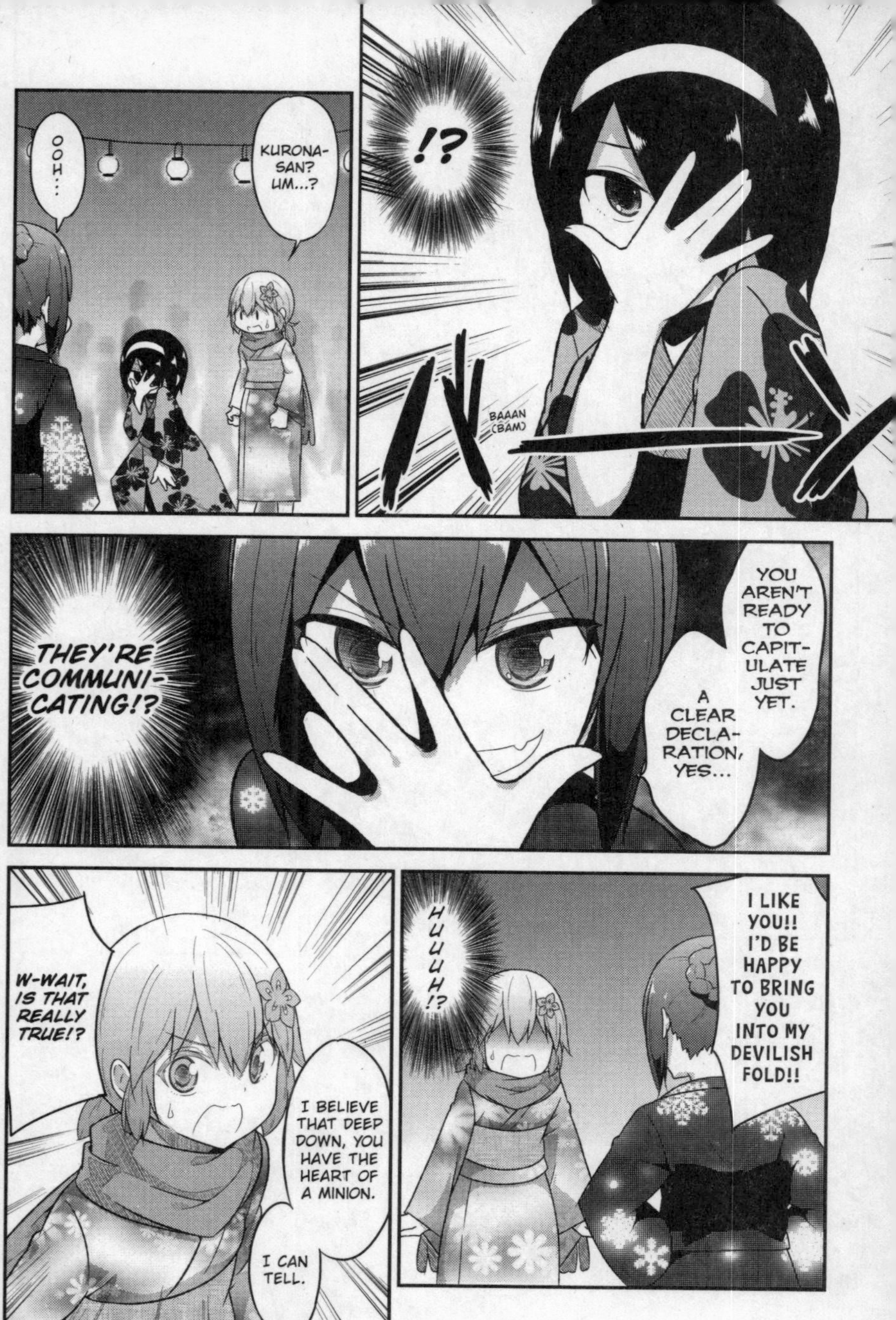
!?
BAAAN (BAM)
KURONA-SAN? UM...?
OOH...
YOU AREN'T READY TO CAPITULATE JUST YET.
A CLEAR DECLARATION, YES...
THEY'RE COMMUNICATING!?
I LIKE YOU!! I'D BE HAPPY TO BRING YOU INTO MY DEVILISH FOLD!!
HUUUH!?
W-WAIT, IS THAT REALLY TRUE!?
I BELIEVE THAT DEEP DOWN, YOU HAVE THE HEART OF A MINION.
I CAN TELL.

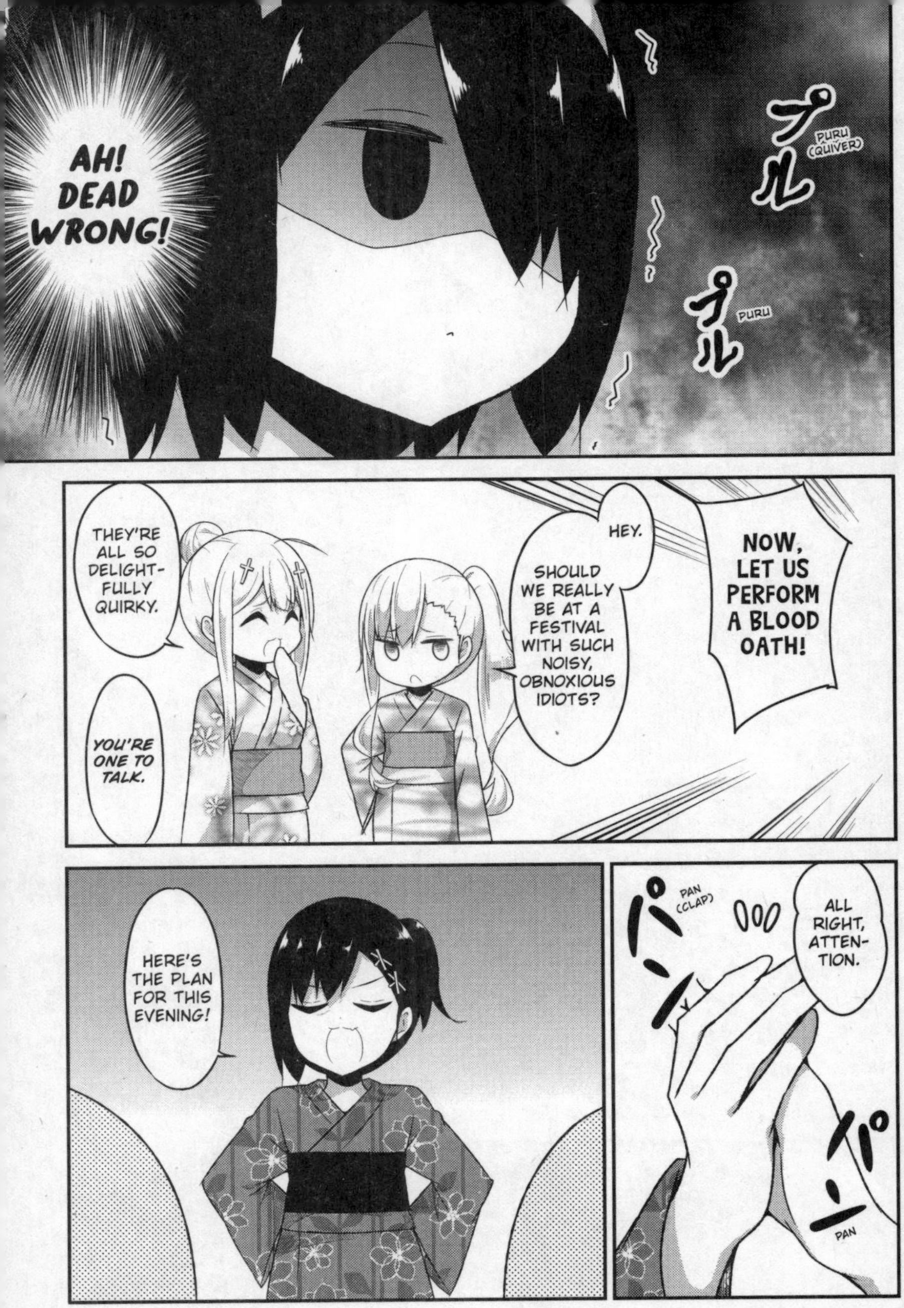
PURU (QUIVER)
PURU
AH! DEAD WRONG!
NOW, LET US PERFORM A BLOOD OATH!
HEY.
SHOULD WE REALLY BE AT A FESTIVAL WITH SUCH NOISY, OBNOXIOUS IDIOTS?
THEY'RE ALL SO DELIGHT-FULLY QUIRKY.
YOU'RE ONE TO TALK.
ALL RIGHT, ATTEN-TION.
PAN (CLAP)
PAN
HERE'S THE PLAN FOR THIS EVENING!

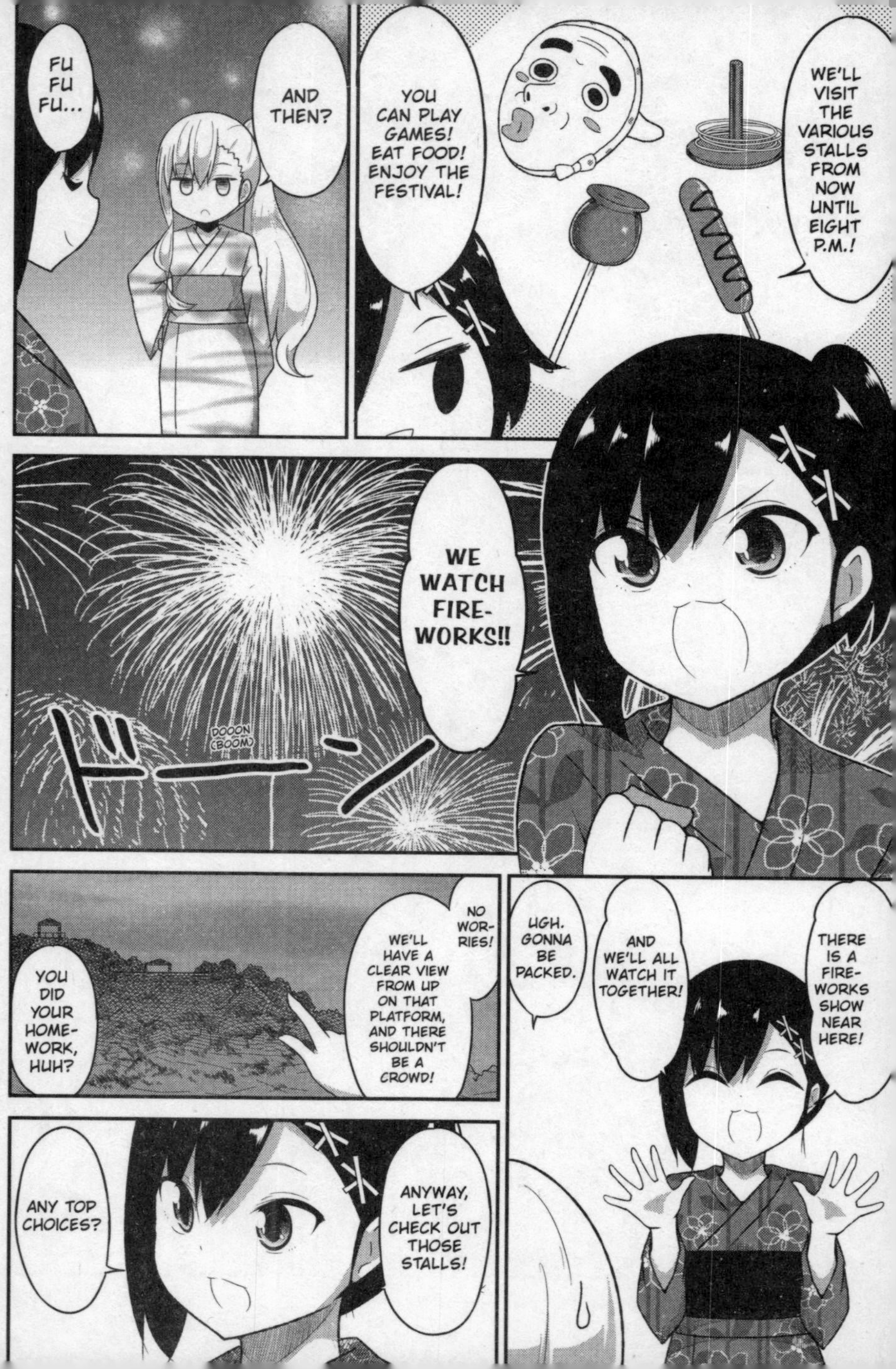
WE'LL VISIT THE VARIOUS STALLS FROM NOW UNTIL EIGHT P.M.!
YOU CAN PLAY GAMES! EAT FOOD! ENJOY THE FESTIVAL!
AND THEN?
FU FU FU...
WE WATCH FIRE-WORKS!!
DOOON (BOOM)
THERE IS A FIRE-WORKS SHOW NEAR HERE!
AND WE'LL ALL WATCH IT TOGETHER!
UGH. GONNA BE PACKED.
NO WOR-RIES!
WE'LL HAVE A CLEAR VIEW FROM UP ON THAT PLATFORM, AND THERE SHOULDN'T BE A CROWD!
YOU DID YOUR HOME-WORK, HUH?
ANYWAY, LET'S CHECK OUT THOSE STALLS!
ANY TOP CHOICES?

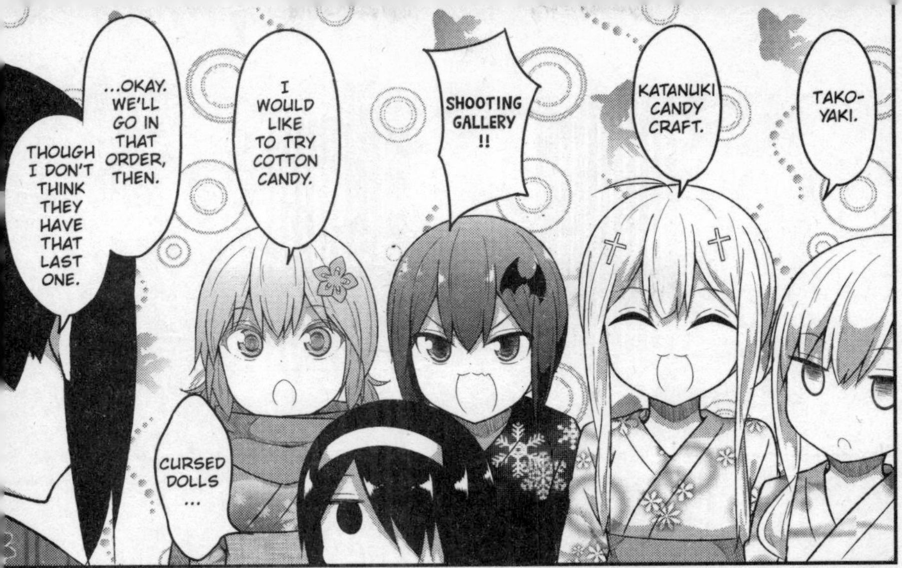
TAKO-YAKI.
KATANUKI CANDY CRAFT.
SHOOTING GALLERY !!
I WOULD LIKE TO TRY COTTON CANDY.
CURSED DOLLS ...
...OKAY. WE'LL GO IN THAT ORDER, THEN.
THOUGH I DON'T THINK THEY HAVE THAT LAST ONE.

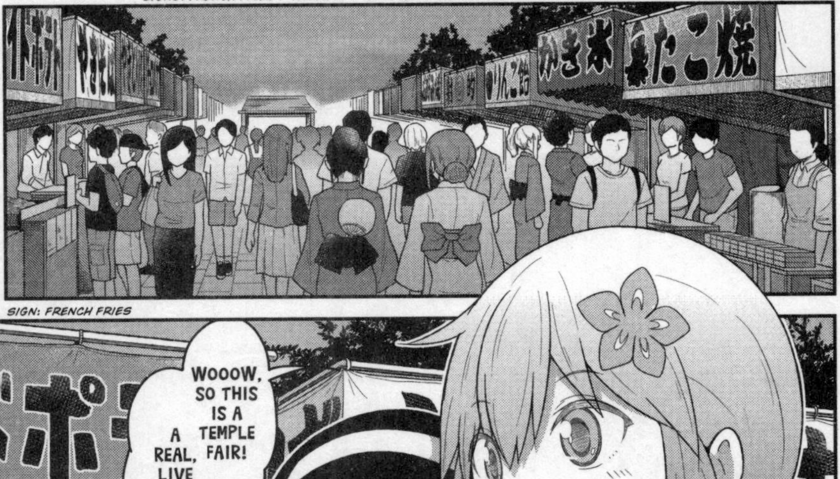
かき氷
たこ焼
りんご飴
SIGNS: FRENCH FRIES / TAKOYAKI / YAKISOBA / SHAVED ICE / CANDY APPLES

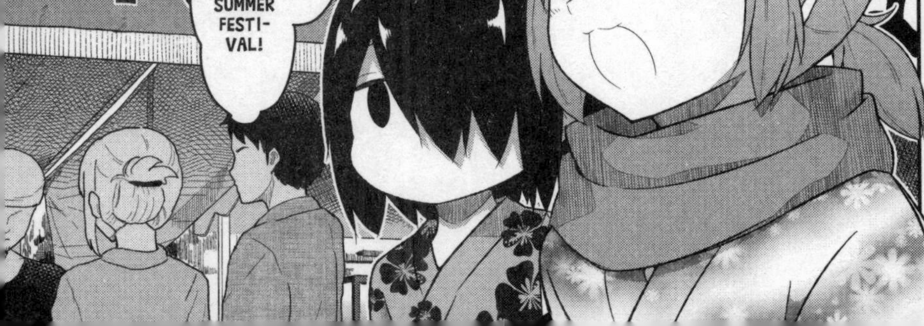
WOOOW, SO THIS IS A TEMPLE FAIR!
A REAL, LIVE SUMMER FESTI-VAL!
SIGN: FRENCH FRIES

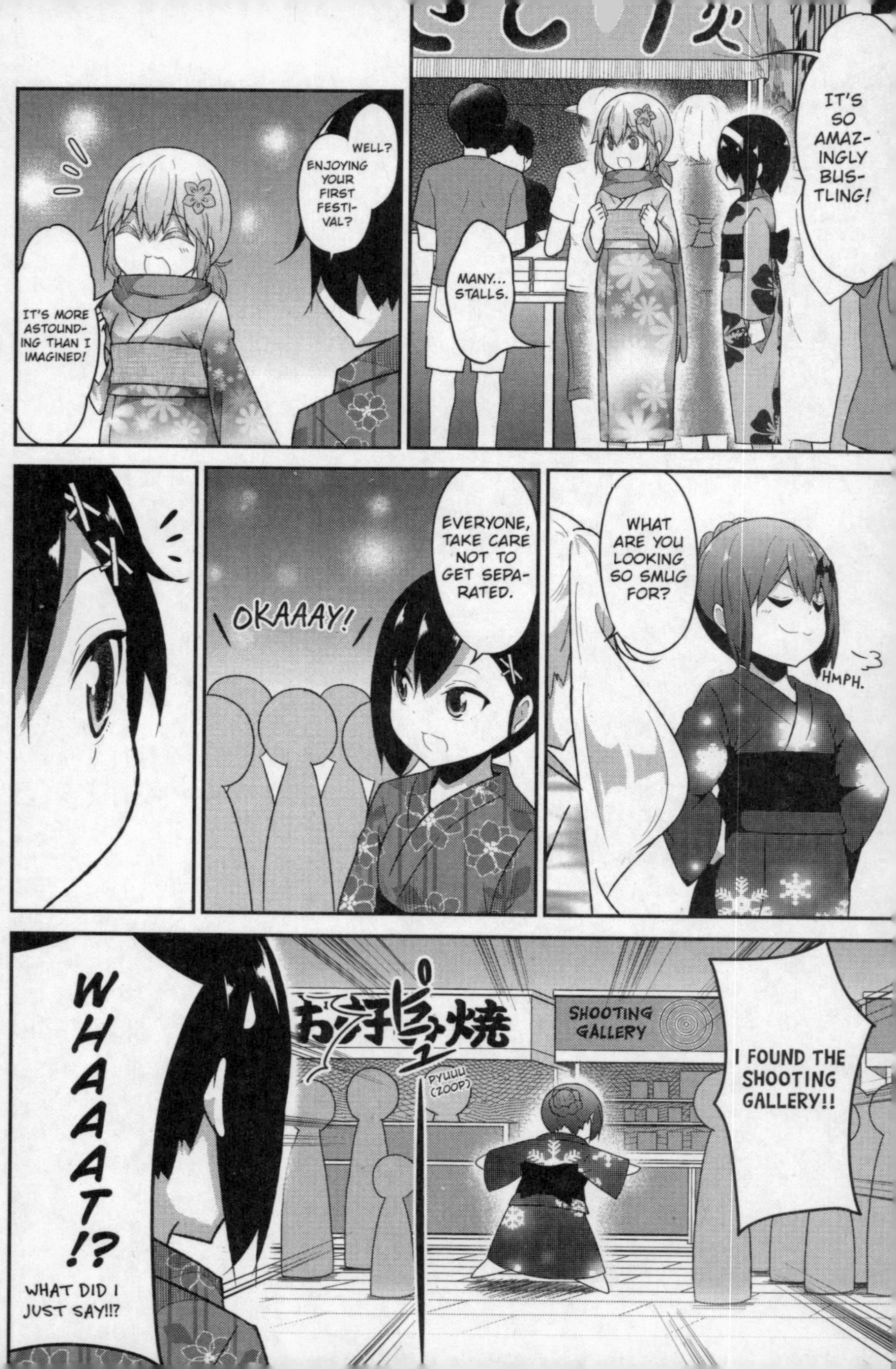
IT'S SO AMAZINGLY BUSTLING!
MANY... STALLS.
WELL? ENJOYING YOUR FIRST FESTIVAL?
IT'S MORE ASTOUNDING THAN I IMAGINED!
WHAT ARE YOU LOOKING SO SMUG FOR?
HMPH.
EVERYONE, TAKE CARE NOT TO GET SEPARATED.
OKAAAY!
I FOUND THE SHOOTING GALLERY!!
SHOOTING GALLERY
PYUUU (ZOOP)
WHAAAAT!?
WHAT DID I JUST SAY!!?

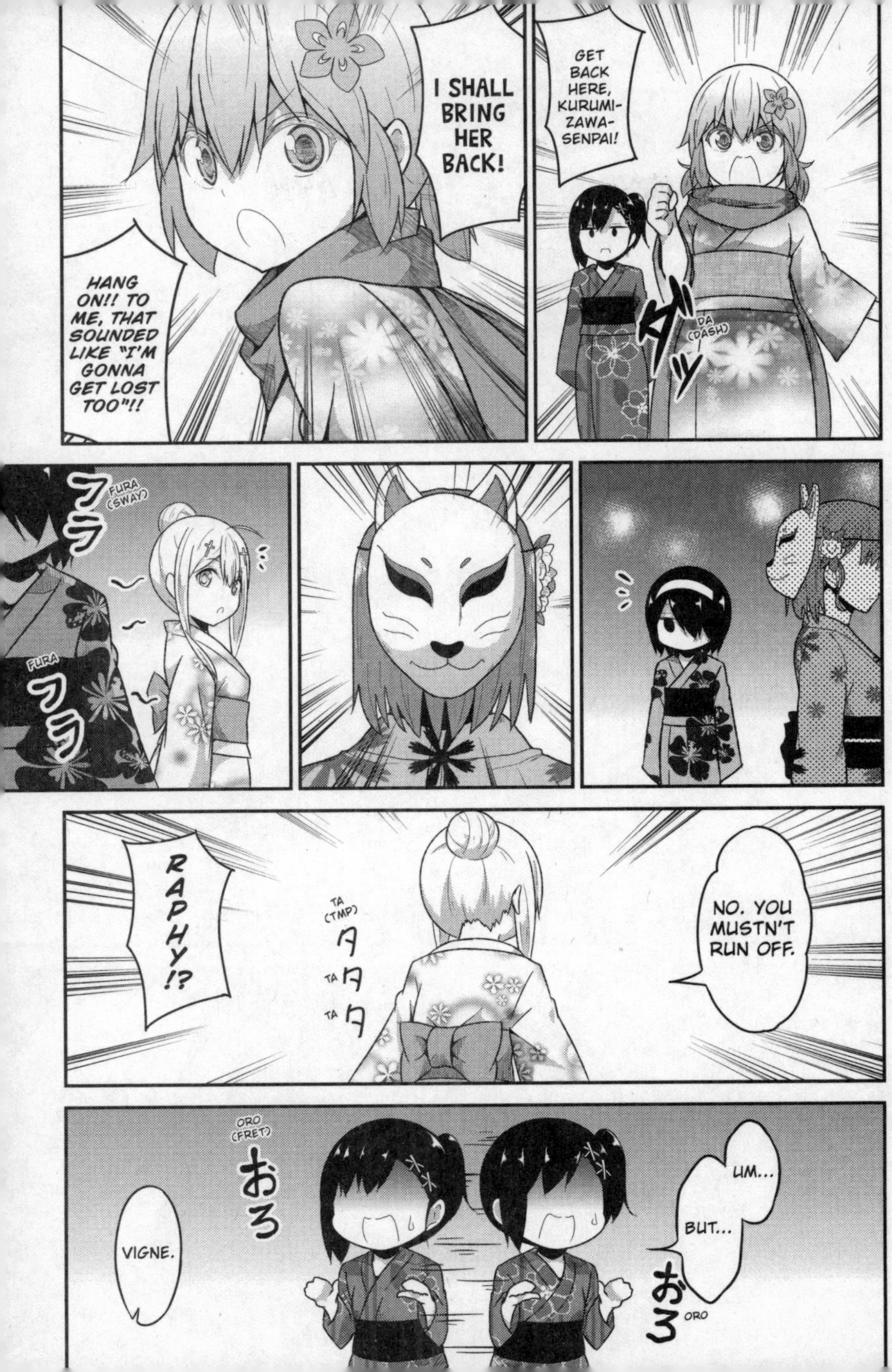
GET BACK HERE, KURUMIZAWA-SENPAI!
DA (DASH)
ダッ
I SHALL BRING HER BACK!
HANG ON!! TO ME, THAT SOUNDED LIKE "I'M GONNA GET LOST TOO"!!
FURA (SWAY)
フラ
FURA
フラ
NO. YOU MUSTN'T RUN OFF.
TA (TMP)
タ
TA
タ
TA
タ
RAPHY!?
UM...
BUT...
おろ
ORO
ORO (FRET)
おろ
VIGNE.

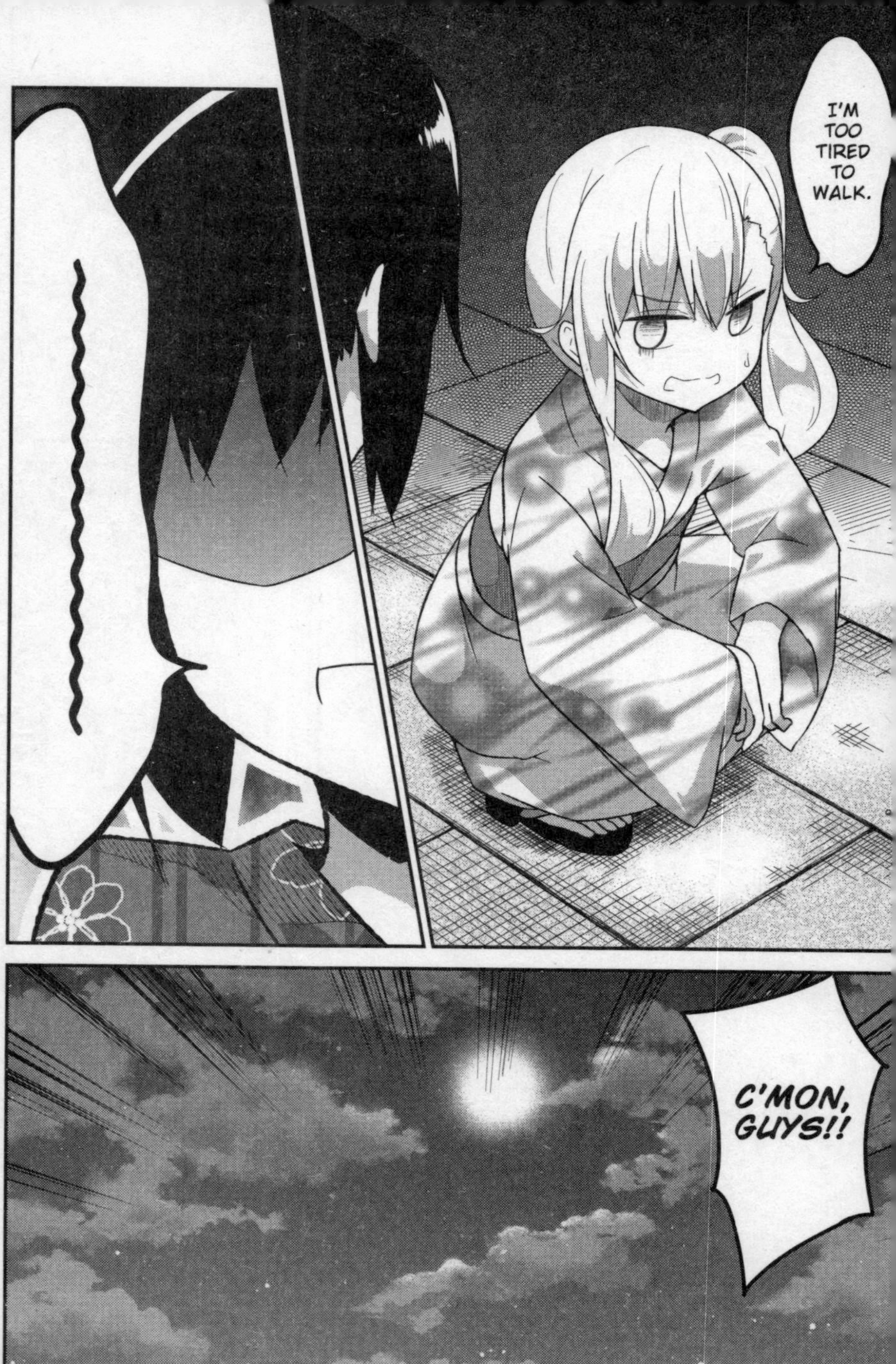
I'M TOO TIRED TO WALK.
C'MON, GUYS!!

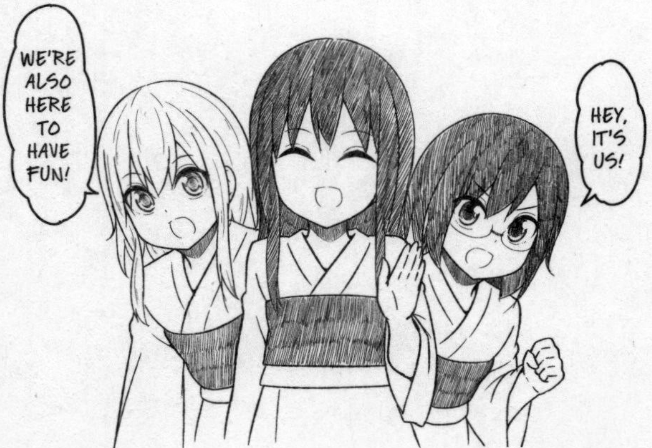
HEY, IT'S US!
WE'RE ALSO HERE TO HAVE FUN!

Gabriel DropOut

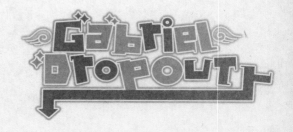

CHAPTER 66

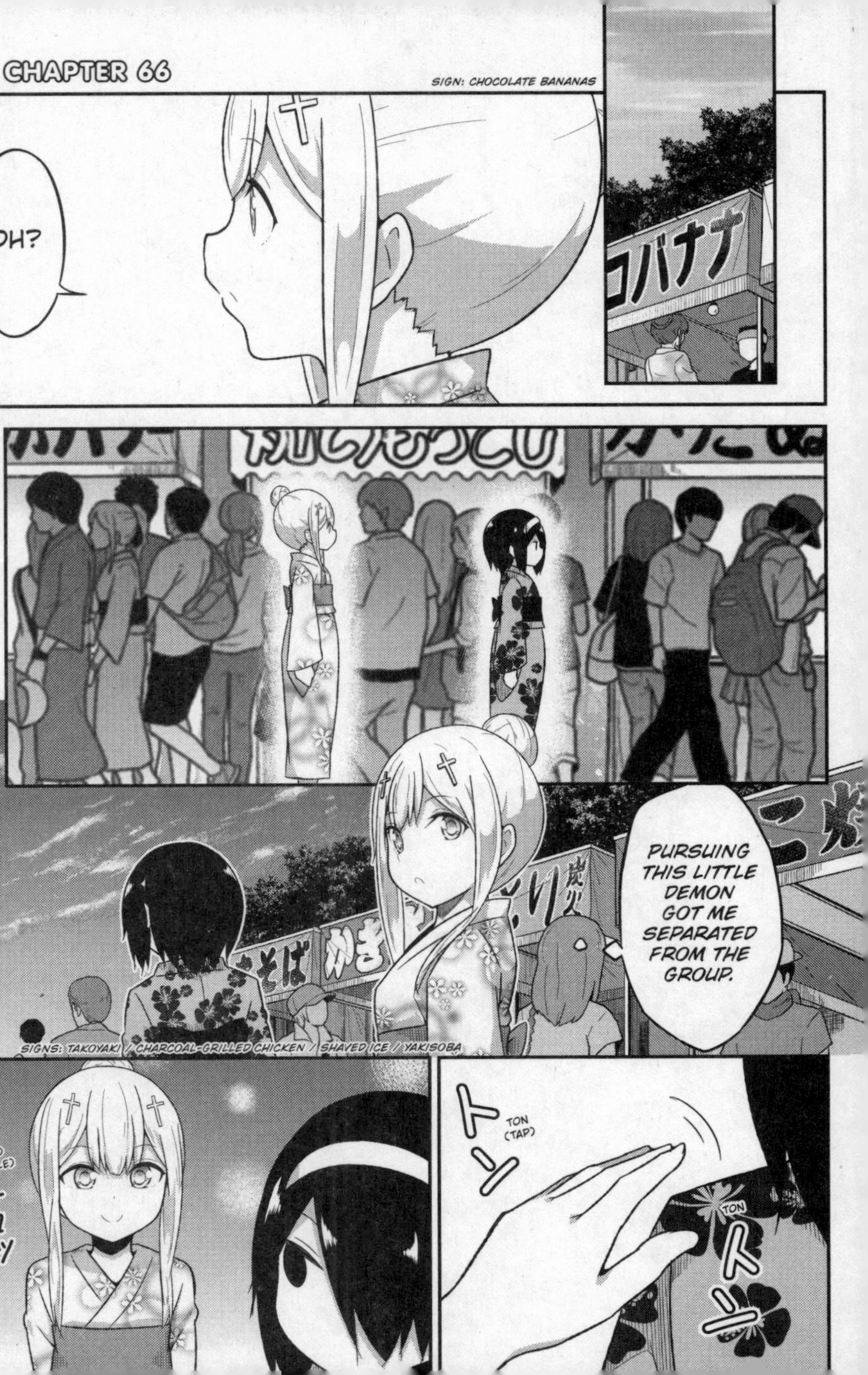

SIGN: CHOCOLATE BANANAS
チョコバナナ
OH?
PURSUING THIS LITTLE DEMON GOT ME SEPARATED FROM THE GROUP.
SIGNS: TAKOYAKI / CHARCOAL-GRILLED CHICKEN / SHAVED ICE / YAKISOBA
TON (TAP)
トン
TON
トン
NIKO (SMILE)
ニコッ

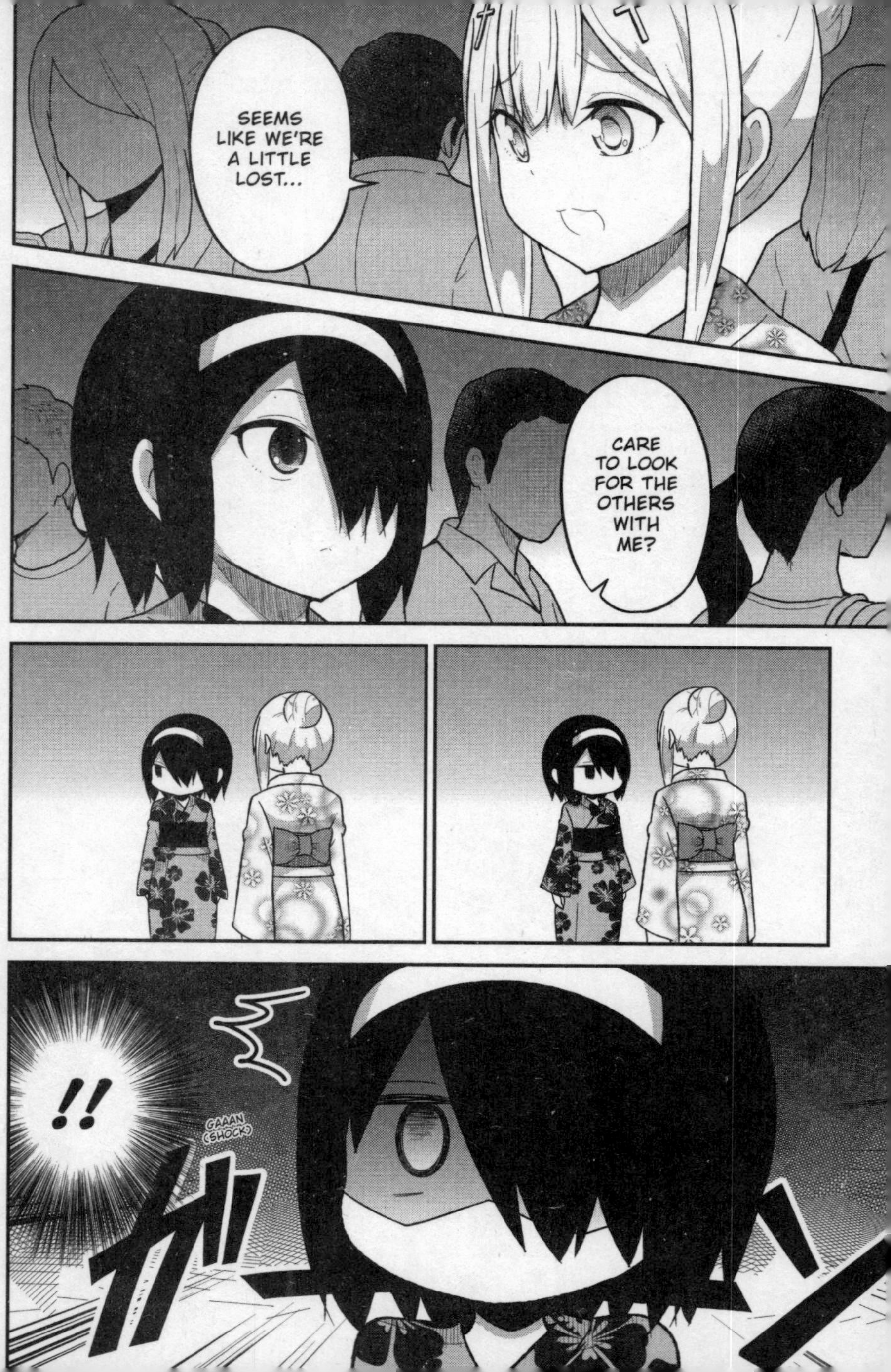
SEEMS LIKE WE'RE A LITTLE LOST...
CARE TO LOOK FOR THE OTHERS WITH ME?
!!
GAAAN (SHOCK)

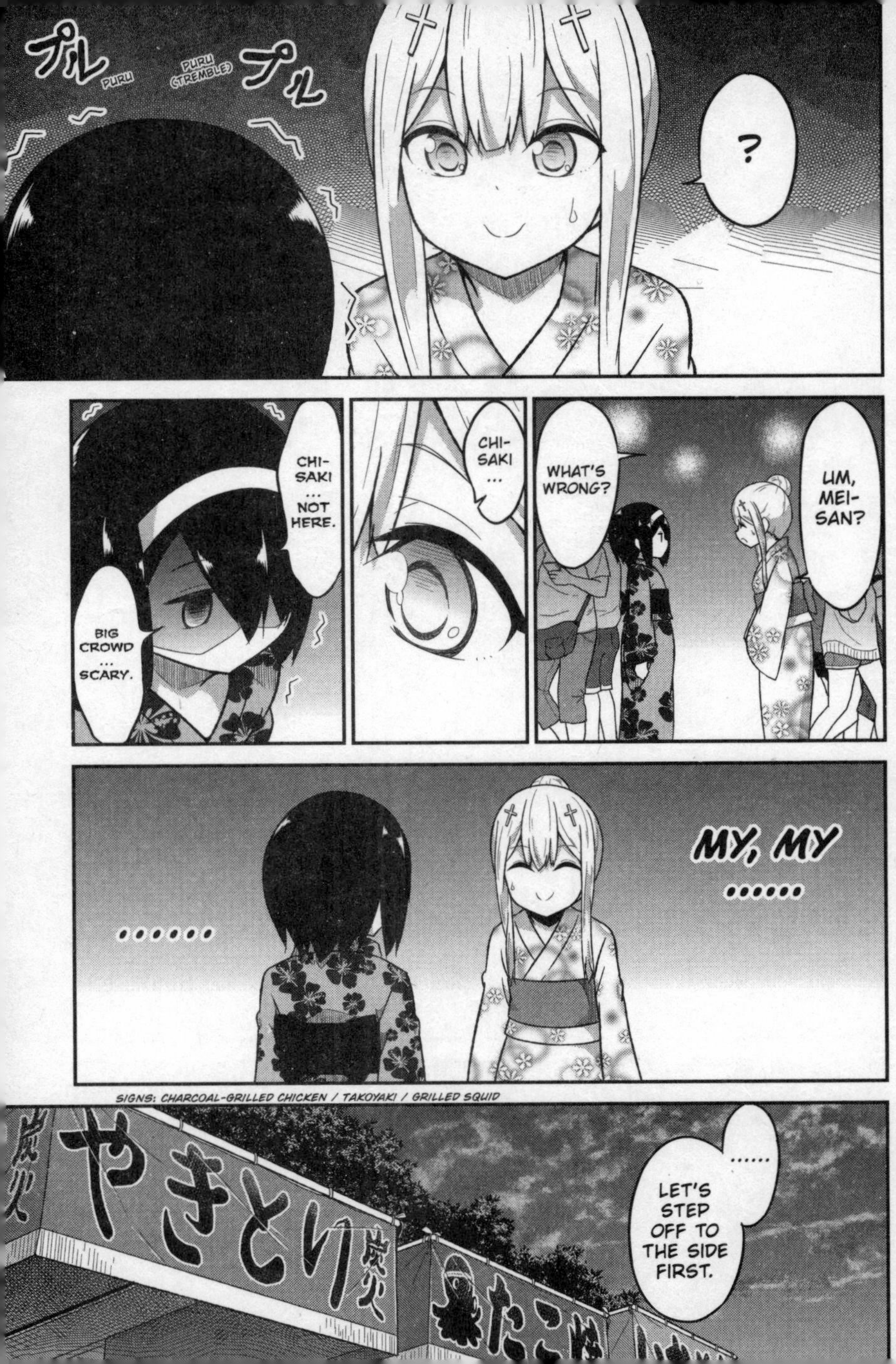

プル
PURU (TREMBLE)
プル
PURU
?
UM, MEI-SAN?
WHAT'S WRONG?
CHI-SAKI ...
CHI-SAKI ... NOT HERE.
BIG CROWD ... SCARY.
MY, MY ......
......
SIGNS: CHARCOAL-GRILLED CHICKEN / TAKOYAKI / GRILLED SQUID
炭火
やきとり
炭火
...... LET'S STEP OFF TO THE SIDE FIRST.

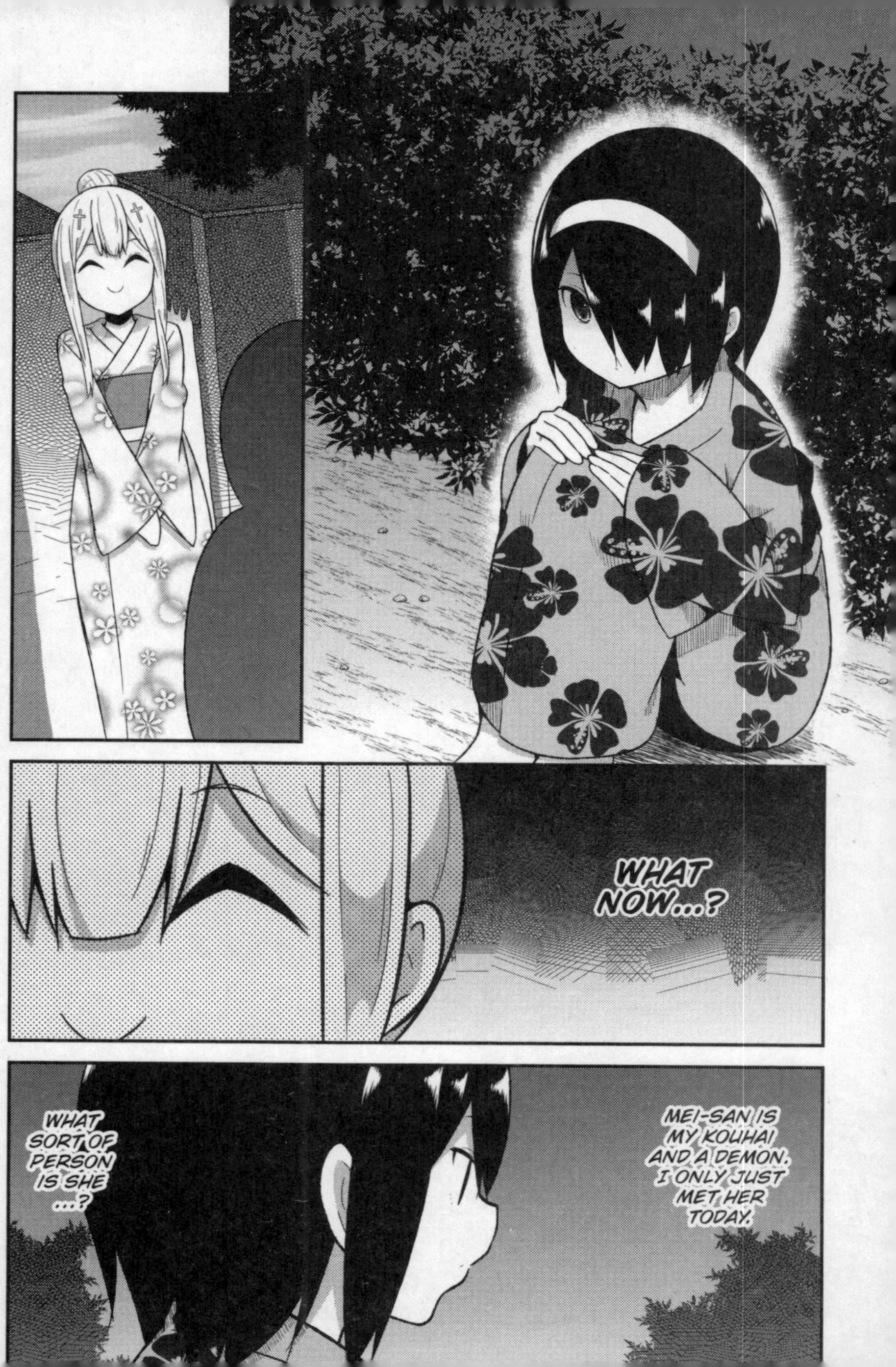
WHAT NOW...?
MEI-SAN IS MY KOUHAI AND A DEMON. I ONLY JUST MET HER TODAY.
WHAT SORT OF PERSON IS SHE ...?

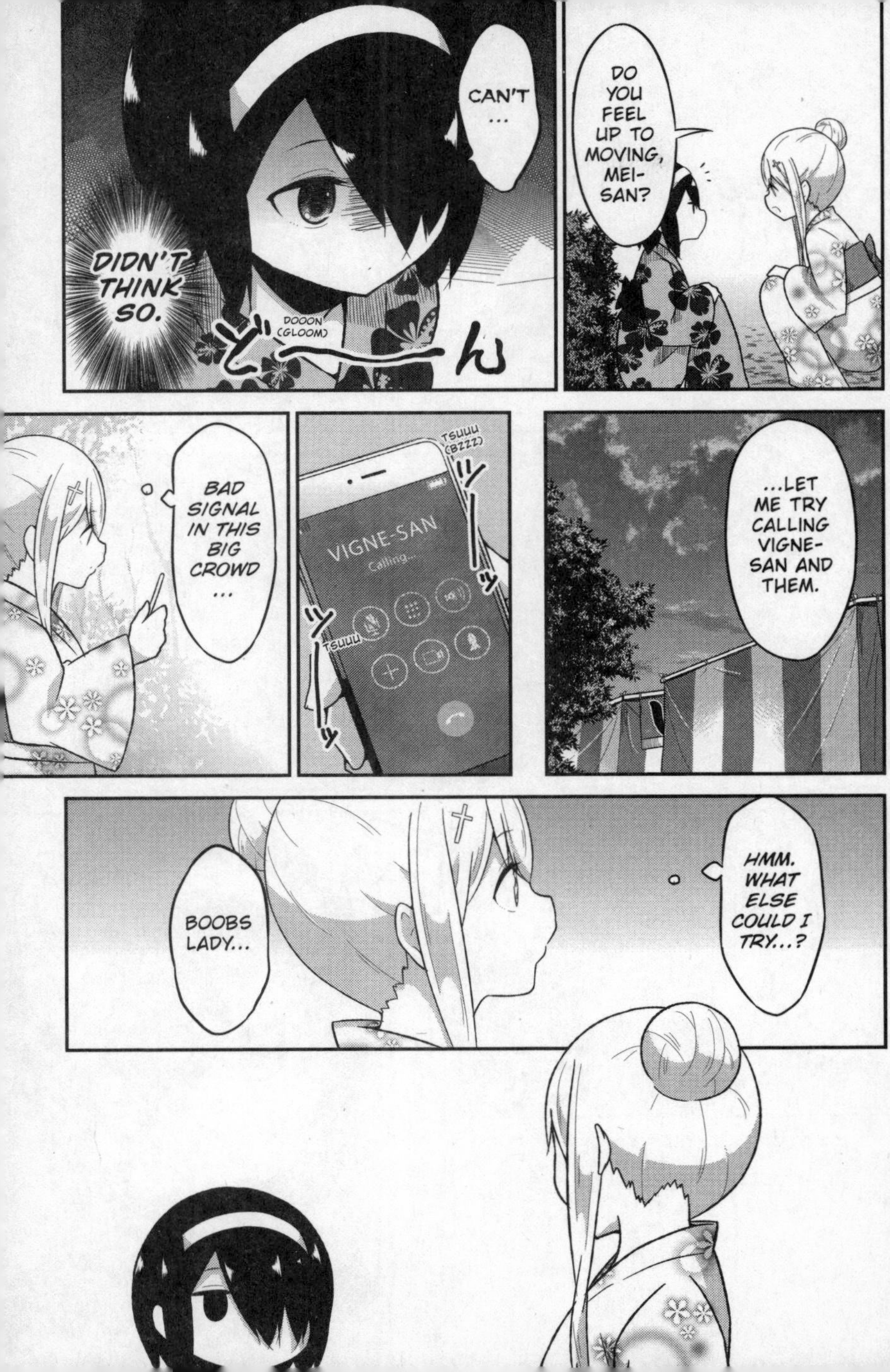
DO YOU FEEL UP TO MOVING, MEI-SAN?
CAN'T ...
DIDN'T THINK SO.
DOOON (GLOOM)
...LET ME TRY CALLING VIGNE-SAN AND THEM.
TSUUU (BZZZ)
VIGNE-SAN
Calling...
TSUUU
BAD SIGNAL IN THIS BIG CROWD ...
HMM. WHAT ELSE COULD I TRY...?
BOOBS LADY...

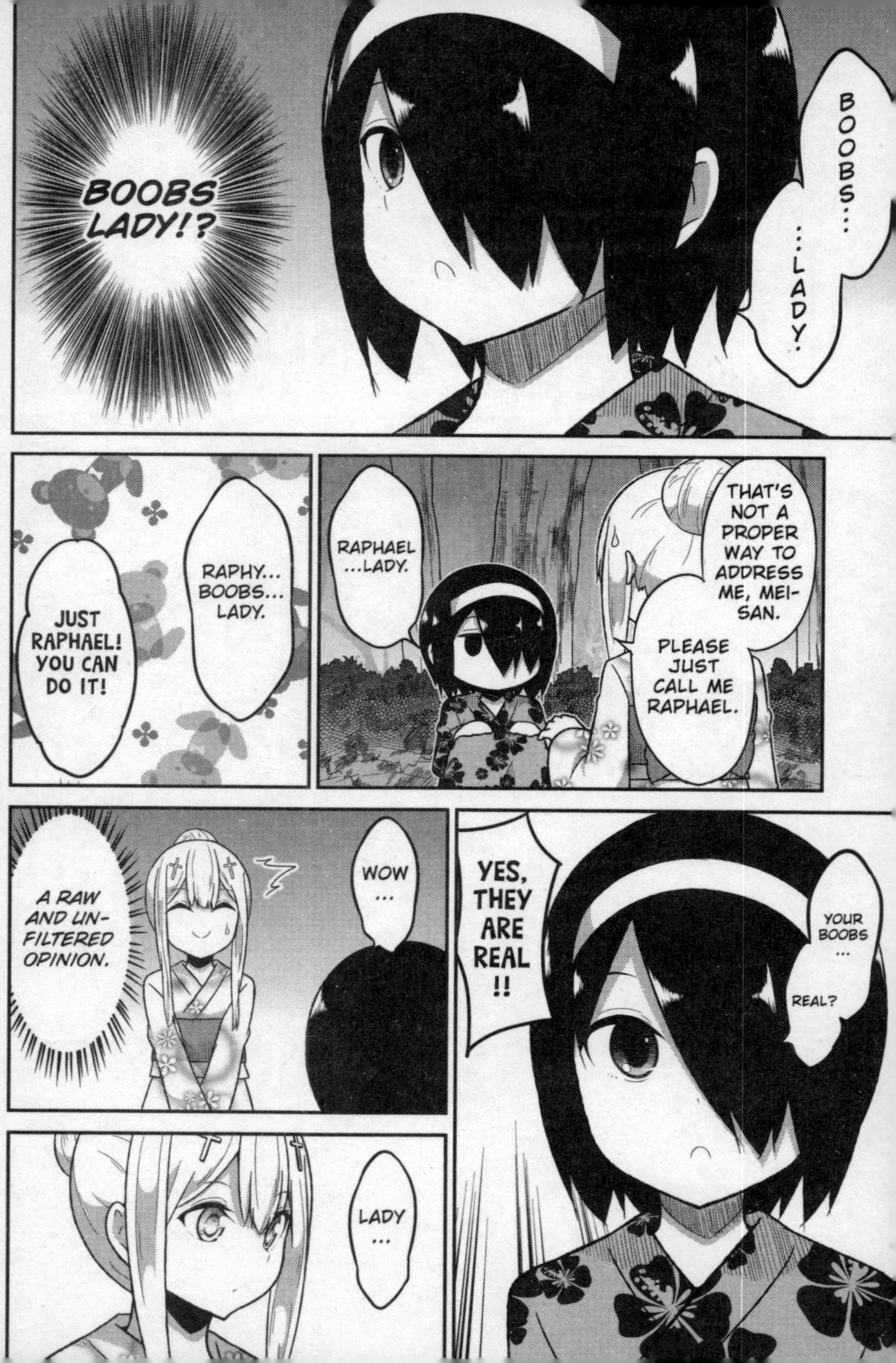
BOOBS...
...LADY.
BOOBS LADY!?
THAT'S NOT A PROPER WAY TO ADDRESS ME, MEI-SAN.
PLEASE JUST CALL ME RAPHAEL.
RAPHAEL ...LADY.
RAPHY... BOOBS... LADY.
JUST RAPHAEL! YOU CAN DO IT!
YOUR BOOBS ...
REAL?
YES, THEY ARE REAL !!
WOW ...
A RAW AND UN-FILTERED OPINION.
LADY ...

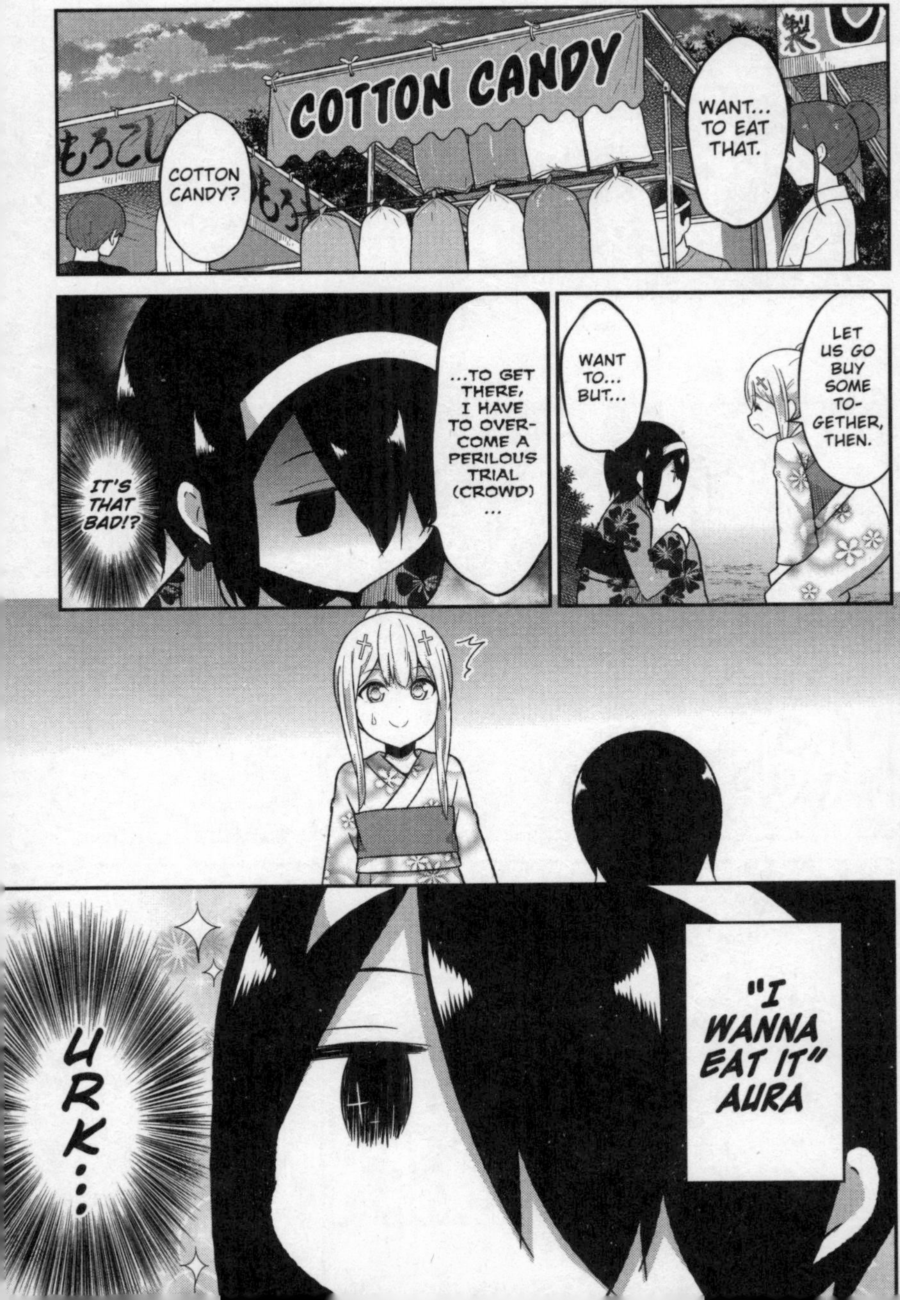
COTTON CANDY
もろこし
WANT... TO EAT THAT.
COTTON CANDY?
LET US GO BUY SOME TO-GETHER, THEN.
WANT TO... BUT...
...TO GET THERE, I HAVE TO OVER-COME A PERILOUS TRIAL (CROWD) ...
IT'S THAT BAD!?
"I WANNA EAT IT" AURA
URK...

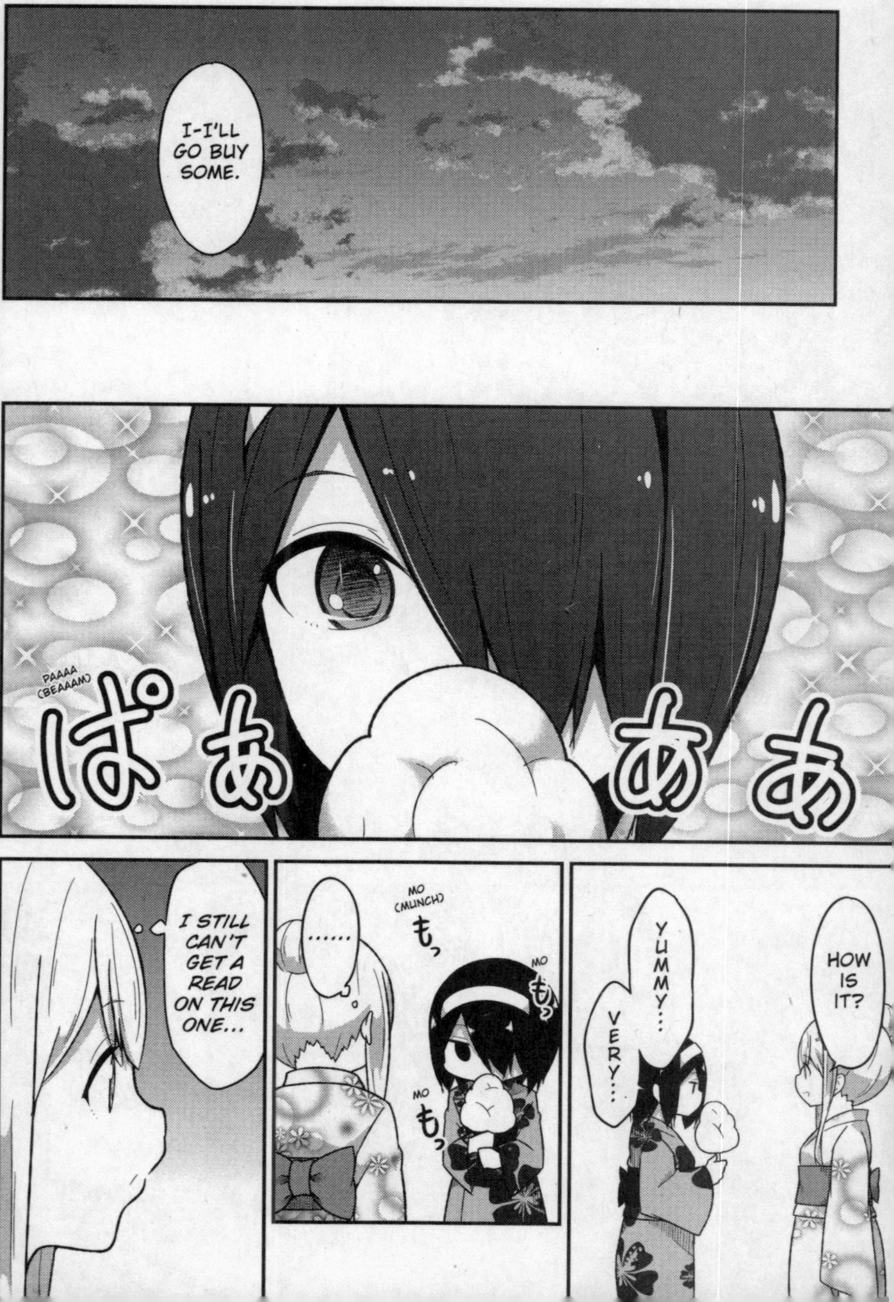
I-I'LL GO BUY SOME.
PAAAA (BEAAAM)
ぱぁああ
HOW IS IT?
YUMMY... VERY...
MO (MUNCH)
もっ
MO
もっ
MO
もっ
......
I STILL CAN'T GET A READ ON THIS ONE...

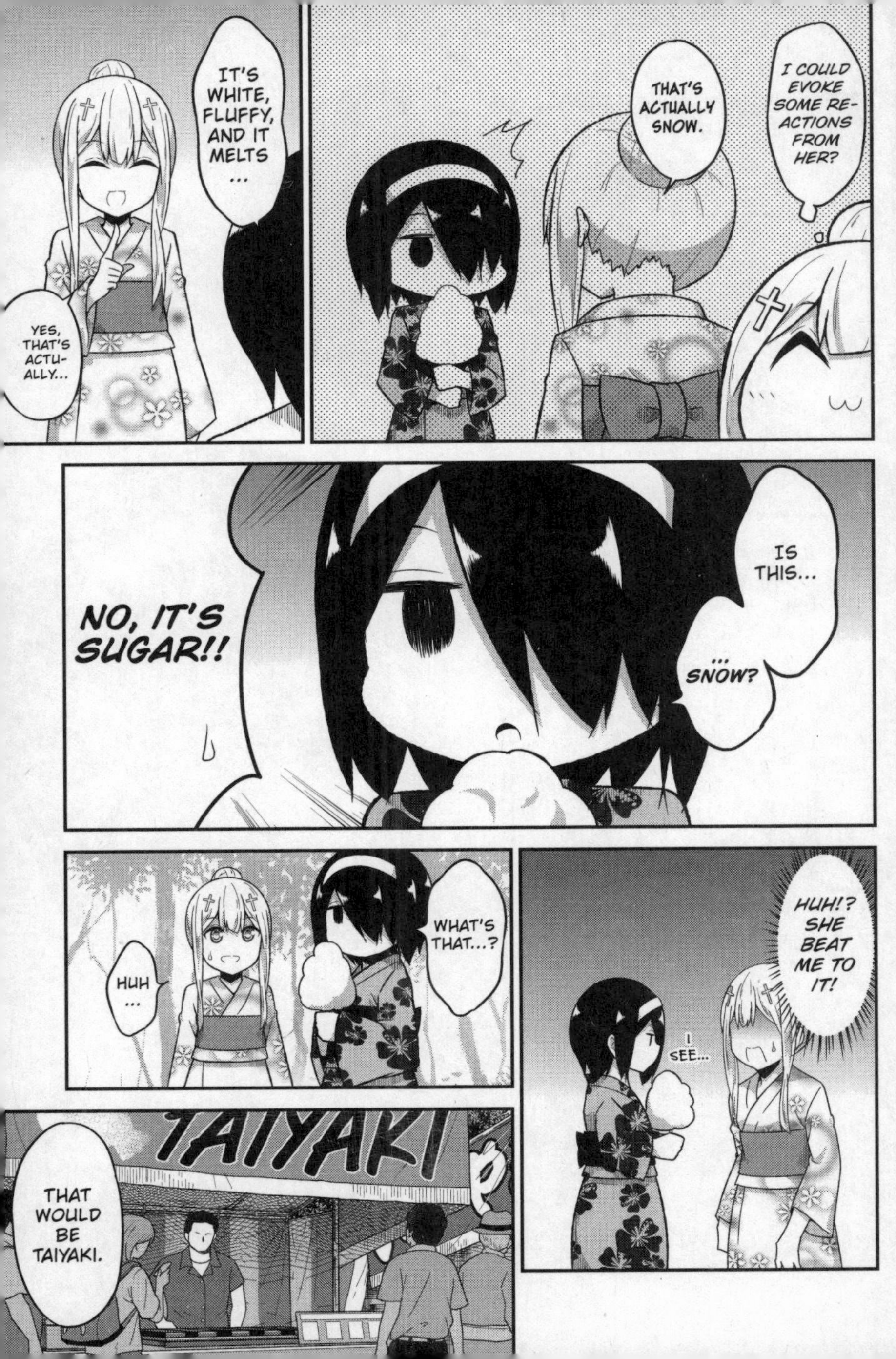
I COULD EVOKE SOME RE-ACTIONS FROM HER?
THAT'S ACTUALLY SNOW.
IT'S WHITE, FLUFFY, AND IT MELTS ...
YES, THAT'S ACTU-ALLY...
IS THIS...
... SNOW?
NO, IT'S SUGAR!!
HUH!? SHE BEAT ME TO IT!
I SEE...
WHAT'S THAT...?
HUH ...
TAIYAKI
THAT WOULD BE TAIYAKI.

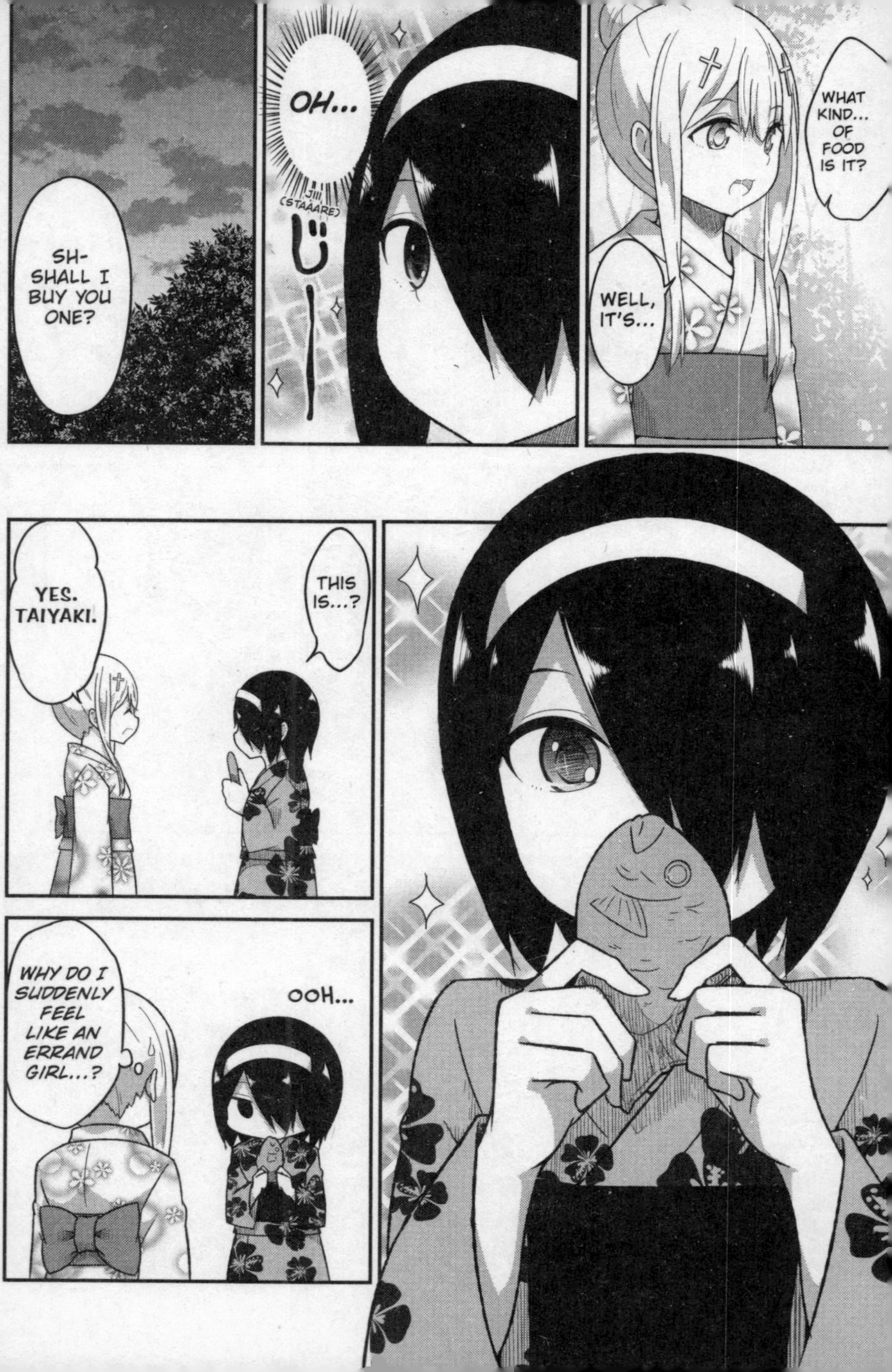
WHAT KIND... OF FOOD IS IT?
WELL, IT'S...
OH...
じー
JIII (STAAARE)
SH-SHALL I BUY YOU ONE?
THIS IS...?
YES. TAIYAKI.
OOH...
WHY DO I SUDDENLY FEEL LIKE AN ERRAND GIRL...?

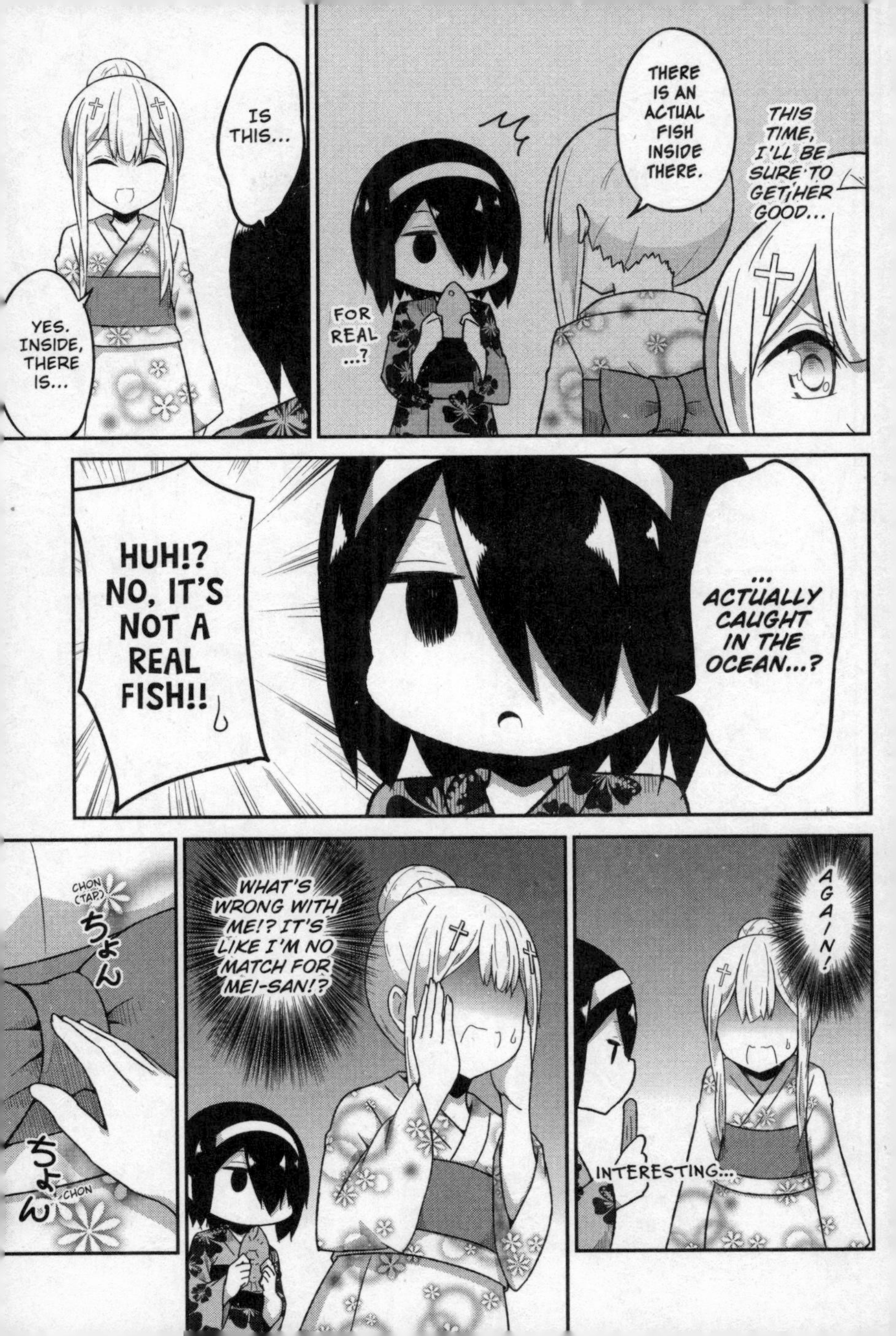
THIS TIME, I'LL BE SURE TO GET HER GOOD...
THERE IS AN ACTUAL FISH INSIDE THERE.
FOR REAL ...?
IS THIS...
YES. INSIDE, THERE IS...
... ACTUALLY CAUGHT IN THE OCEAN...?
HUH!? NO, IT'S NOT A REAL FISH!!
AGAIN!
INTERESTING...
WHAT'S WRONG WITH ME!? IT'S LIKE I'M NO MATCH FOR MEI-SAN!?
CHON (TAP)
ちょん
ちょん
CHON

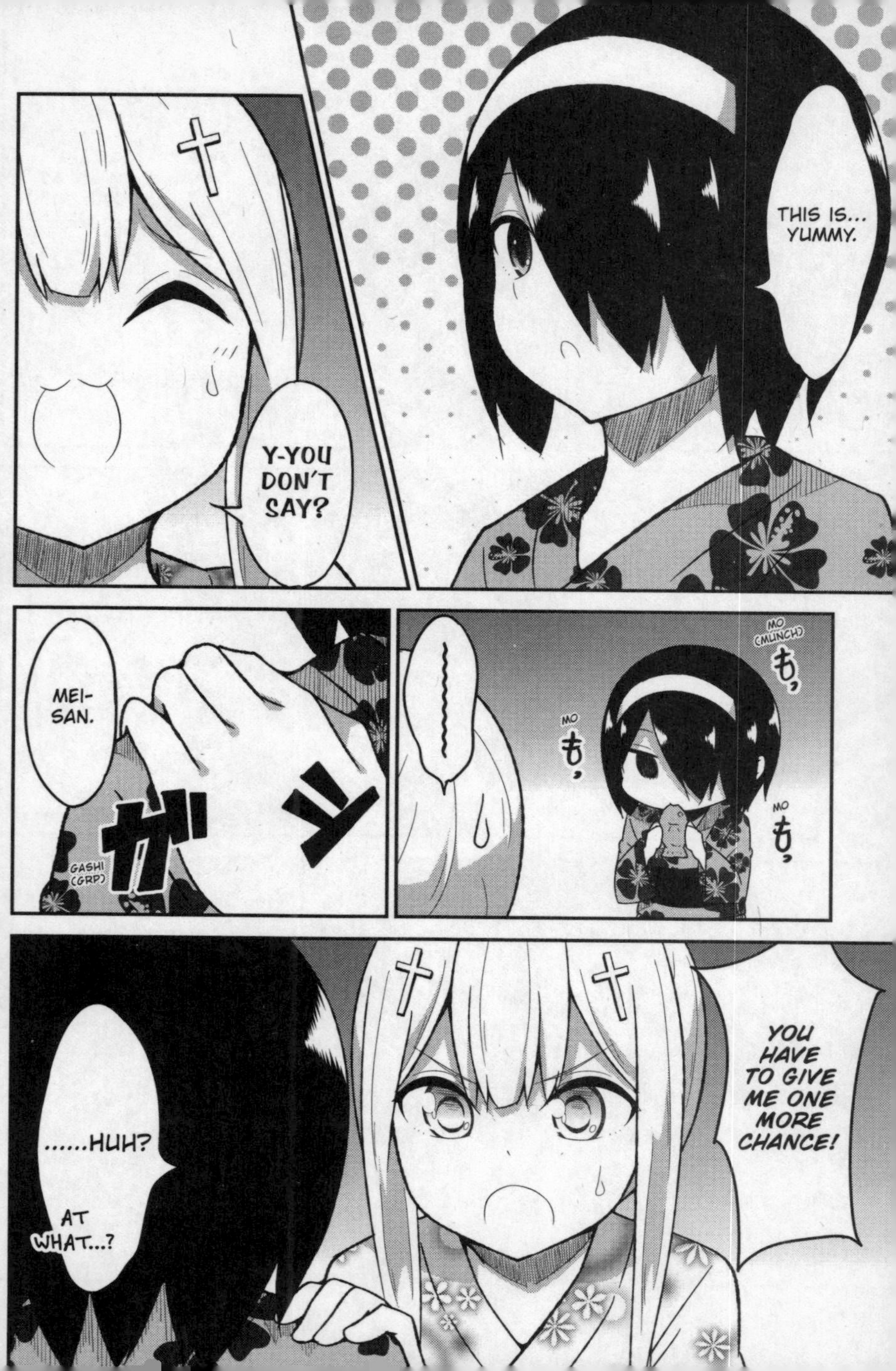
THIS IS... YUMMY.
Y-YOU DON'T SAY?
MO (MUNCH) も,
MO も,
MO も,
MEI-SAN.
ガッ
GASHI (GRP)
YOU HAVE TO GIVE ME ONE MORE CHANCE!
......HUH?
AT WHAT...?

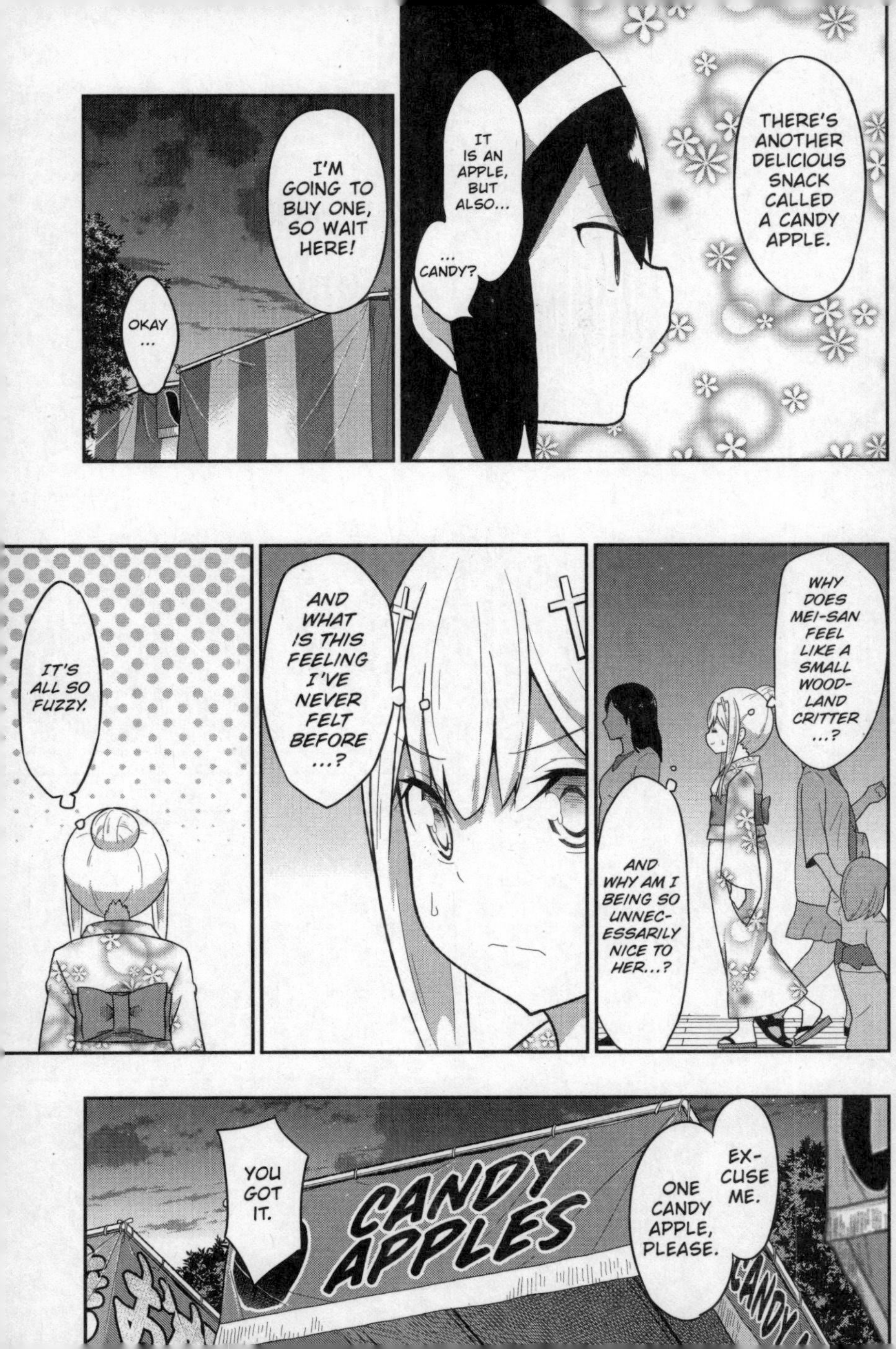
THERE'S ANOTHER DELICIOUS SNACK CALLED A CANDY APPLE.
IT IS AN APPLE, BUT ALSO...
... CANDY?
I'M GOING TO BUY ONE, SO WAIT HERE!
OKAY ...
WHY DOES MEI-SAN FEEL LIKE A SMALL WOOD-LAND CRITTER ...?
AND WHY AM I BEING SO UNNEC-ESSARILY NICE TO HER...?
AND WHAT IS THIS FEELING I'VE NEVER FELT BEFORE ...?
IT'S ALL SO FUZZY.
EX-CUSE ME.
ONE CANDY APPLE, PLEASE.
YOU GOT IT.
CANDY APPLES

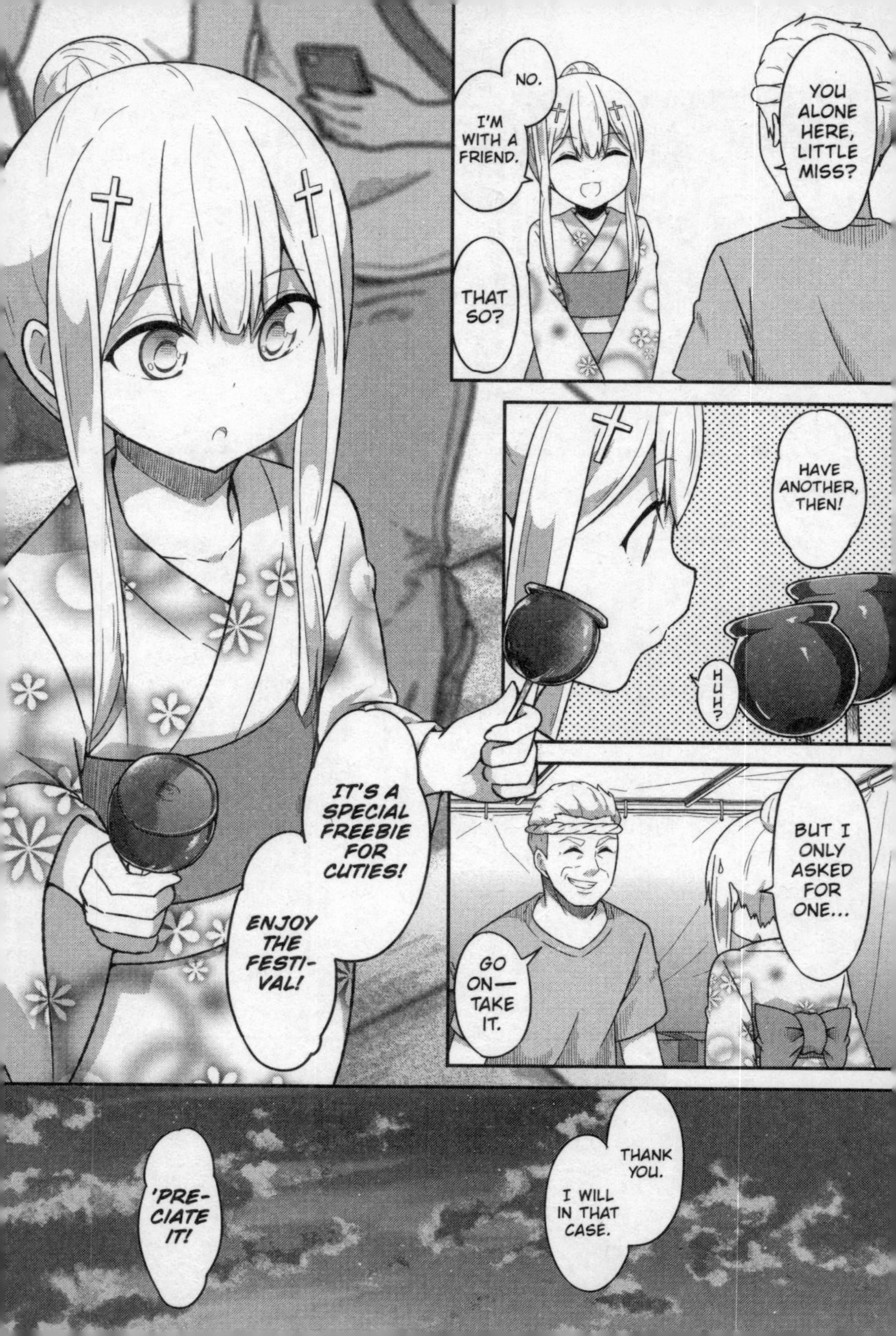
YOU ALONE HERE, LITTLE MISS?
NO.
I'M WITH A FRIEND.
THAT SO?
HAVE ANOTHER, THEN!
HUH?
BUT I ONLY ASKED FOR ONE...
GO ON—TAKE IT.
IT'S A SPECIAL FREEBIE FOR CUTIES!
ENJOY THE FESTI-VAL!
THANK YOU.
I WILL IN THAT CASE.
'PRE-CIATE IT!

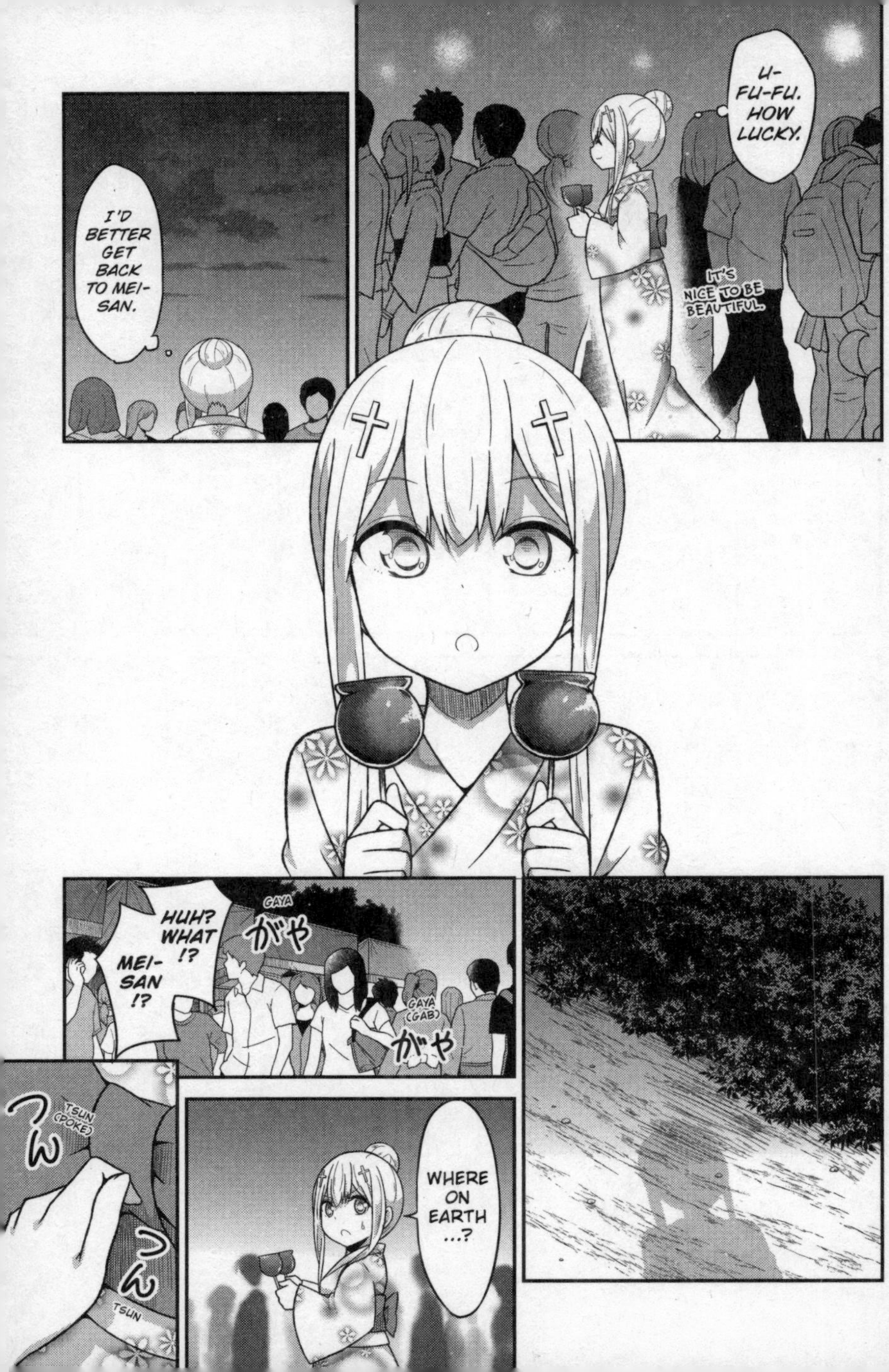
U-FU-FU. HOW LUCKY.
IT'S NICE TO BE BEAUTIFUL.
I'D BETTER GET BACK TO MEI-SAN.
GAYA
がや
HUH? WHAT!?
MEI-SAN!?
GAYA (GAB)
がや
WHERE ON EARTH ...?
TSUN (POKE)
つん
つん
TSUN

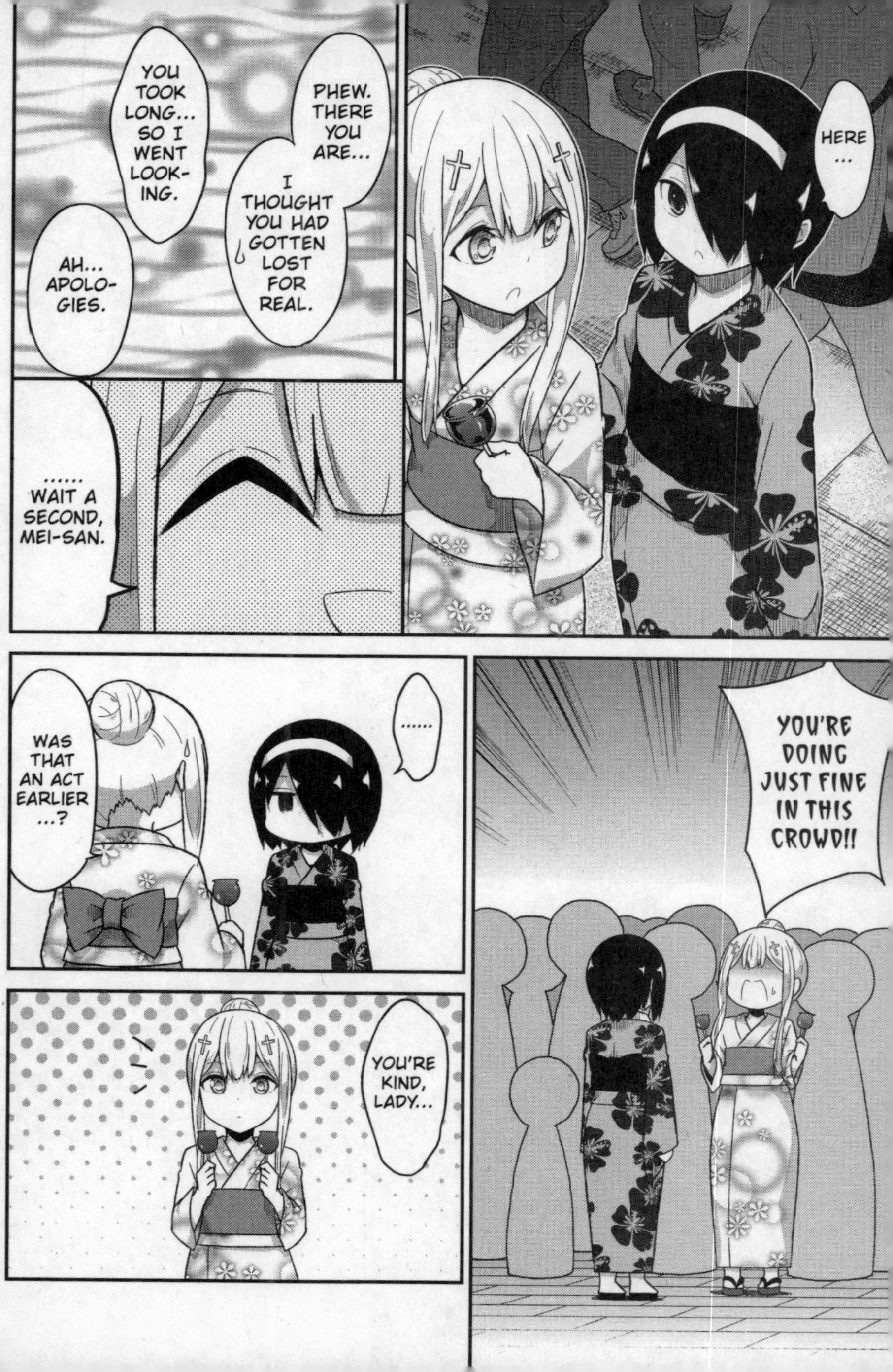
HERE ...
PHEW. THERE YOU ARE...
I THOUGHT YOU HAD GOTTEN LOST FOR REAL.
YOU TOOK LONG... SO I WENT LOOKING.
AH... APOLOGIES.
...... WAIT A SECOND, MEI-SAN.
YOU'RE DOING JUST FINE IN THIS CROWD!!
......
WAS THAT AN ACT EARLIER ...?
YOU'RE KIND, LADY...

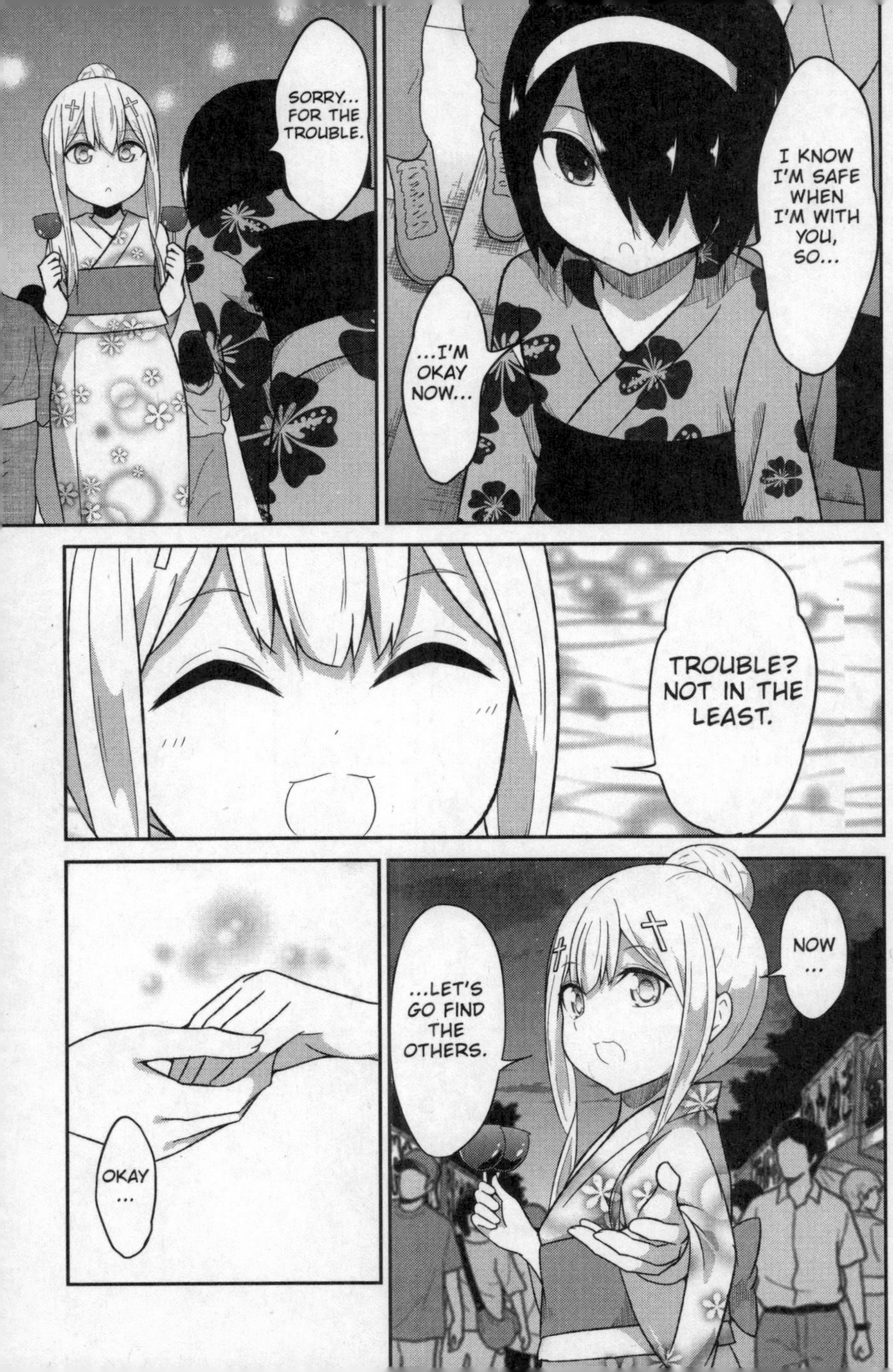
I KNOW I'M SAFE WHEN I'M WITH YOU, SO...
...I'M OKAY NOW...
SORRY... FOR THE TROUBLE.
TROUBLE? NOT IN THE LEAST.
NOW ...
...LET'S GO FIND THE OTHERS.
OKAY ...

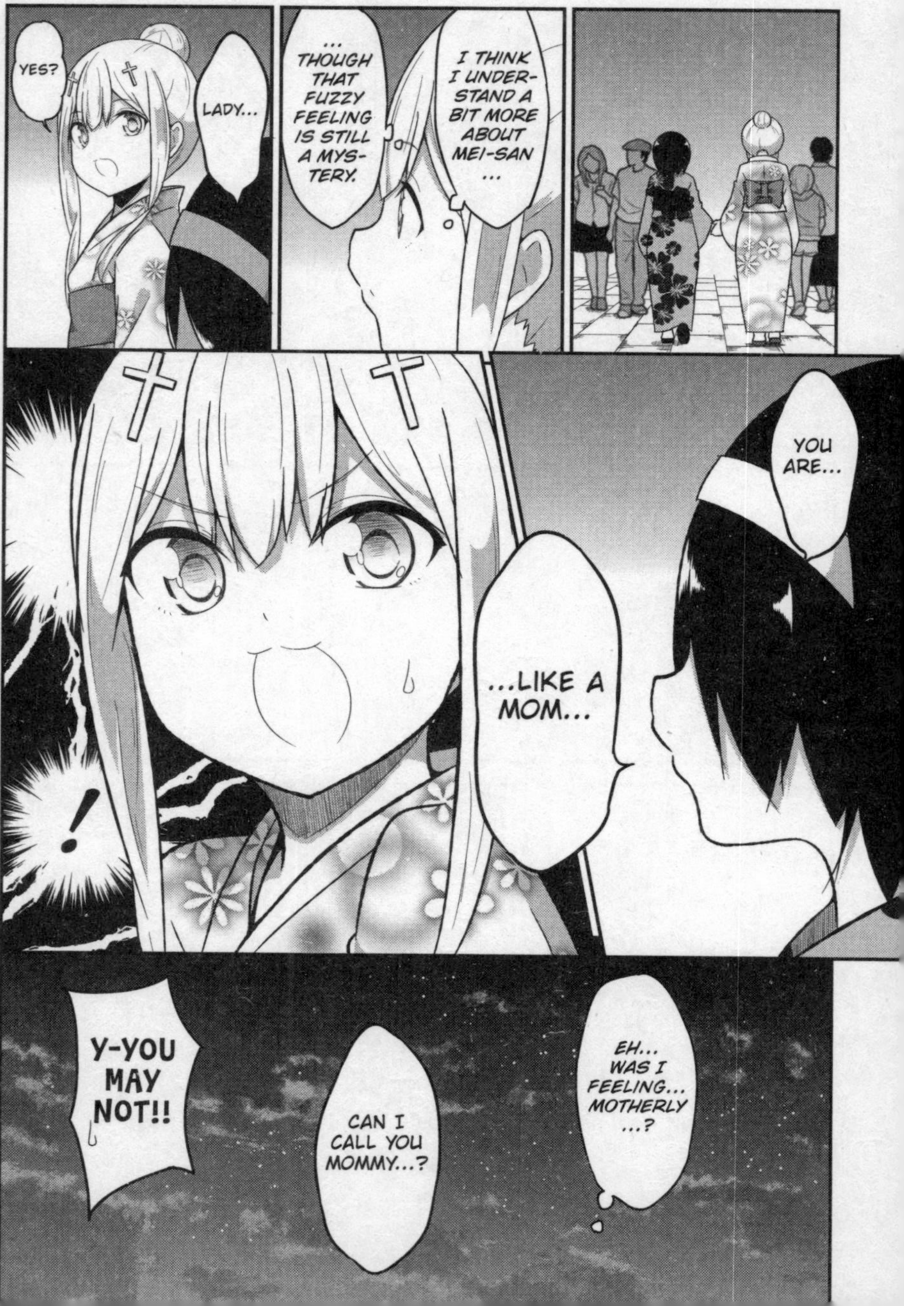
I THINK I UNDER-STAND A BIT MORE ABOUT MEI-SAN...
...THOUGH THAT FUZZY FEELING IS STILL A MYS-TERY.
LADY...
YES?
YOU ARE...
...LIKE A MOM...
!
EH... WAS I FEELING... MOTHERLY...?
CAN I CALL YOU MOMMY...?
Y-YOU MAY NOT!!

MAMA RAPHY

DINNER'S ALMOST READY.

Gabriel DropOut

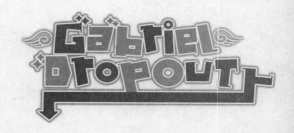

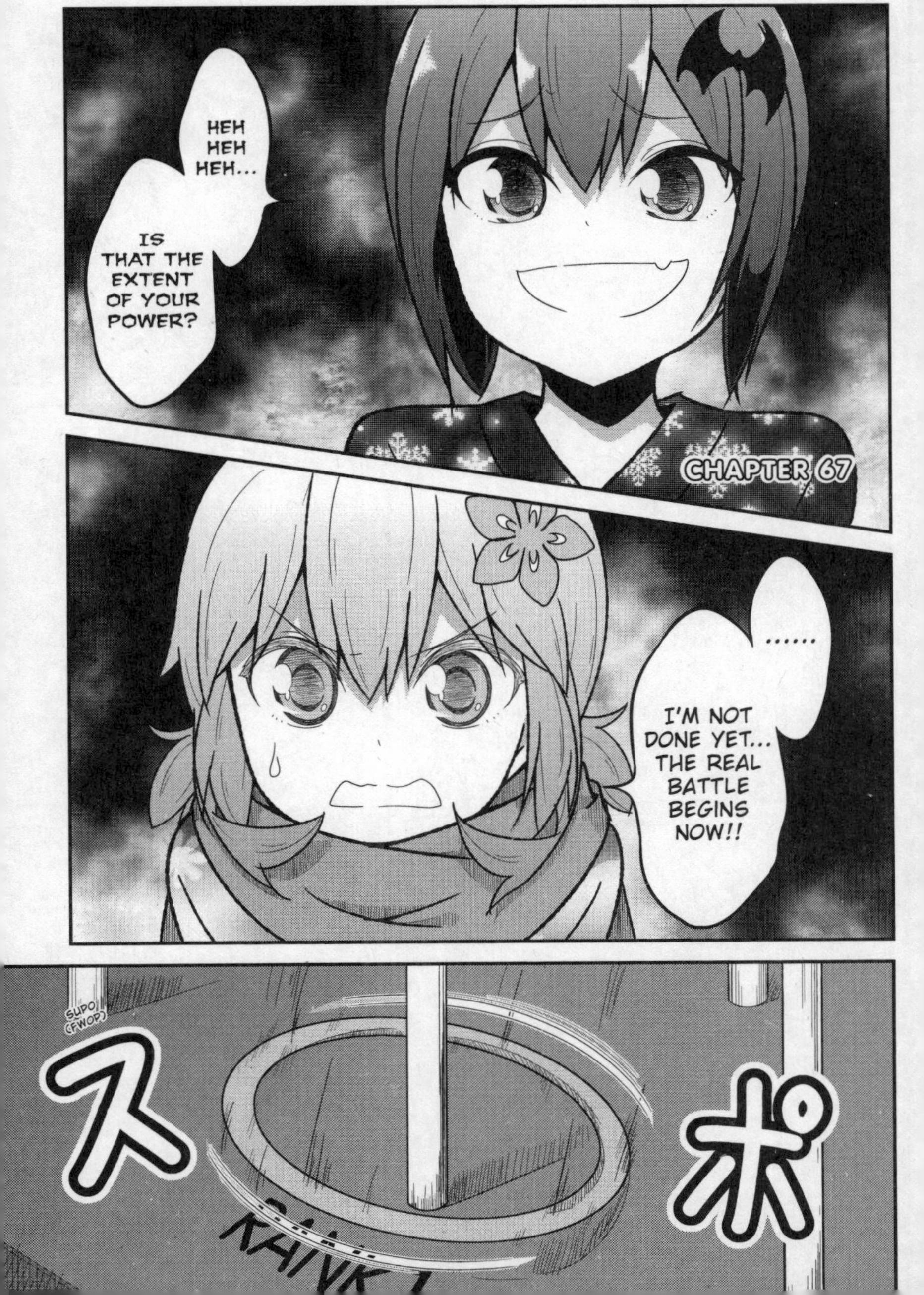
HEH HEH HEH...
IS THAT THE EXTENT OF YOUR POWER?
CHAPTER 67
......
I'M NOT DONE YET... THE REAL BATTLE BEGINS NOW!!
SUPO (FWOP)
スポ

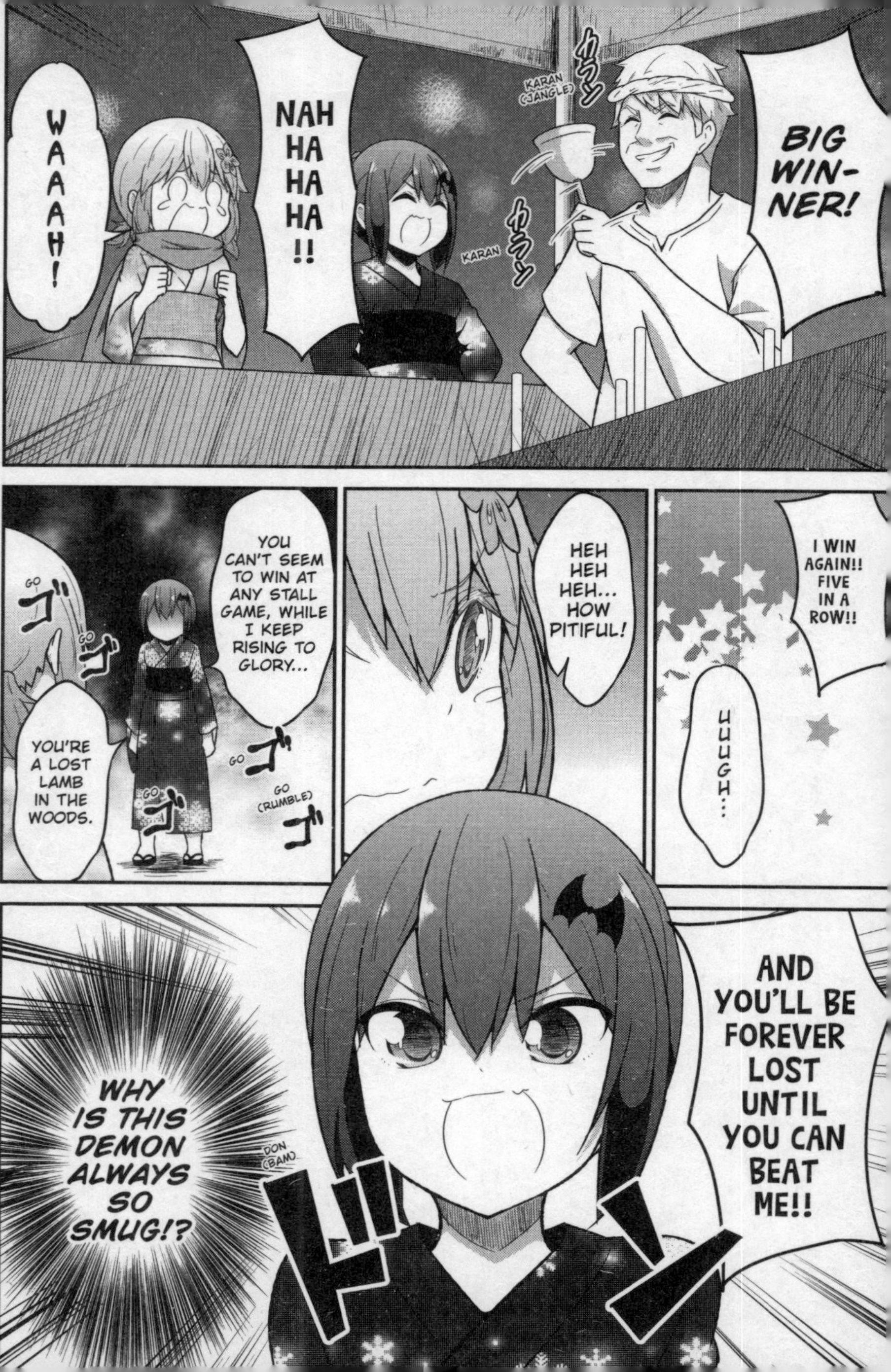

BIG WIN-NER!
KARAN (JANGLE)
KARAN
NAH HA HA HA!!
WAAAAH!
I WIN AGAIN!! FIVE IN A ROW!!
UUUGH...
HEH HEH HEH... HOW PITIFUL!
YOU CAN'T SEEM TO WIN AT ANY STALL GAME, WHILE I KEEP RISING TO GLORY...
GO
GO
YOU'RE A LOST LAMB IN THE WOODS.
GO
GO
GO (RUMBLE)
AND YOU'LL BE FOREVER LOST UNTIL YOU CAN BEAT ME!!
DON (BAM)
WHY IS THIS DEMON ALWAYS SO SMUG!?

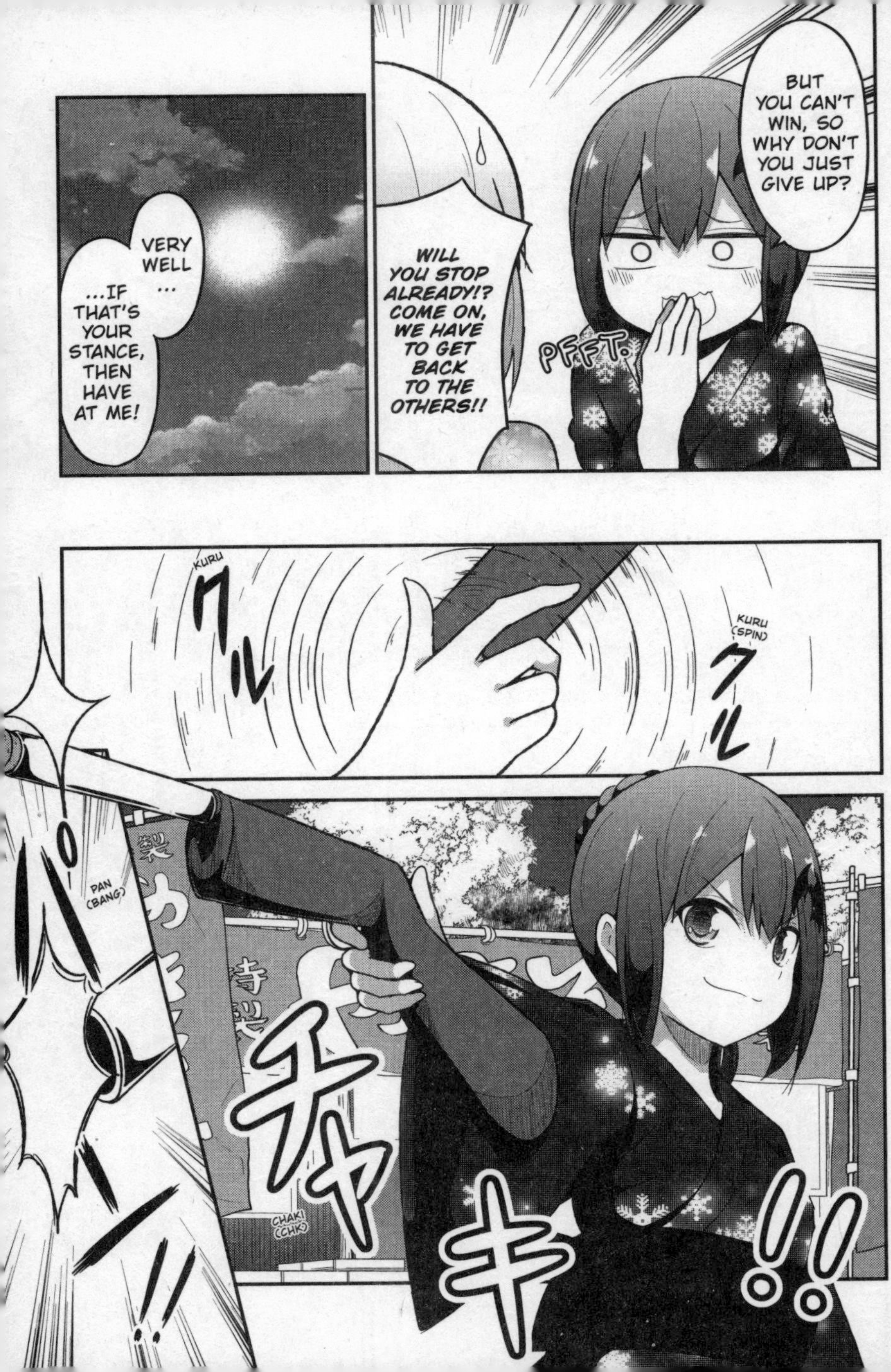
BUT YOU CAN'T WIN, SO WHY DON'T YOU JUST GIVE UP?
WILL YOU STOP ALREADY!? COME ON, WE HAVE TO GET BACK TO THE OTHERS!!
PFFT.
VERY WELL...
...IF THAT'S YOUR STANCE, THEN HAVE AT ME!
KURU (SPIN)
KURU
CHAKI (CHK)
PAN (BANG)

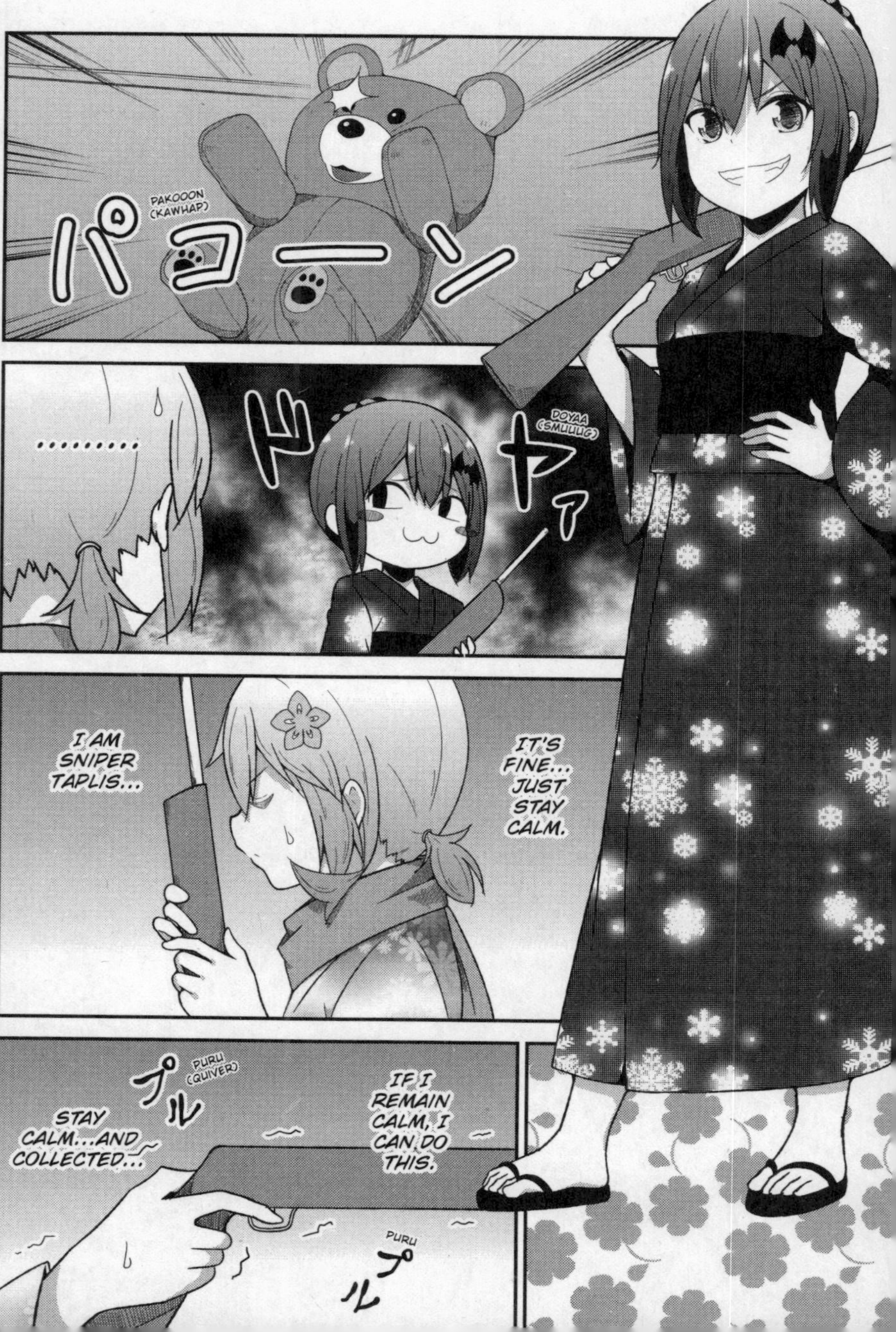
PAKOOON (KAWHAP)
パコーーン
DOYAA (SMUUUG)
ドヤァ
....
IT'S FINE... JUST STAY CALM.
I AM SNIPER TAPLIS...
IF I REMAIN CALM, I CAN DO THIS.
PURU (QUIVER)
プル
STAY CALM...AND COLLECTED...
PURU
プル

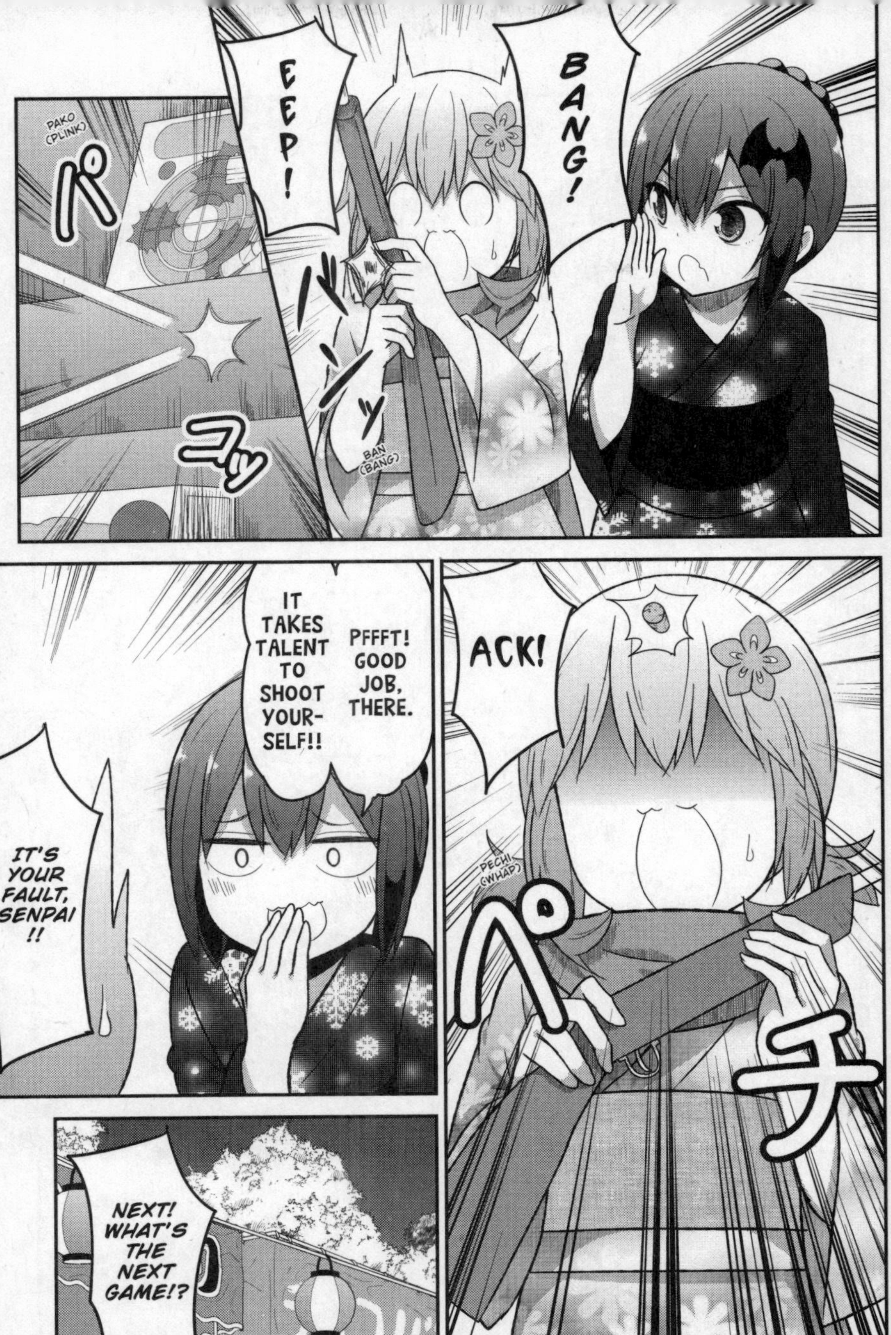
BANG!
EEP!
PAKO (PLINK)
BAN (BANG)
ACK!
PECHI (WHAP)
PFFFT! GOOD JOB, THERE.
IT TAKES TALENT TO SHOOT YOURSELF!!
IT'S YOUR FAULT, SENPAI!!
NEXT! WHAT'S THE NEXT GAME!?

OKAY! I'M FEELING GOOD ABOUT THIS...

パキ...
(PAK!)

パキ...
(PAK! KRK)

KATANUKI

プル
(PURU QUIVER)

プル
(PURU)

JUST A LITTLE MORE...

F
W
A
A
A
A
H.

F
W
U
U
U
U
H.

ベキッ
(BAKI KRAK)

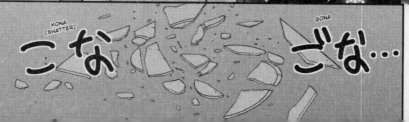

こな
(KONA SHATTER)

ごな...
(GONA)

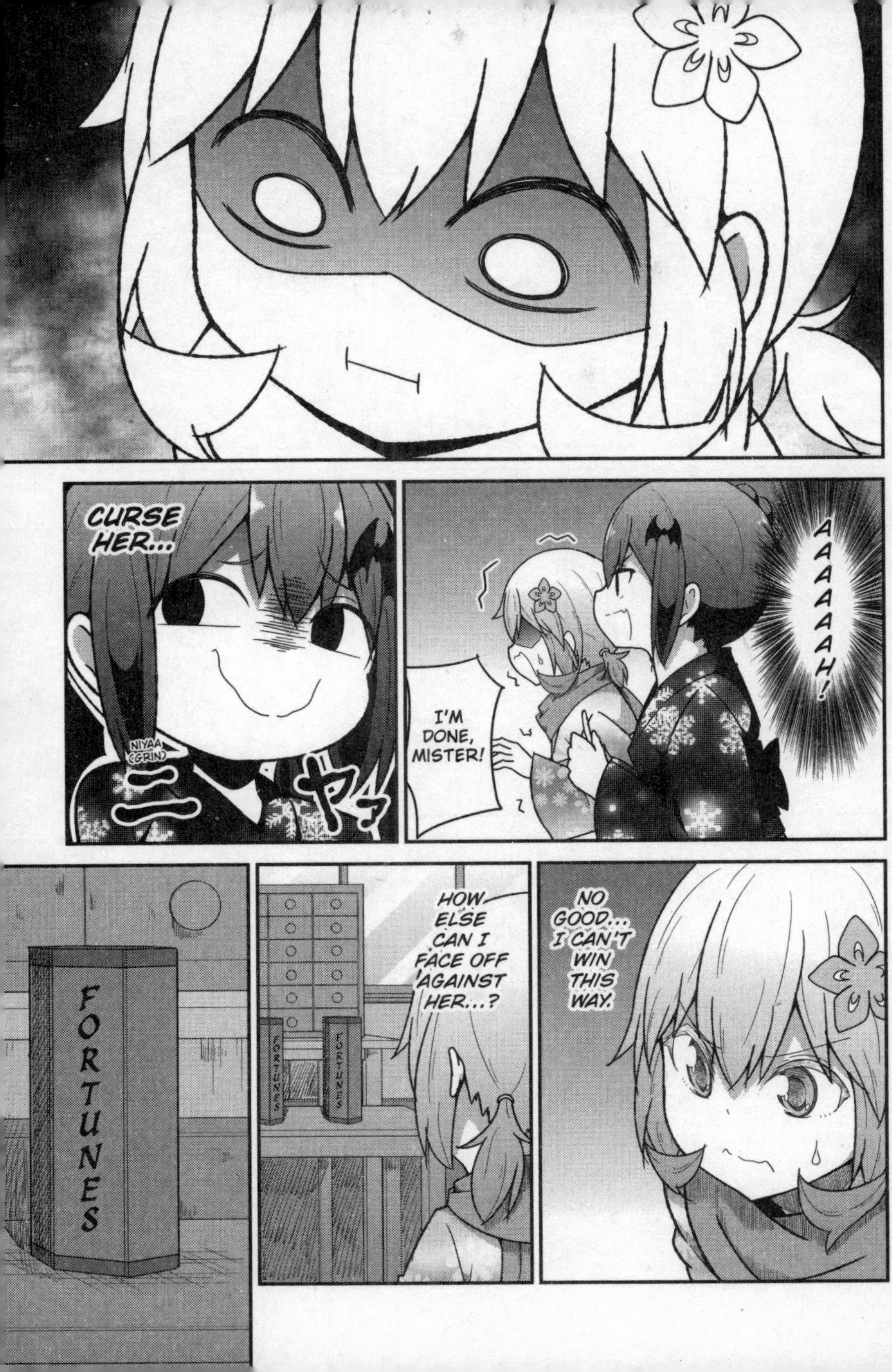
AAAAAAAH!
I'M DONE, MISTER!
CURSE HER...
ニヤッ
NIYAA (GRIN)
NO GOOD... I CAN'T WIN THIS WAY.
HOW ELSE CAN I FACE OFF AGAINST HER...?
FORTUNES
FORTUNES
FORTUNES

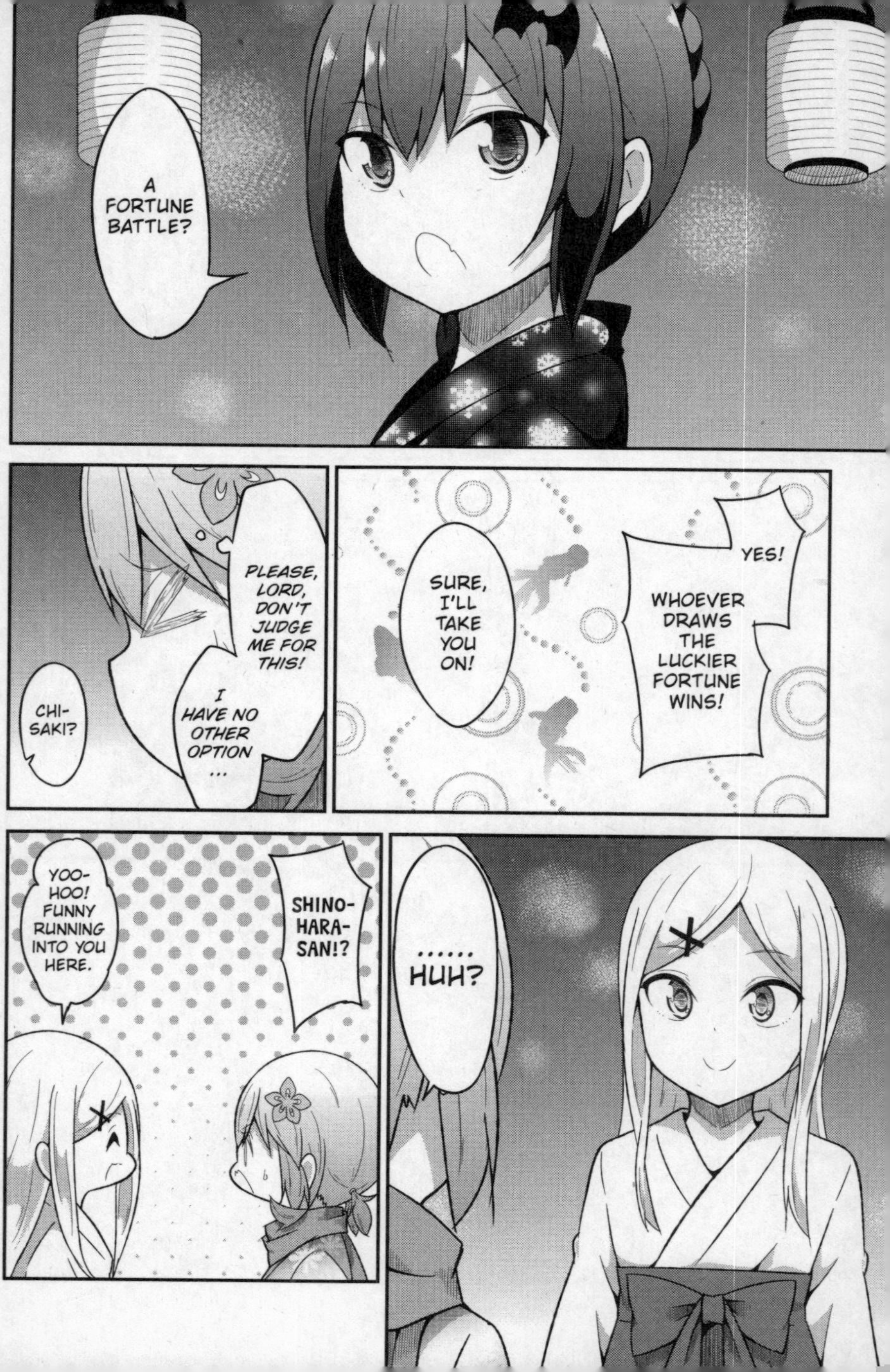
A FORTUNE BATTLE?
YES!
WHOEVER DRAWS THE LUCKIER FORTUNE WINS!
SURE, I'LL TAKE YOU ON!
PLEASE, LORD, DON'T JUDGE ME FOR THIS!
I HAVE NO OTHER OPTION...
CHI-SAKI?
......HUH?
SHINO-HARA-SAN!?
YOO-HOO! FUNNY RUNNING INTO YOU HERE.

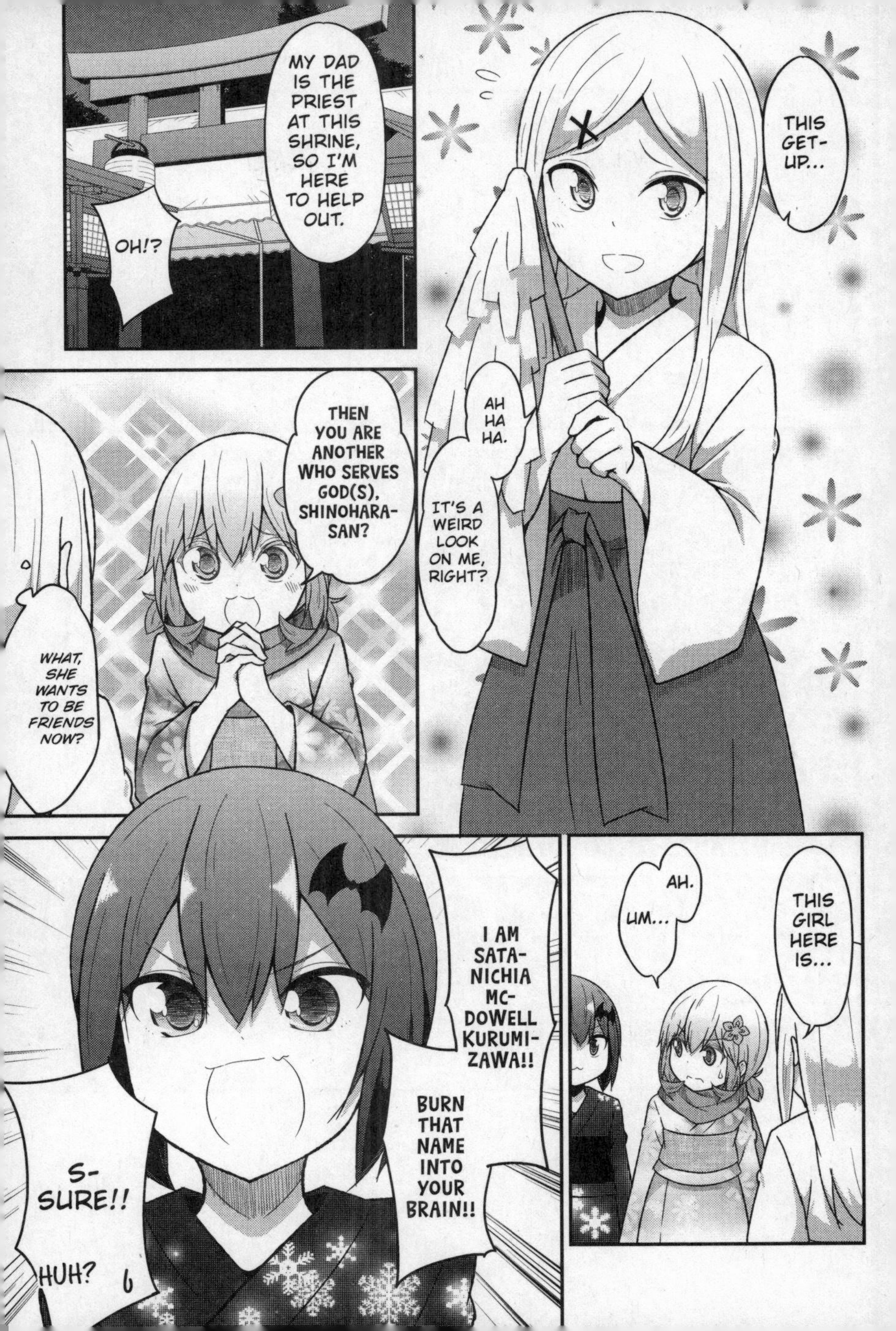
THIS GET-UP...
AH HA HA.
IT'S A WEIRD LOOK ON ME, RIGHT?
MY DAD IS THE PRIEST AT THIS SHRINE, SO I'M HERE TO HELP OUT.
OH!?
THEN YOU ARE ANOTHER WHO SERVES GOD(S), SHINOHARA-SAN?
WHAT, SHE WANTS TO BE FRIENDS NOW?
THIS GIRL HERE IS...
AH.
UM...
I AM SATANICHIA MCDOWELL KURUMIZAWA!!
BURN THAT NAME INTO YOUR BRAIN!!
S-SURE!!
HUH?

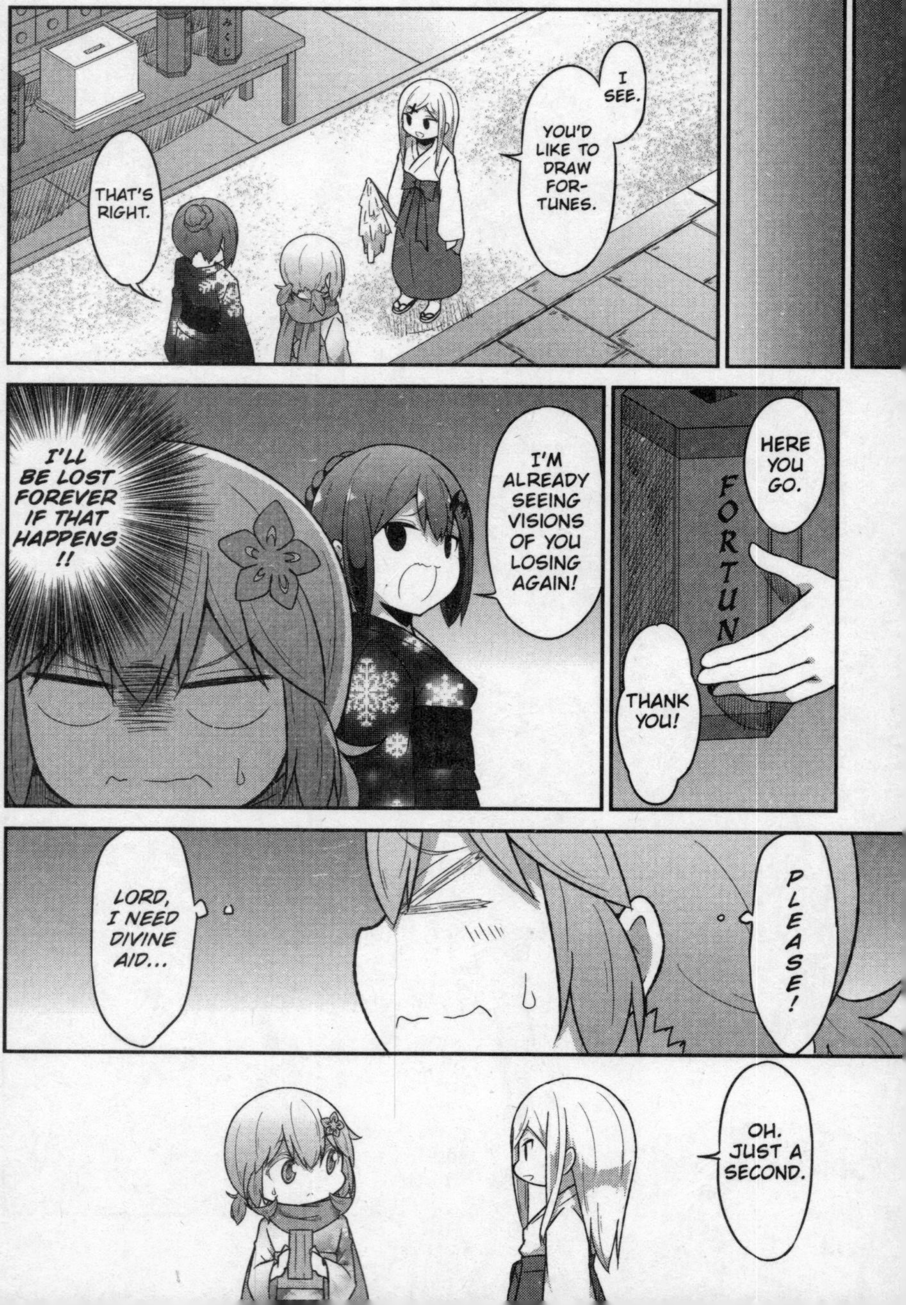

I SEE.
YOU'D LIKE TO DRAW FOR-TUNES.
THAT'S RIGHT.
HERE YOU GO.
FORTUN
THANK YOU!
I'M ALREADY SEEING VISIONS OF YOU LOSING AGAIN!
I'LL BE LOST FOREVER IF THAT HAPPENS!!
PLEASE!
LORD, I NEED DIVINE AID...
OH. JUST A SECOND.

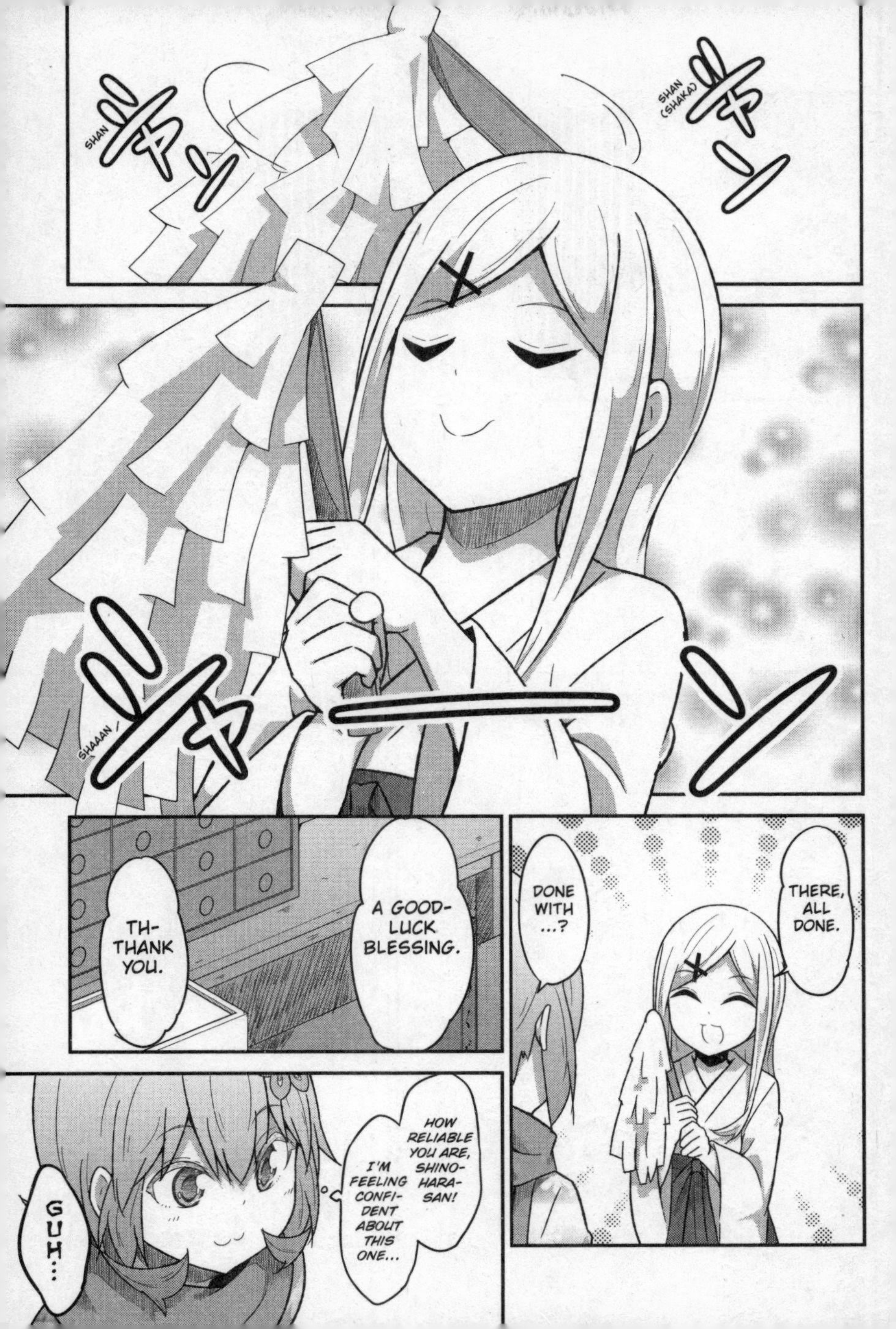
SHAN (SHAKA)
SHAN
SHAAAN
THERE, ALL DONE.
DONE WITH ...?
A GOOD-LUCK BLESSING.
TH-THANK YOU.
HOW RELIABLE YOU ARE, SHINOHARA-SAN!
I'M FEELING CONFIDENT ABOUT THIS ONE...
GUH...

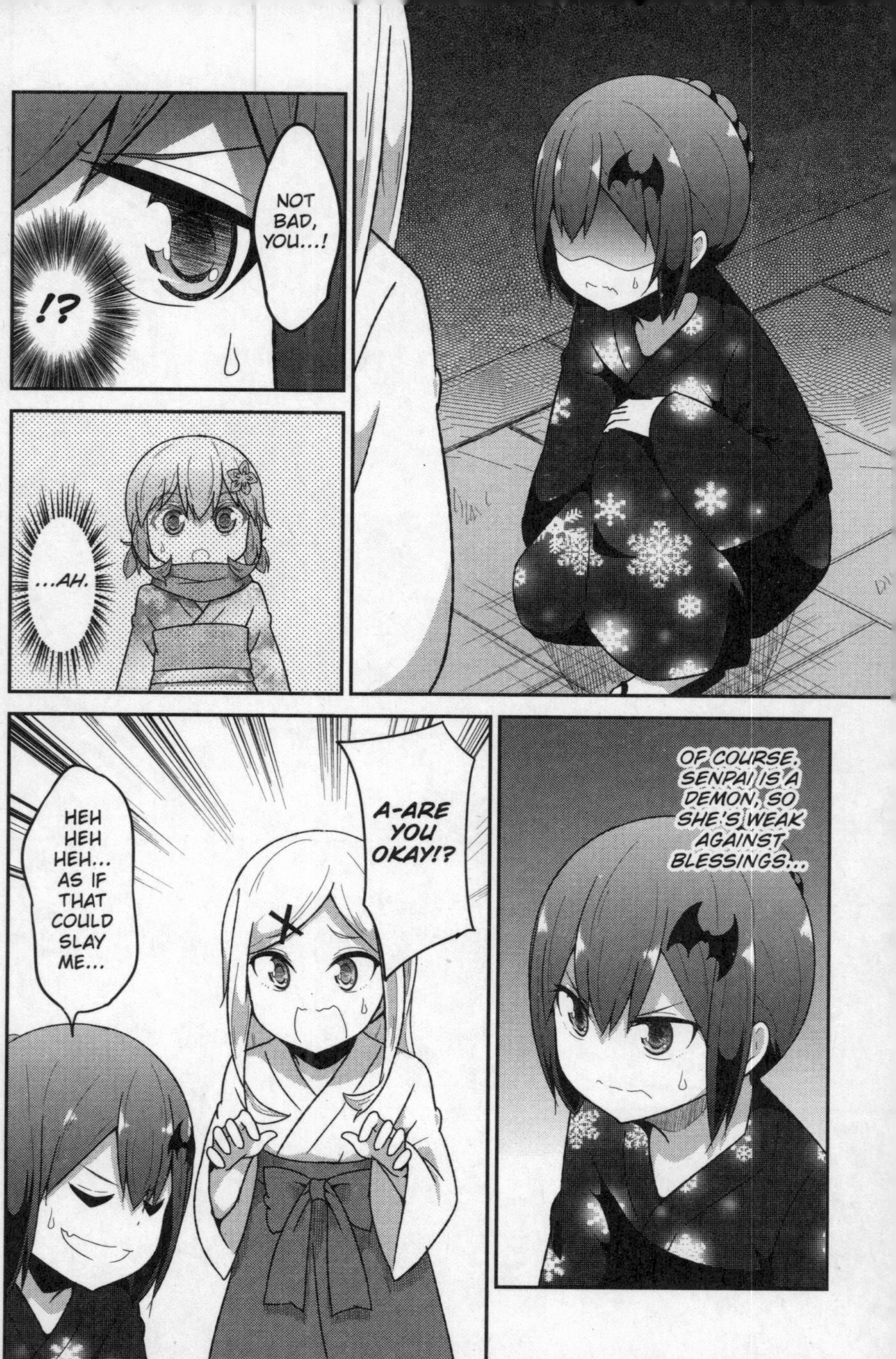
NOT BAD, YOU...!
!?
...AH.
OF COURSE. SENPAI IS A DEMON, SO SHE'S WEAK AGAINST BLESSINGS...
A-ARE YOU OKAY!?
HEH HEH HEH... AS IF THAT COULD SLAY ME...

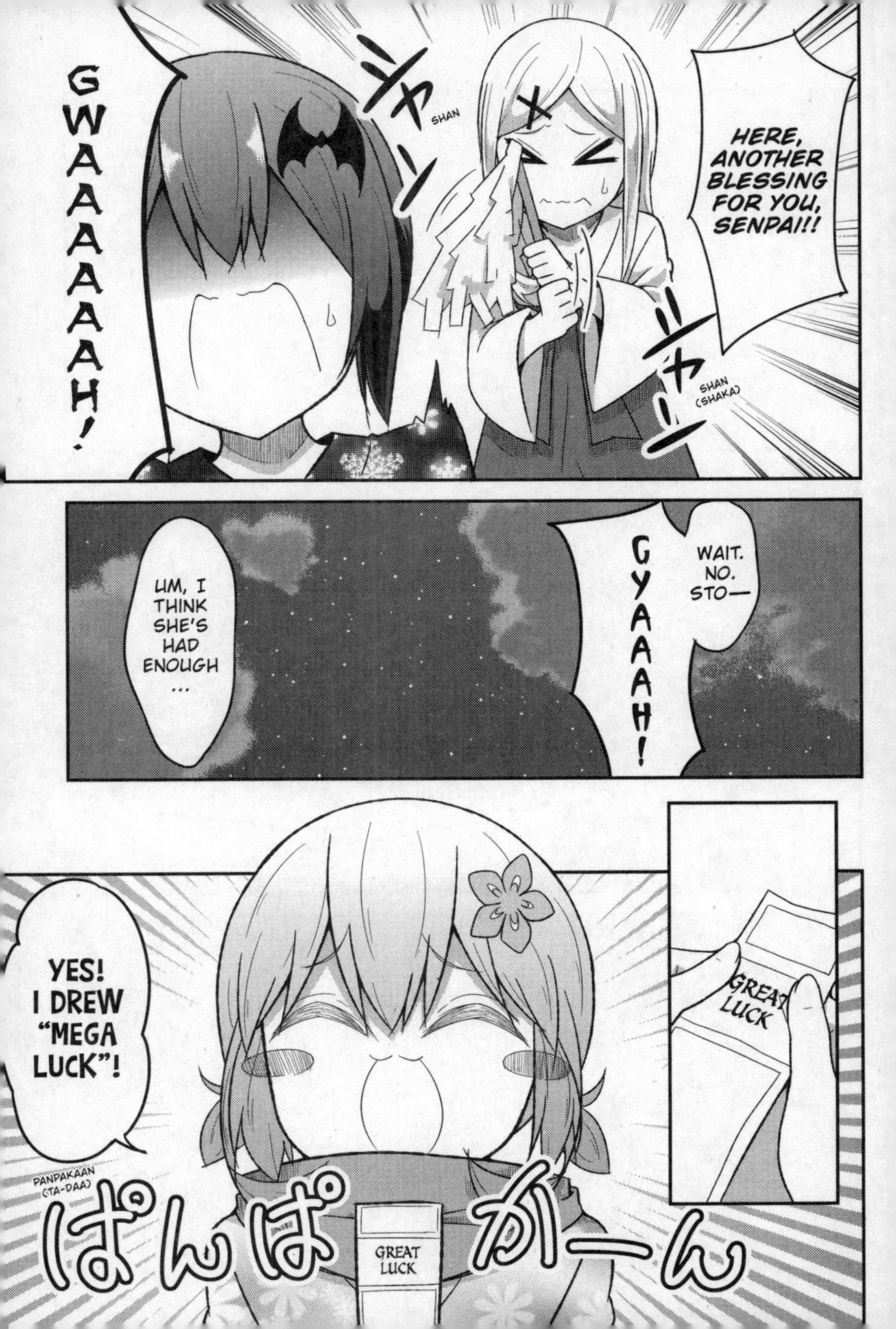
HERE, ANOTHER BLESSING FOR YOU, SENPAI!!
シャーン
SHAN (SHAKA)
シャーン
SHAN
GWAAAAAAAH!
WAIT. NO. STO—
GYAAAAH!
UM, I THINK SHE'S HAD ENOUGH ...
GREAT LUCK
YES! I DREW "MEGA LUCK"!
PANPAKAAN (TA-DAA)
ぱんぱかーん
GREAT LUCK

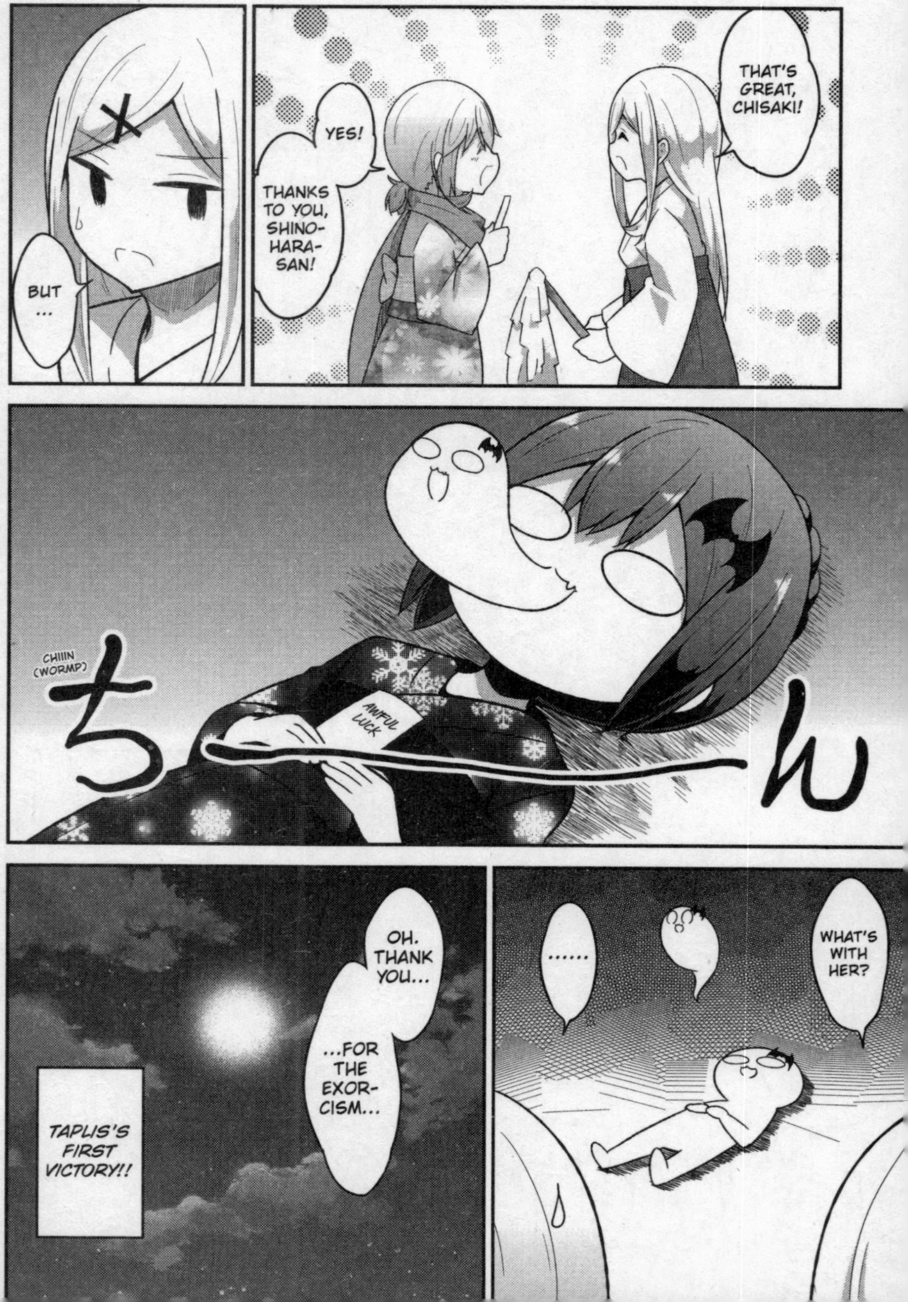
THAT'S GREAT, CHISAKI!
YES!
THANKS TO YOU, SHINOHARA-SAN!
BUT ...
CHIIN (WORMP)
AWFUL LUCK
ち ん
WHAT'S WITH HER?
......
OH. THANK YOU...
...FOR THE EXORCISM...
TAPLIS'S FIRST VICTORY!!

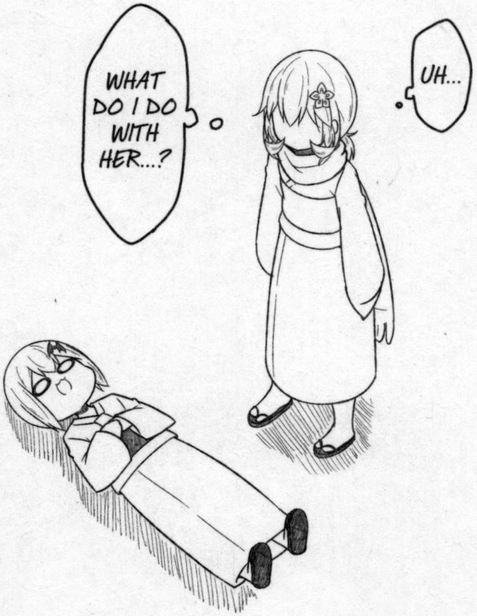
UH...
WHAT DO I DO WITH HER...?

Gabriel Dropout

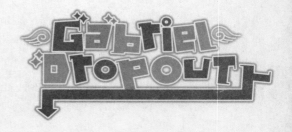

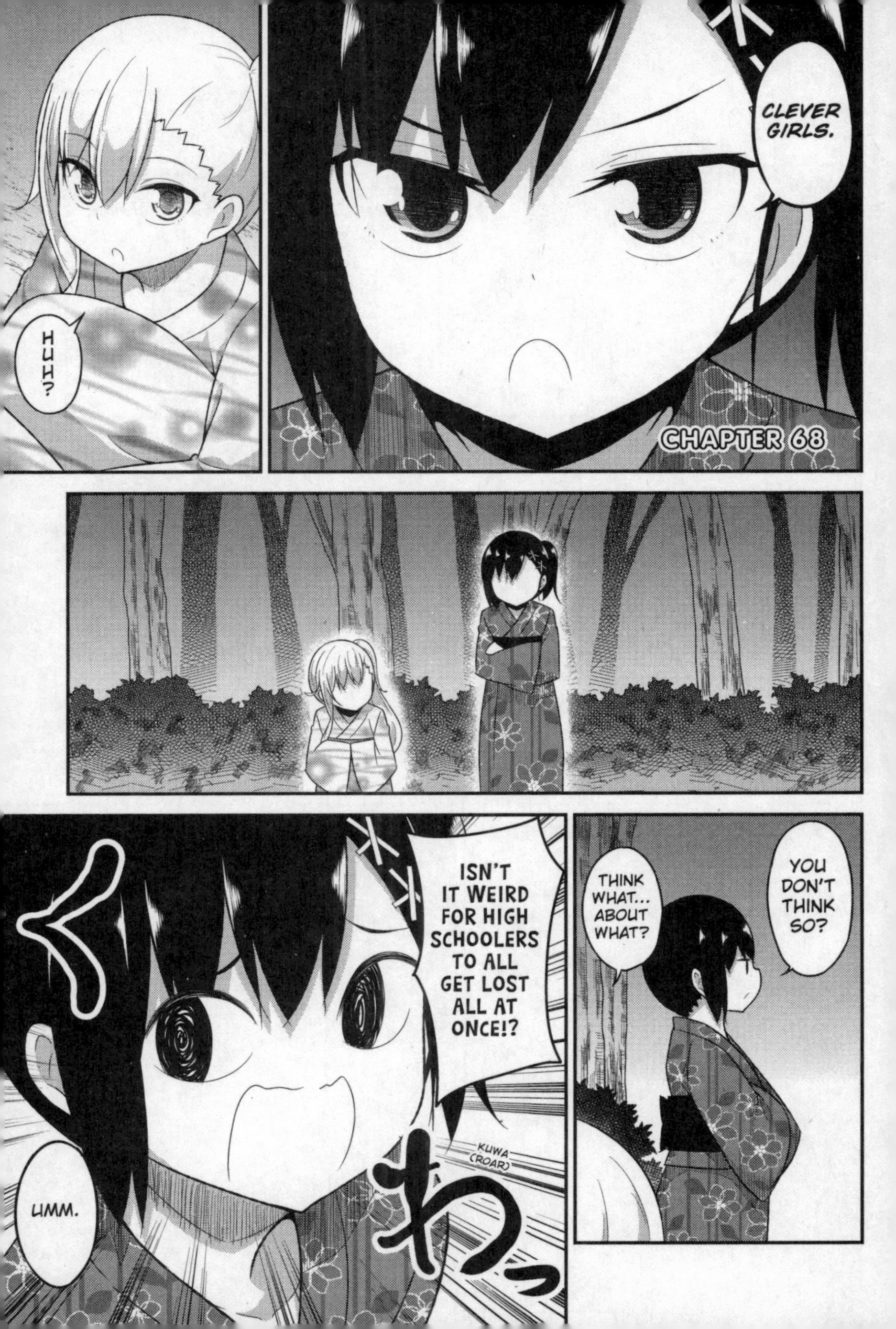
CLEVER GIRLS.
CHAPTER 68
HUH?
YOU DON'T THINK SO?
THINK WHAT... ABOUT WHAT?
ISN'T IT WEIRD FOR HIGH SCHOOLERS TO ALL GET LOST ALL AT ONCE!?
KUWA (ROAR)
UMM.

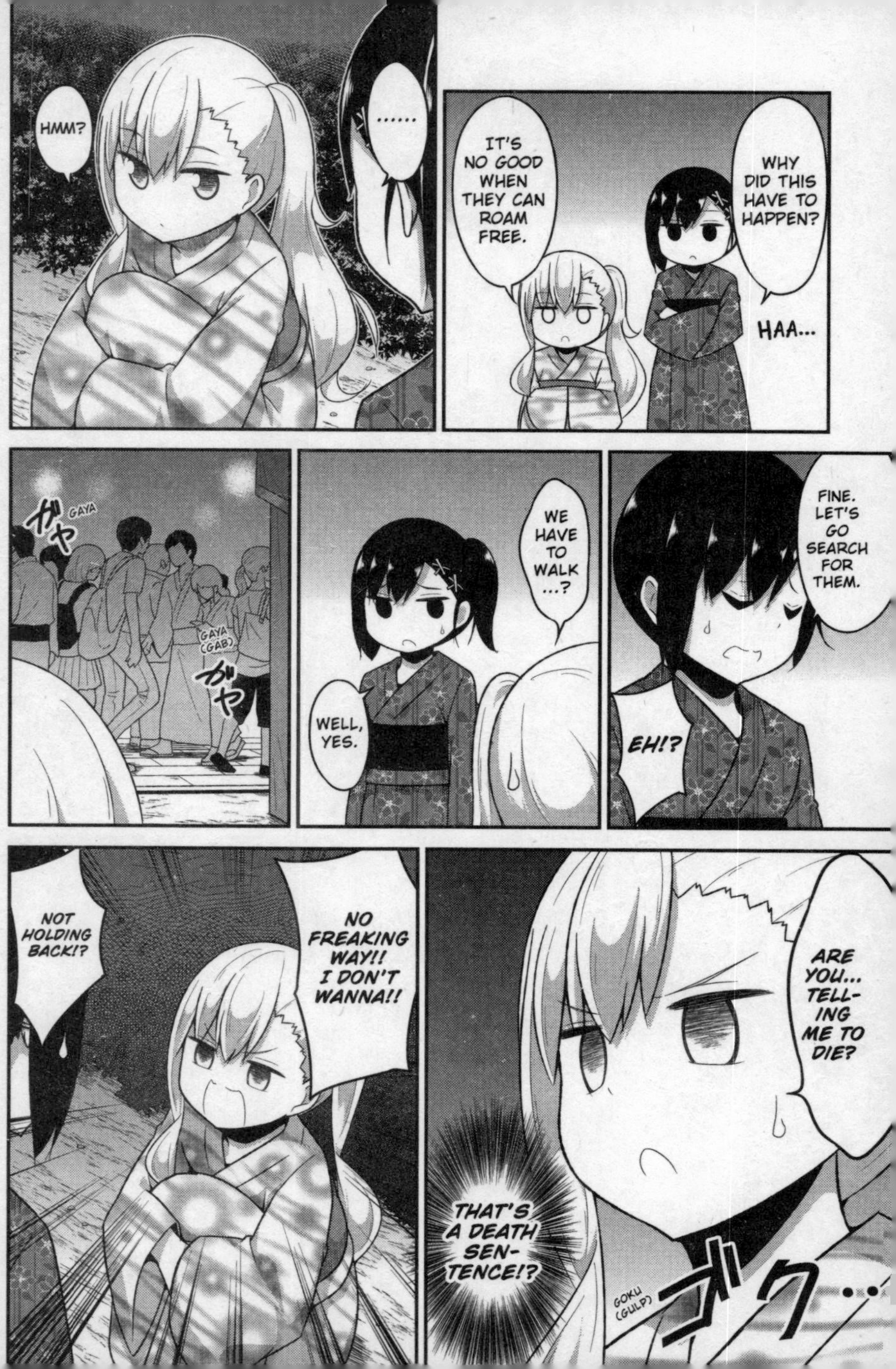
WHY DID THIS HAVE TO HAPPEN?
IT'S NO GOOD WHEN THEY CAN ROAM FREE.
HAA...
......
HMM?
FINE. LET'S GO SEARCH FOR THEM.
EH!?
WE HAVE TO WALK ...?
WELL, YES.
ガヤ
GAYA
GAYA (GAB)
ガヤ
ARE YOU... TELL-ING ME TO DIE?
THAT'S A DEATH SEN-TENCE!?
ゴク
GOKU (GULP)
NO FREAKING WAY!! I DON'T WANNA!!
NOT HOLDING BACK!?

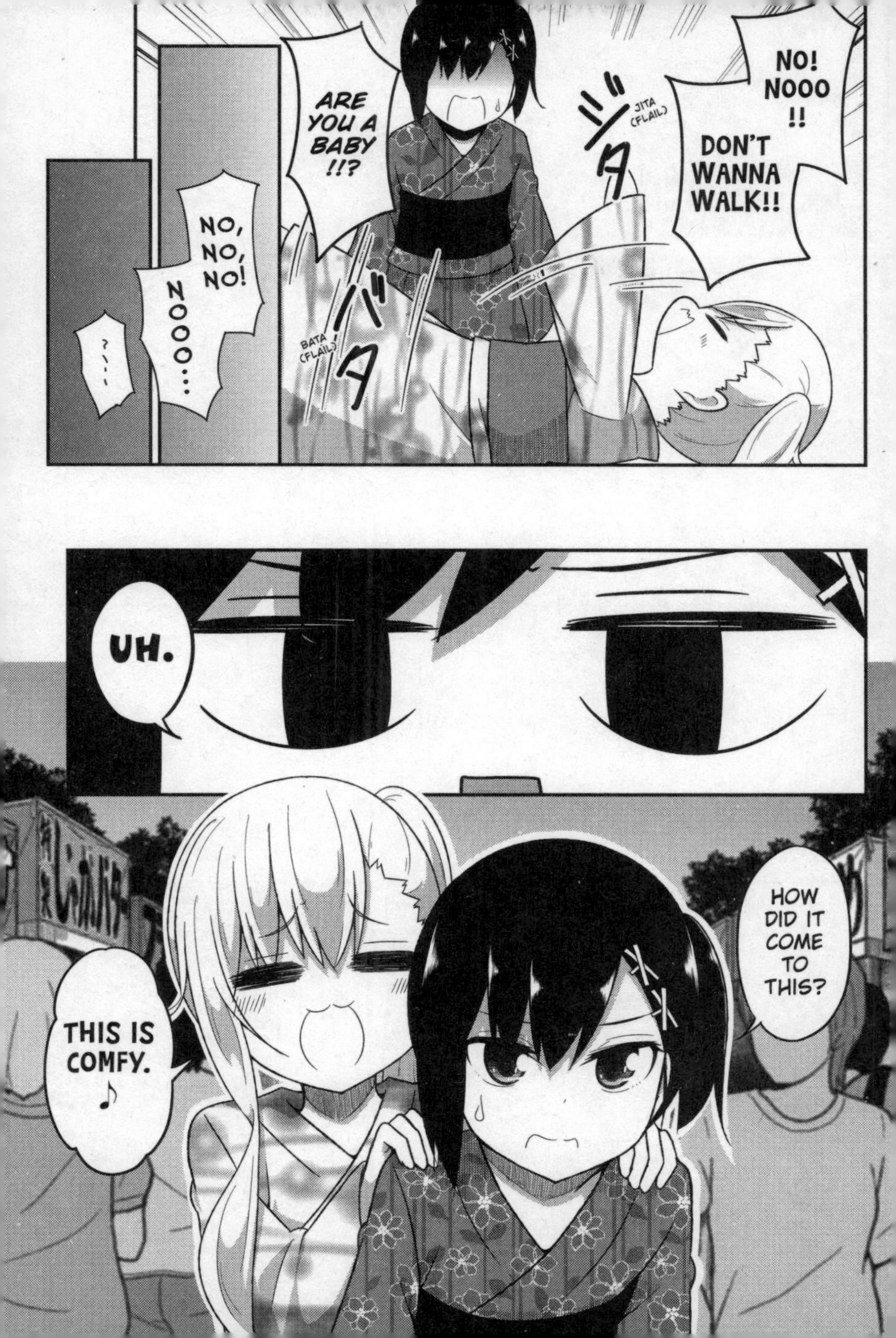
NO! NOOO!! DON'T WANNA WALK!!
JITA (FLAIL)
ARE YOU A BABY!!?
BATA (FLAIL)
NO, NO, NO! NOOO...
...?
UH.
HOW DID IT COME TO THIS?
THIS IS COMFY. ♪

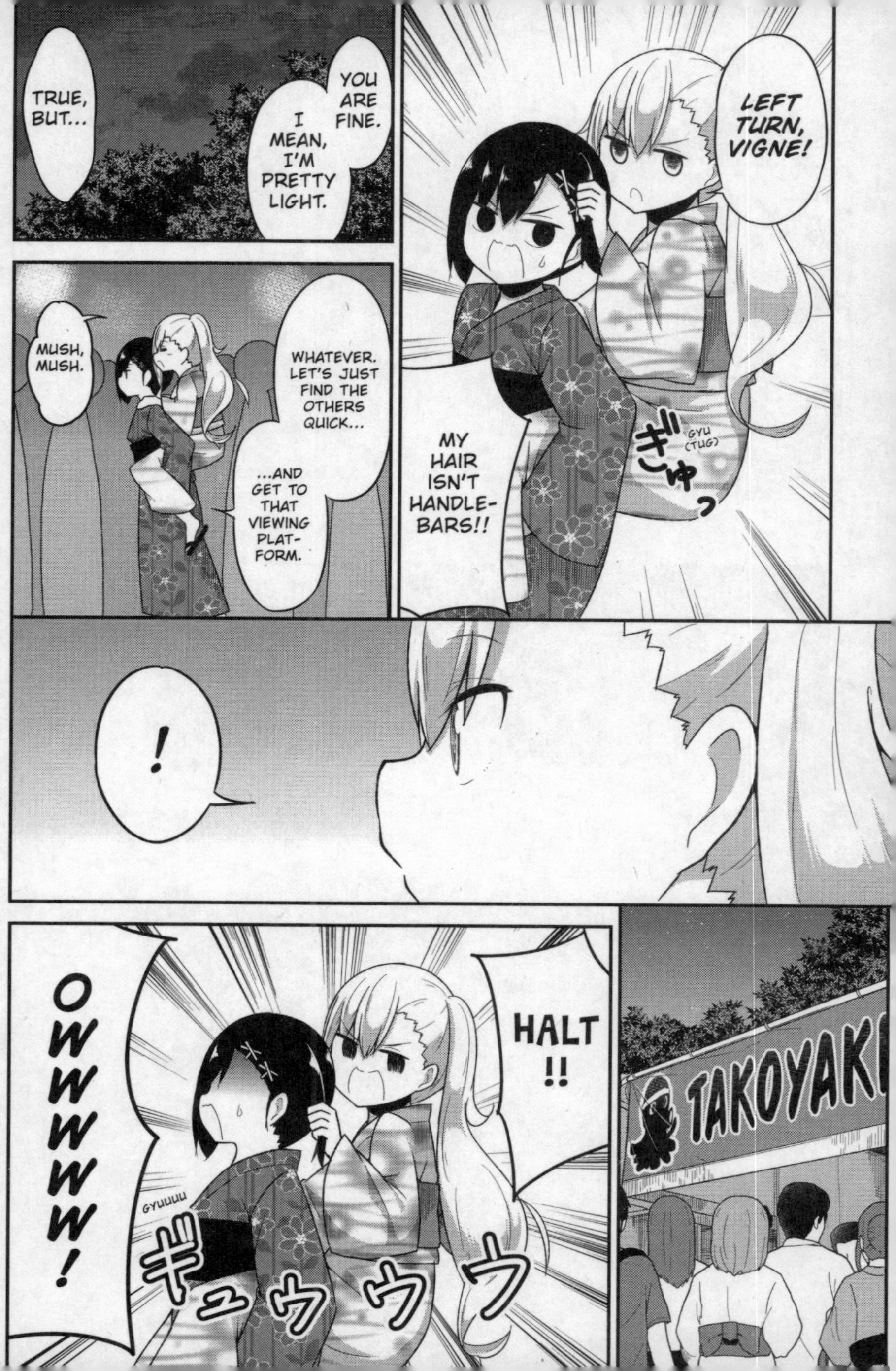
LEFT TURN, VIGNE!
GYU (TUG)
ぎゅっ
MY HAIR ISN'T HANDLE-BARS!!
YOU ARE FINE.
I MEAN, I'M PRETTY LIGHT.
TRUE, BUT...
WHATEVER. LET'S JUST FIND THE OTHERS QUICK...
...AND GET TO THAT VIEWING PLAT-FORM.
MUSH, MUSH.
!
TAKOYAKI
HALT!!
OWWWWWW!
GYUUUU
ギュゥウウ

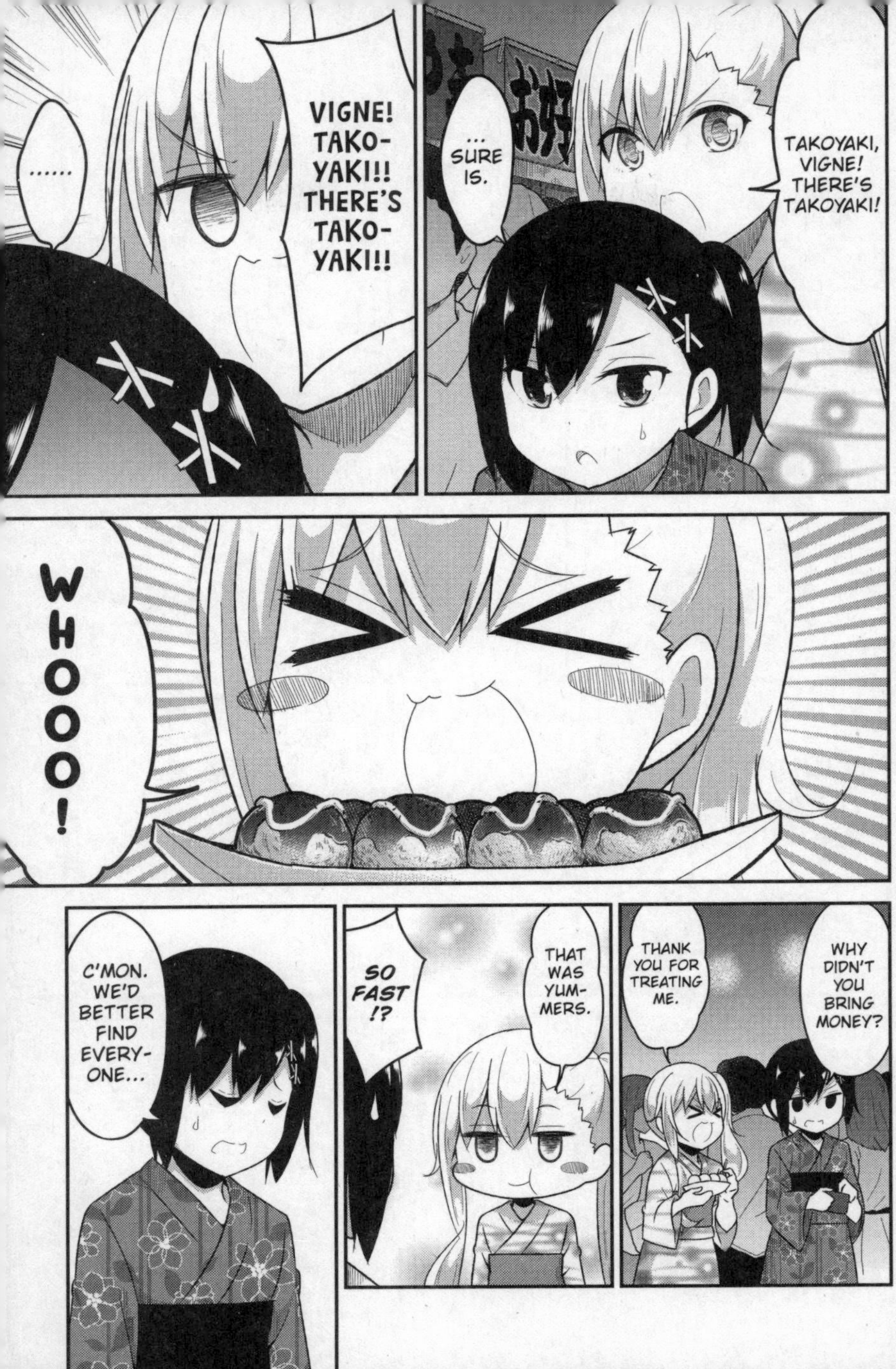
TAKOYAKI, VIGNE! THERE'S TAKOYAKI!
... SURE IS.
VIGNE! TAKO-YAKI!!! THERE'S TAKO-YAKI!!!
......
WHOOOO!
WHY DIDN'T YOU BRING MONEY?
THANK YOU FOR TREATING ME.
THAT WAS YUM-MERS.
SO FAST!?
C'MON. WE'D BETTER FIND EVERY-ONE...

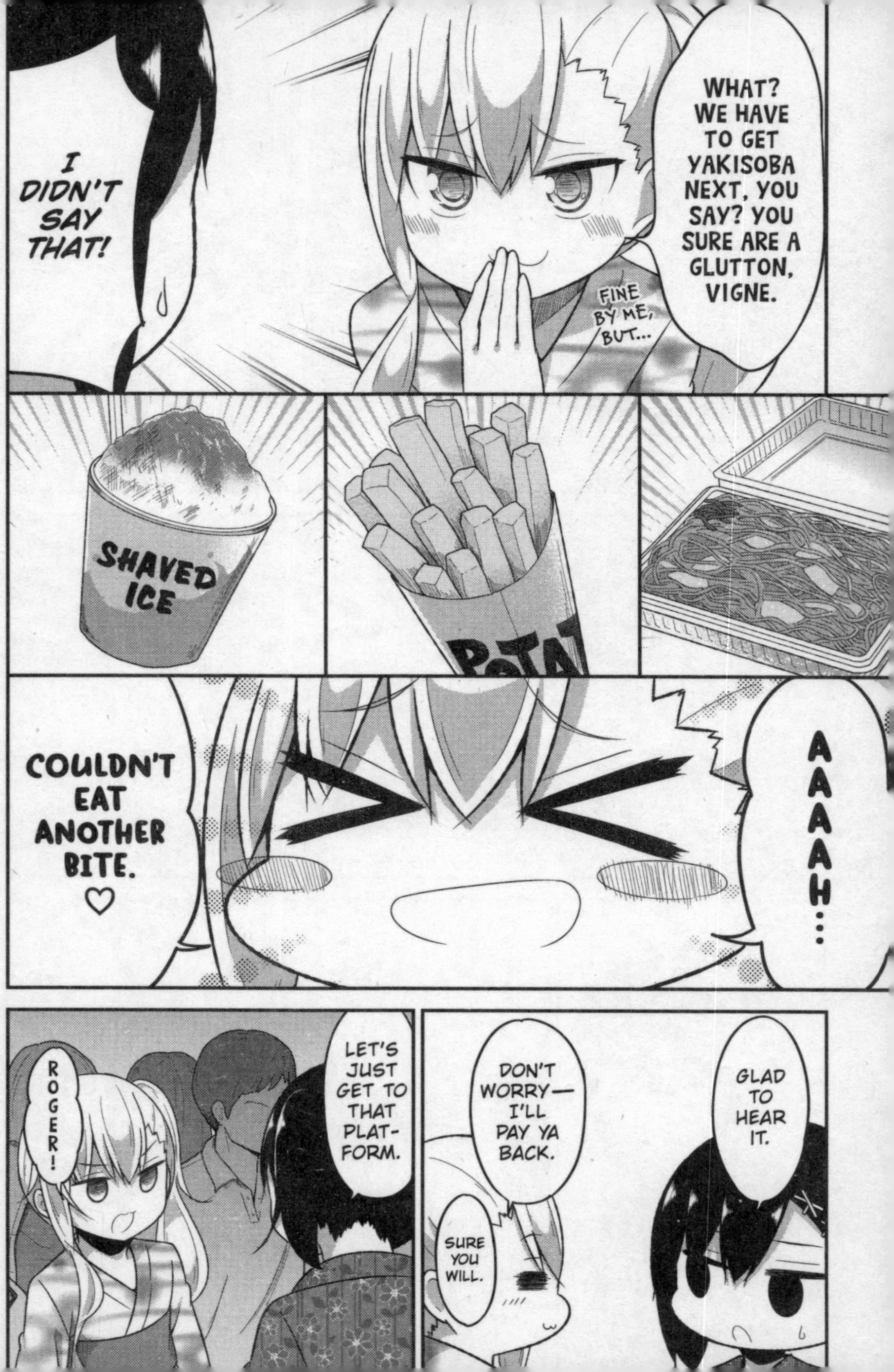
WHAT? WE HAVE TO GET YAKISOBA NEXT, YOU SAY? YOU SURE ARE A GLUTTON, VIGNE.
FINE BY ME, BUT...
I DIDN'T SAY THAT!
POTAT
SHAVED ICE
AAAAAH...
COULDN'T EAT ANOTHER BITE. ♡
GLAD TO HEAR IT.
DON'T WORRY—I'LL PAY YA BACK.
SURE YOU WILL.
LET'S JUST GET TO THAT PLATFORM.
ROGER!

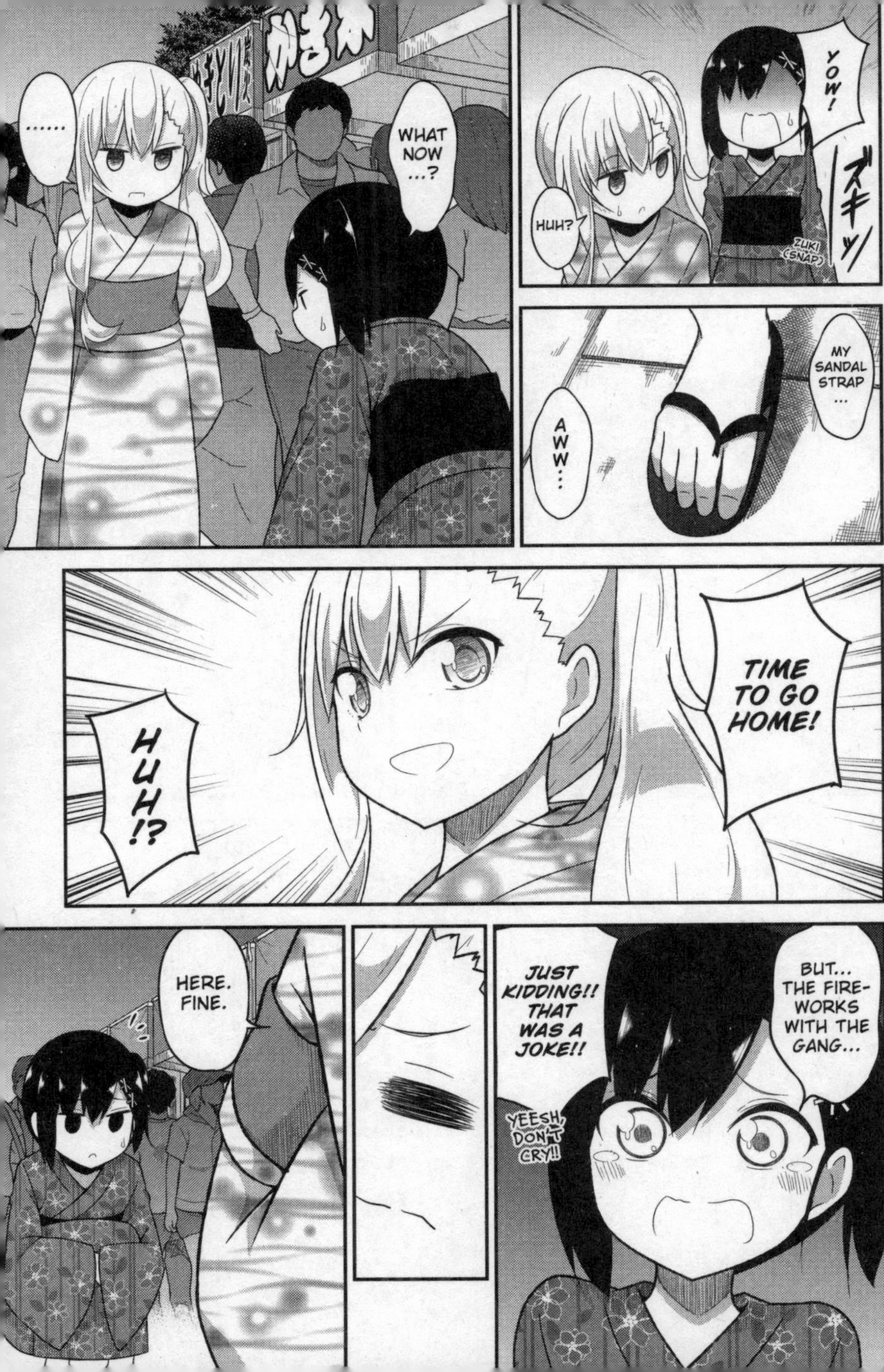
YOW!
ズキッ
ZUKI (SNAP)
HUH?
MY SANDAL STRAP ...
AWW...
WHAT NOW ...?
....
TIME TO GO HOME!
HUH!?
BUT... THE FIRE-WORKS WITH THE GANG...
JUST KIDDING!! THAT WAS A JOKE!!
YEESH, DON'T CRY!!
HERE. FINE.

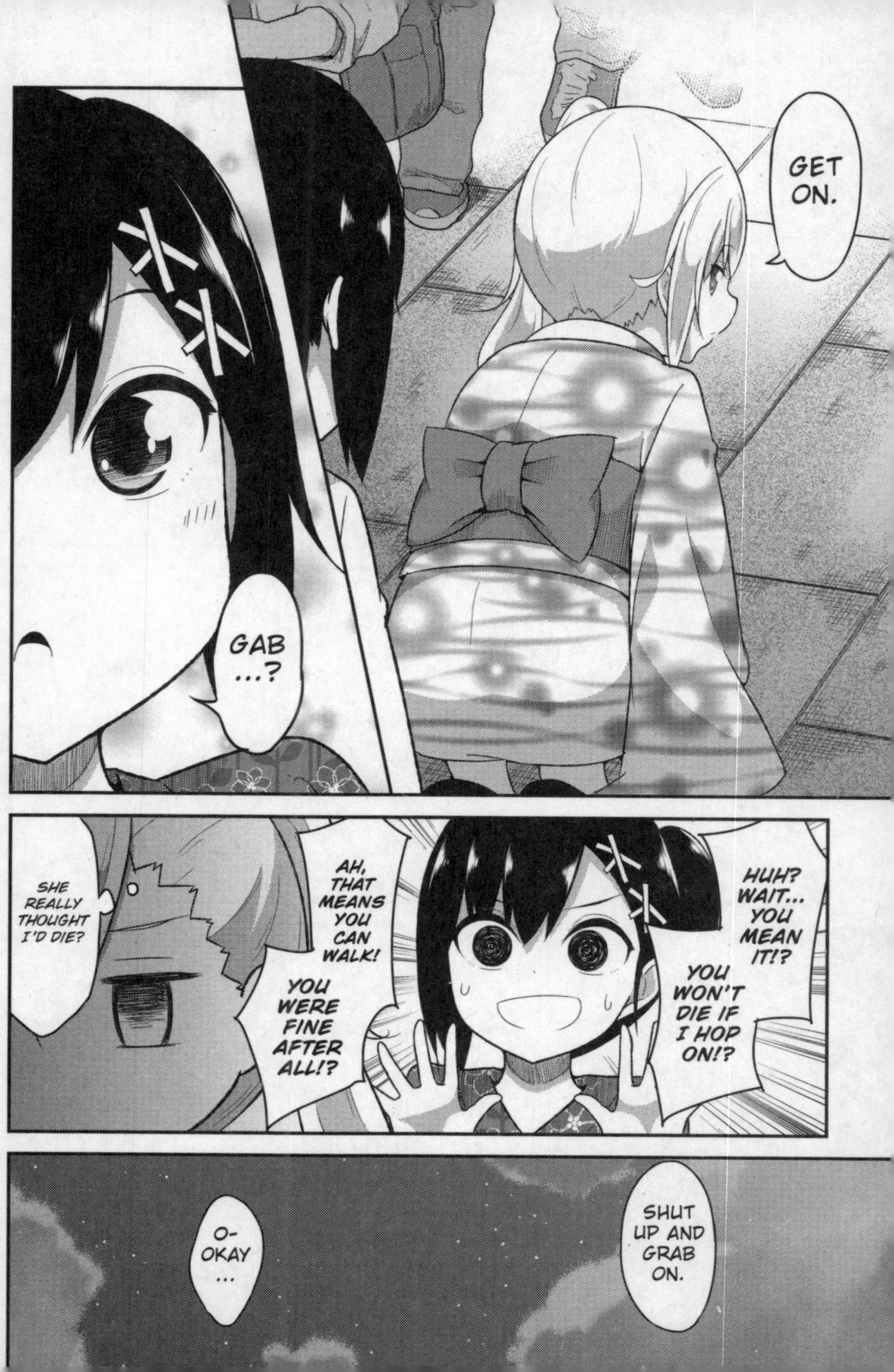
GET ON.
GAB ...?
HUH? WAIT... YOU MEAN IT!?
YOU WON'T DIE IF I HOP ON!?
AH, THAT MEANS YOU CAN WALK!
YOU WERE FINE AFTER ALL!?
SHE REALLY THOUGHT I'D DIE?
SHUT UP AND GRAB ON.
O-OKAY ...

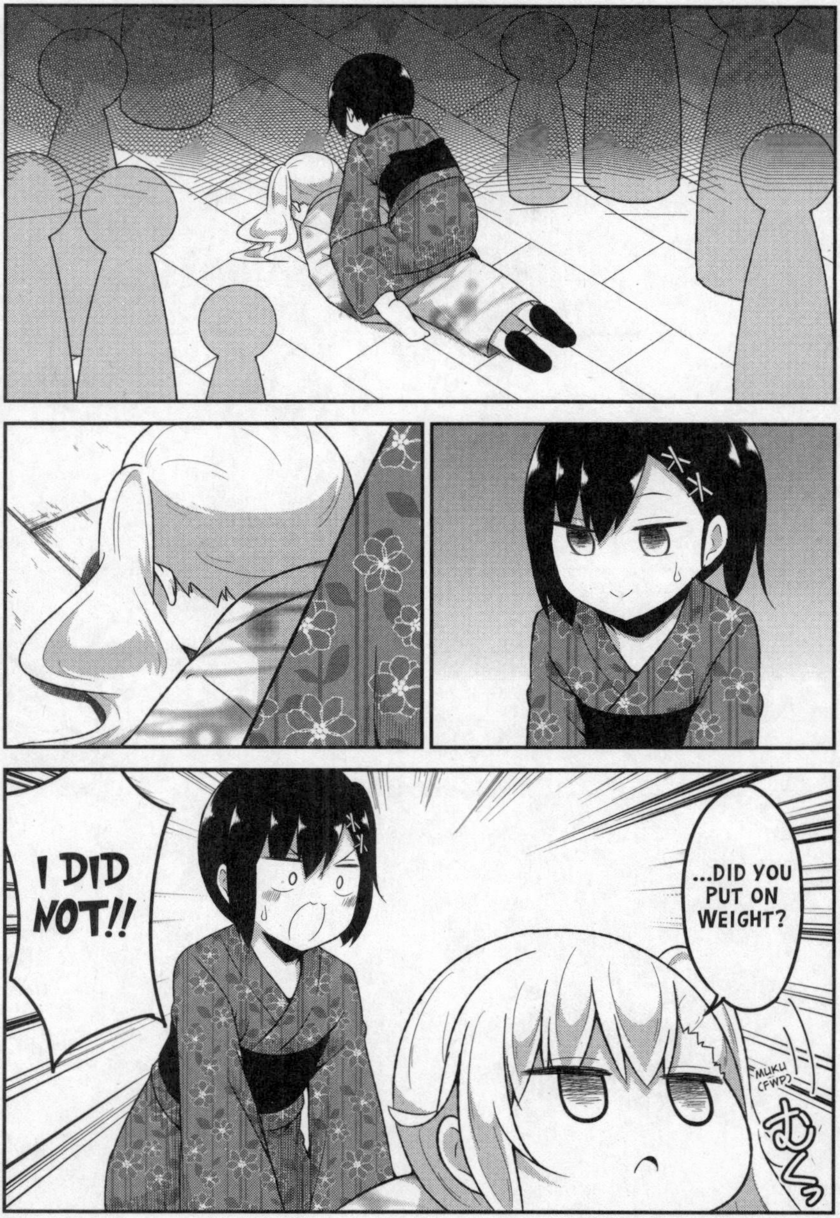
...DID YOU PUT ON WEIGHT?
MUKU (FWP)
むくっ
I DID NOT!!

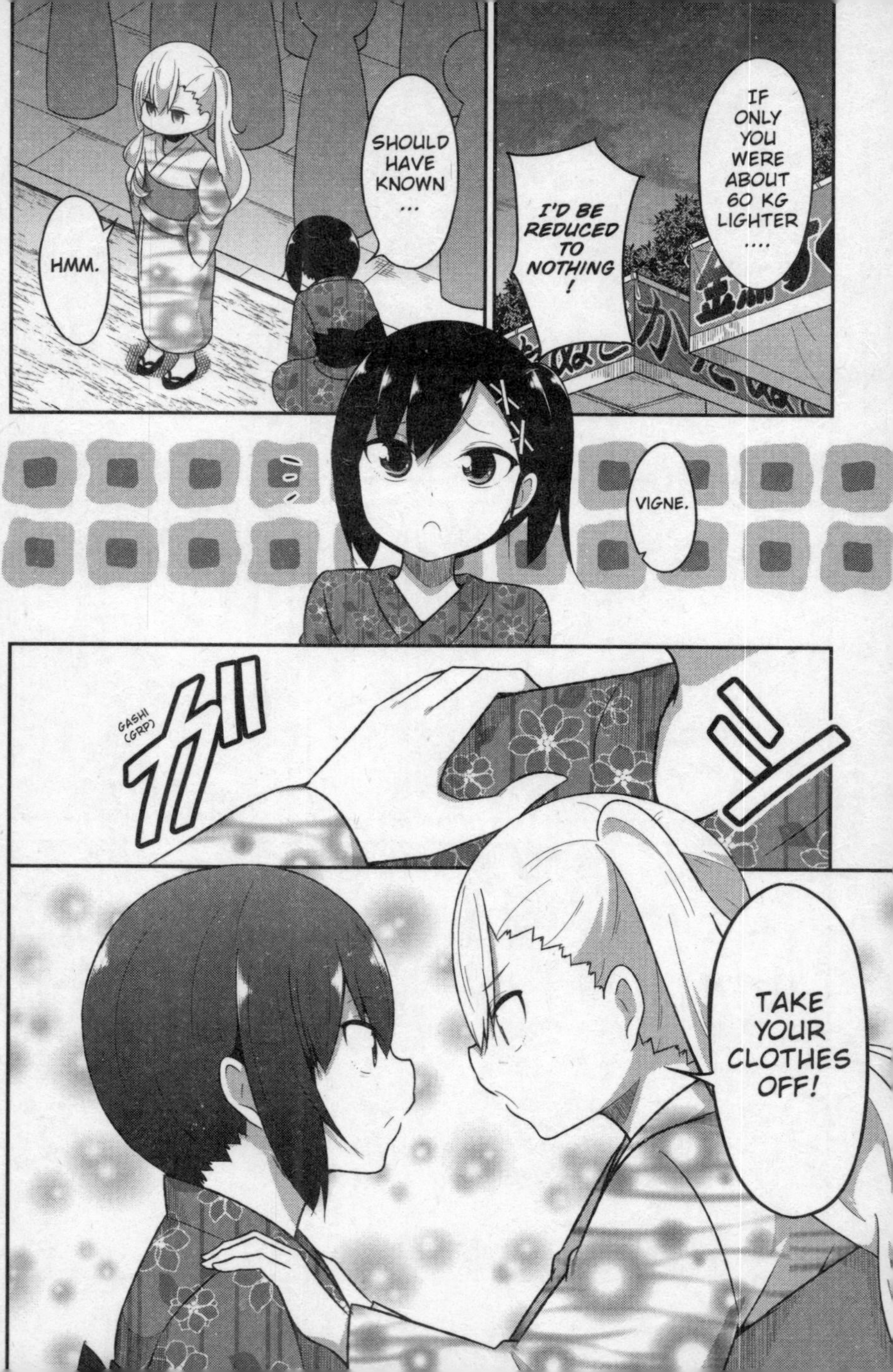
IF ONLY YOU WERE ABOUT 60 KG LIGHTER....
I'D BE REDUCED TO NOTHING!
SHOULD HAVE KNOWN...
HMM.
VIGNE.
GASHI (GRP)
TAKE YOUR CLOTHES OFF!

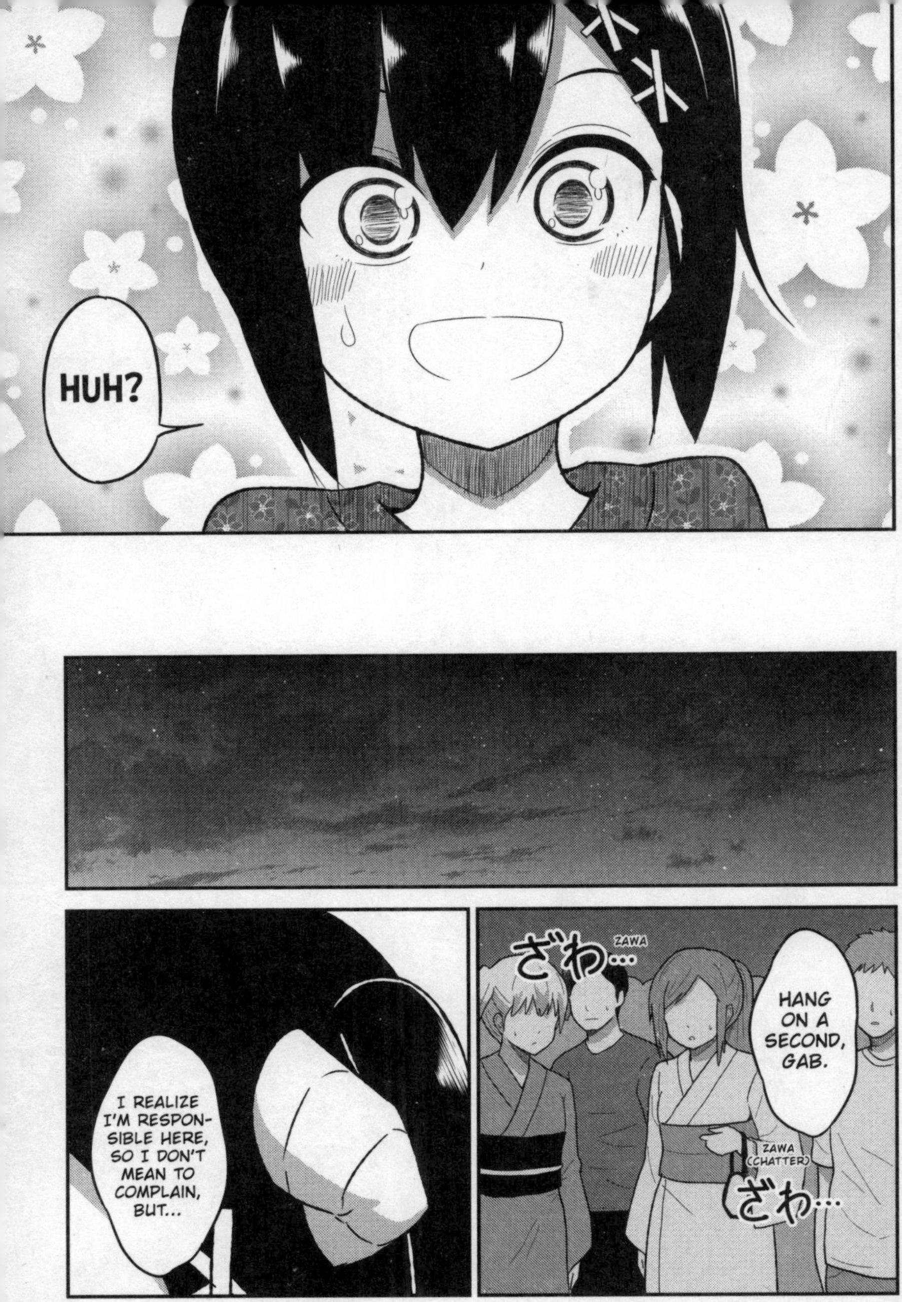
HUH?
HANG ON A SECOND, GAB.
ざわ…
ZAWA
ZAWA (CHATTER)
ざわ…
I REALIZE I'M RESPONSIBLE HERE, SO I DON'T MEAN TO COMPLAIN, BUT...

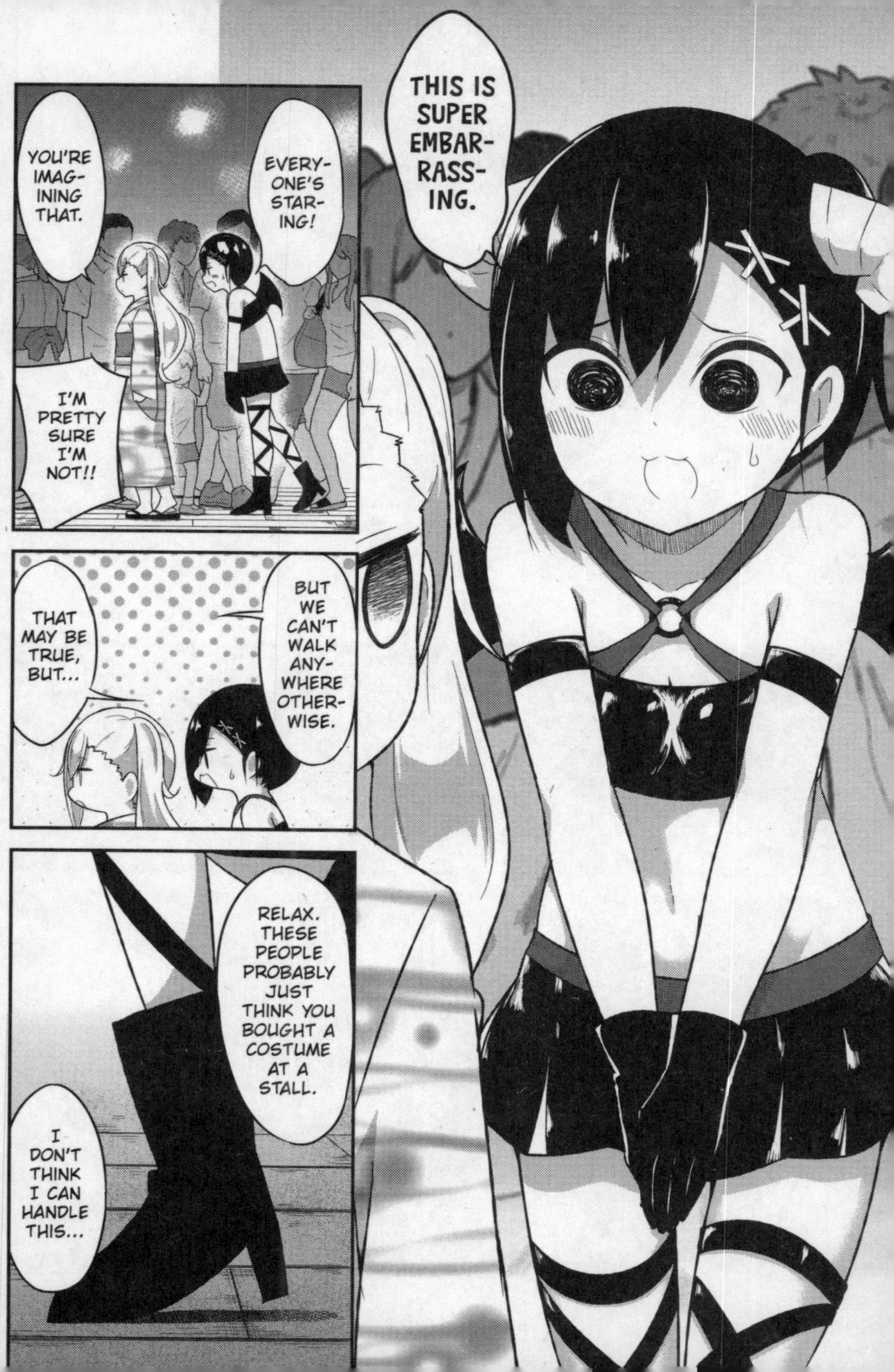
THIS IS SUPER EMBARRASSING.
EVERYONE'S STARING!
YOU'RE IMAGINING THAT.
I'M PRETTY SURE I'M NOT!!
BUT WE CAN'T WALK ANYWHERE OTHERWISE.
THAT MAY BE TRUE, BUT...
RELAX. THESE PEOPLE PROBABLY JUST THINK YOU BOUGHT A COSTUME AT A STALL.
I DON'T THINK I CAN HANDLE THIS...

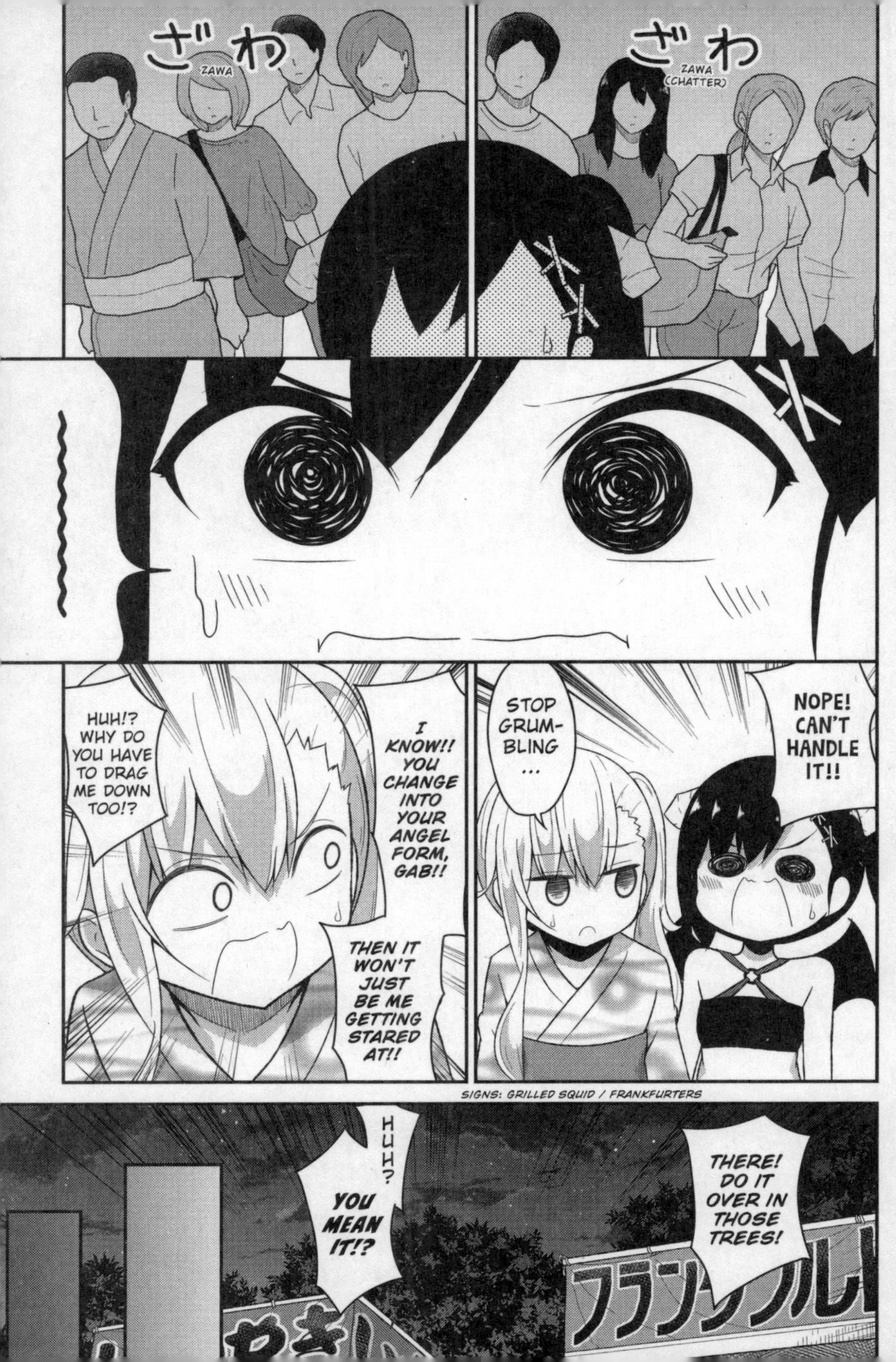
ざわ
ZAWA (CHATTER)
ざわ
ZAWA
NOPE! CAN'T HANDLE IT!!
STOP GRUMBLING...
I KNOW!! YOU CHANGE INTO YOUR ANGEL FORM, GAB!!
THEN IT WON'T JUST BE ME GETTING STARED AT!!
HUH!? WHY DO YOU HAVE TO DRAG ME DOWN TOO!?
SIGNS: GRILLED SQUID / FRANKFURTERS
THERE! DO IT OVER IN THOSE TREES!
HUH?
YOU MEAN IT!?

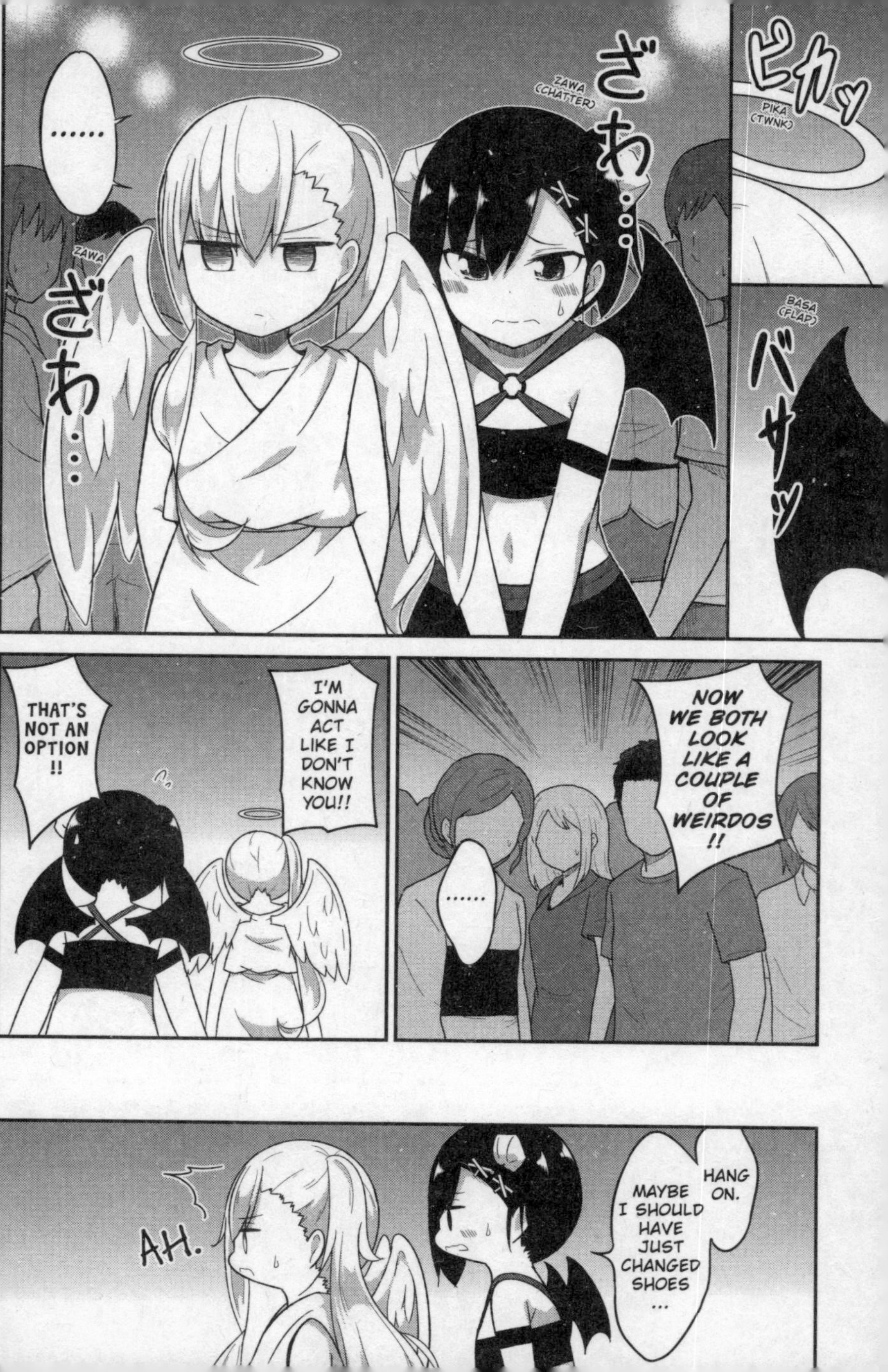
ピカッ
PIKA (TWNK)
バサッ
BASA (FLAP)
ざわ…
ZAWA (CHATTER)
......
ざわ…
ZAWA
NOW WE BOTH LOOK LIKE A COUPLE OF WEIRDOS!!
....
I'M GONNA ACT LIKE I DON'T KNOW YOU!!
THAT'S NOT AN OPTION!!
HANG ON. MAYBE I SHOULD HAVE JUST CHANGED SHOES...
AH.

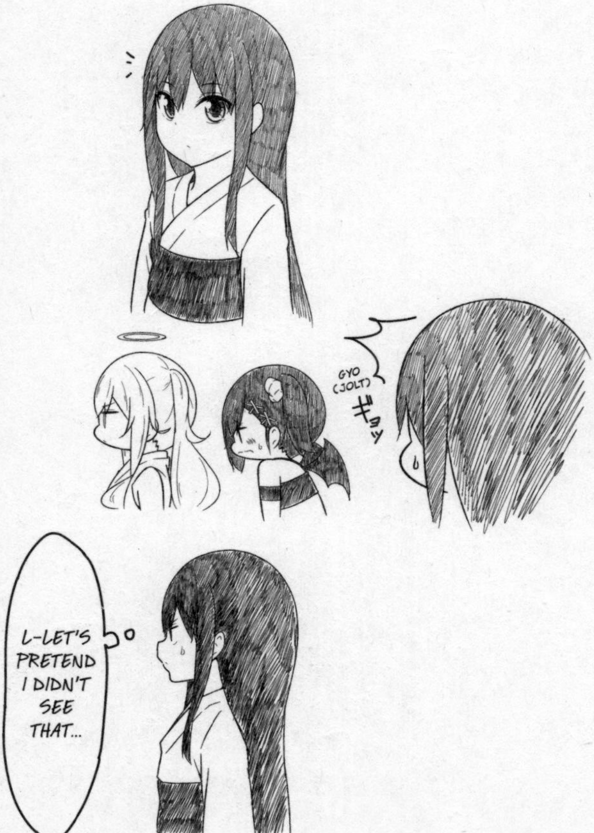
GYO (JOLT)
ギョッ
L-LET'S PRETEND I DIDN'T SEE THAT...

Gabriel Dropout

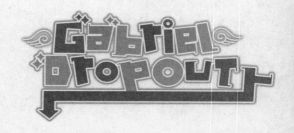

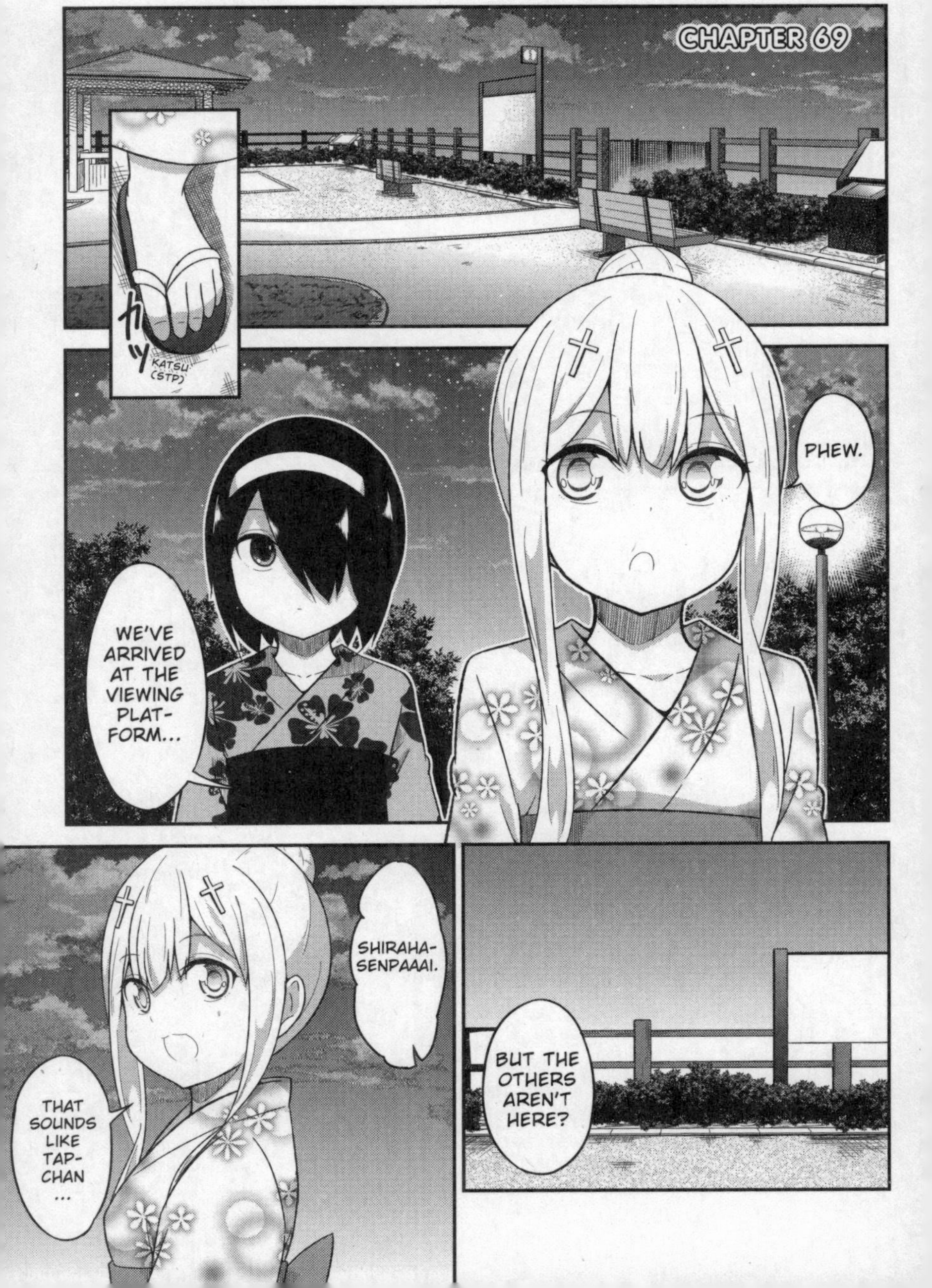
CHAPTER 69
カッ KATSU (STP)
PHEW.
WE'VE ARRIVED AT THE VIEWING PLAT-FORM...
BUT THE OTHERS AREN'T HERE?
SHIRAHA-SENPAAAI.
THAT SOUNDS LIKE TAP-CHAN ...

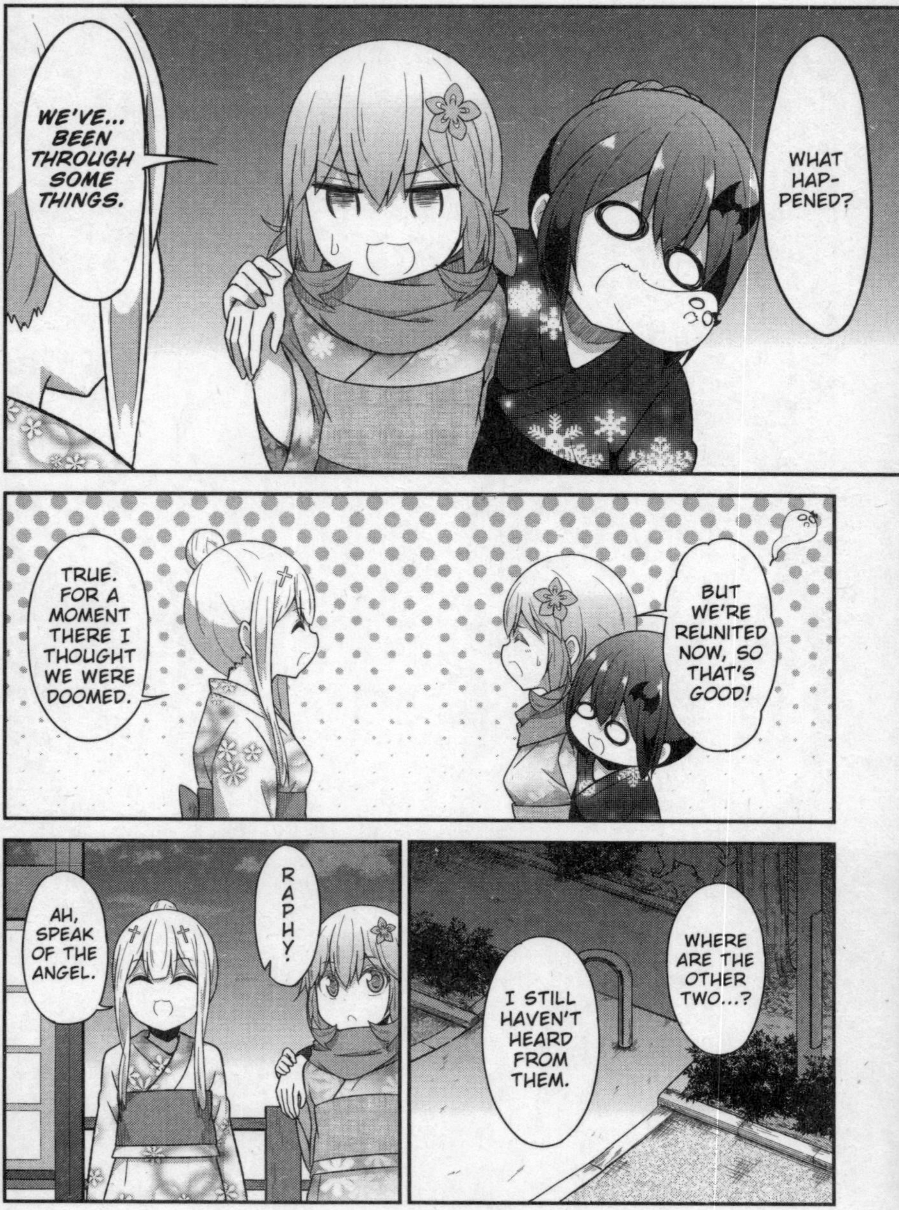
WHAT HAP-PENED?
WE'VE... BEEN THROUGH SOME THINGS.
BUT WE'RE REUNITED NOW, SO THAT'S GOOD!
TRUE. FOR A MOMENT THERE I THOUGHT WE WERE DOOMED.
WHERE ARE THE OTHER TWO...?
I STILL HAVEN'T HEARD FROM THEM.
RAPHY.
AH, SPEAK OF THE ANGEL.

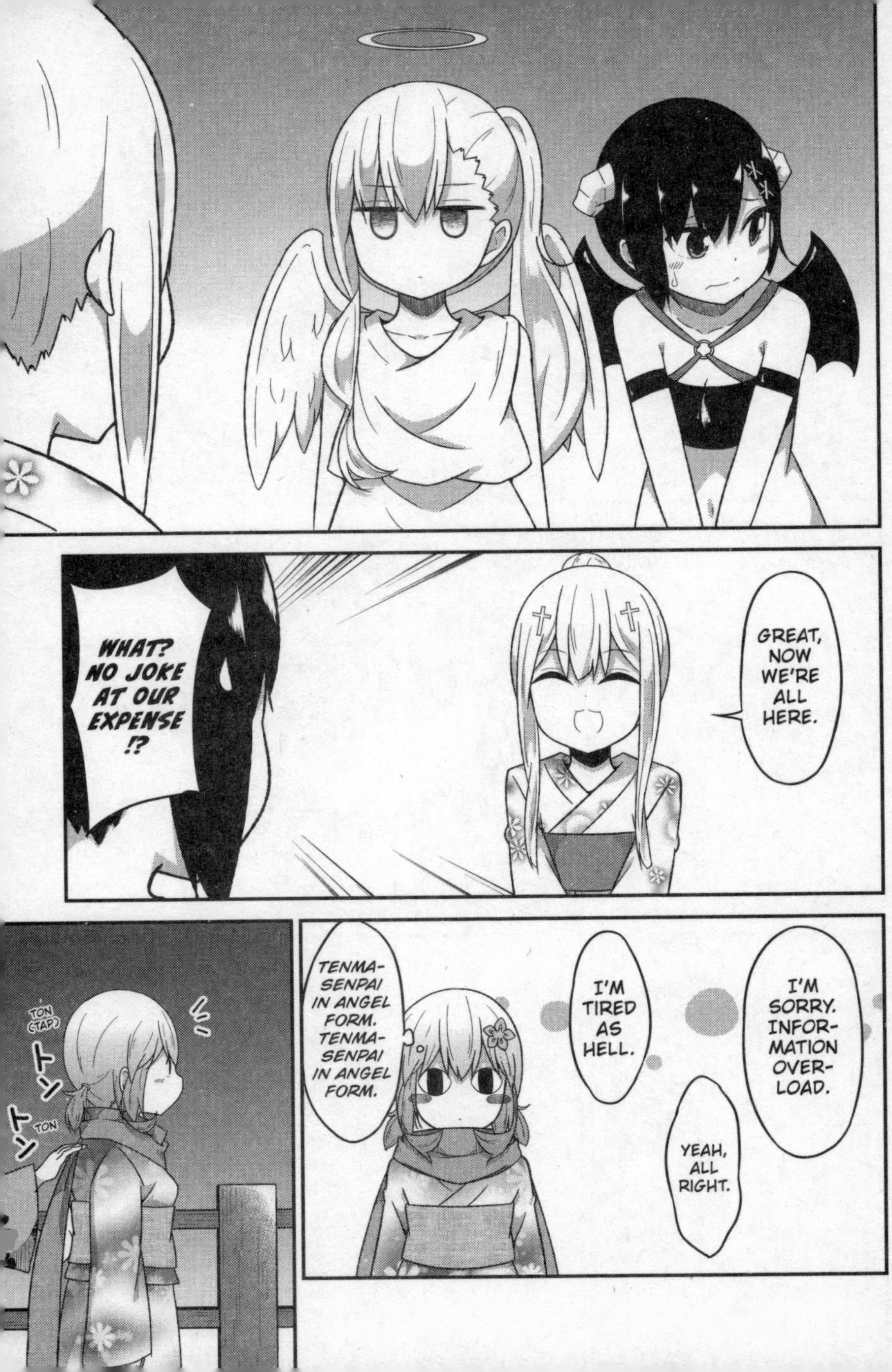
GREAT, NOW WE'RE ALL HERE.
WHAT? NO JOKE AT OUR EXPENSE!?
I'M SORRY. INFORMATION OVERLOAD.
I'M TIRED AS HELL.
YEAH, ALL RIGHT.
TENMA-SENPAI IN ANGEL FORM. TENMA-SENPAI IN ANGEL FORM.
TON (TAP)
TON

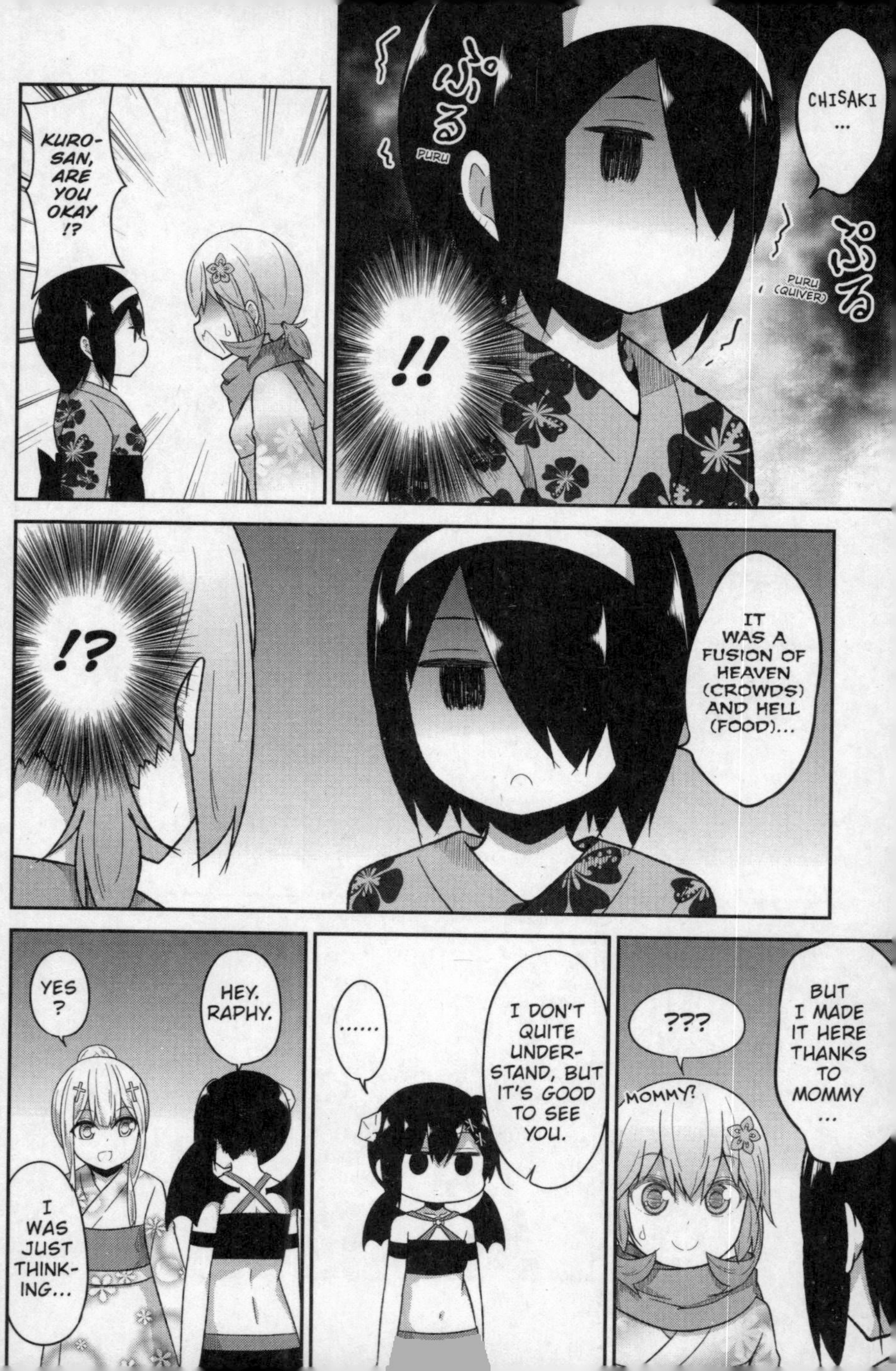
CHISAKI...
ぷる
PURU (QUIVER)
ぷる
PURU
!!
KURO-SAN, ARE YOU OKAY!?
IT WAS A FUSION OF HEAVEN (CROWDS) AND HELL (FOOD)...
!?
BUT I MADE IT HERE THANKS TO MOMMY...
???
MOMMY?
I DON'T QUITE UNDER-STAND, BUT IT'S GOOD TO SEE YOU.
......
HEY. RAPHY.
YES?
I WAS JUST THINK-ING...

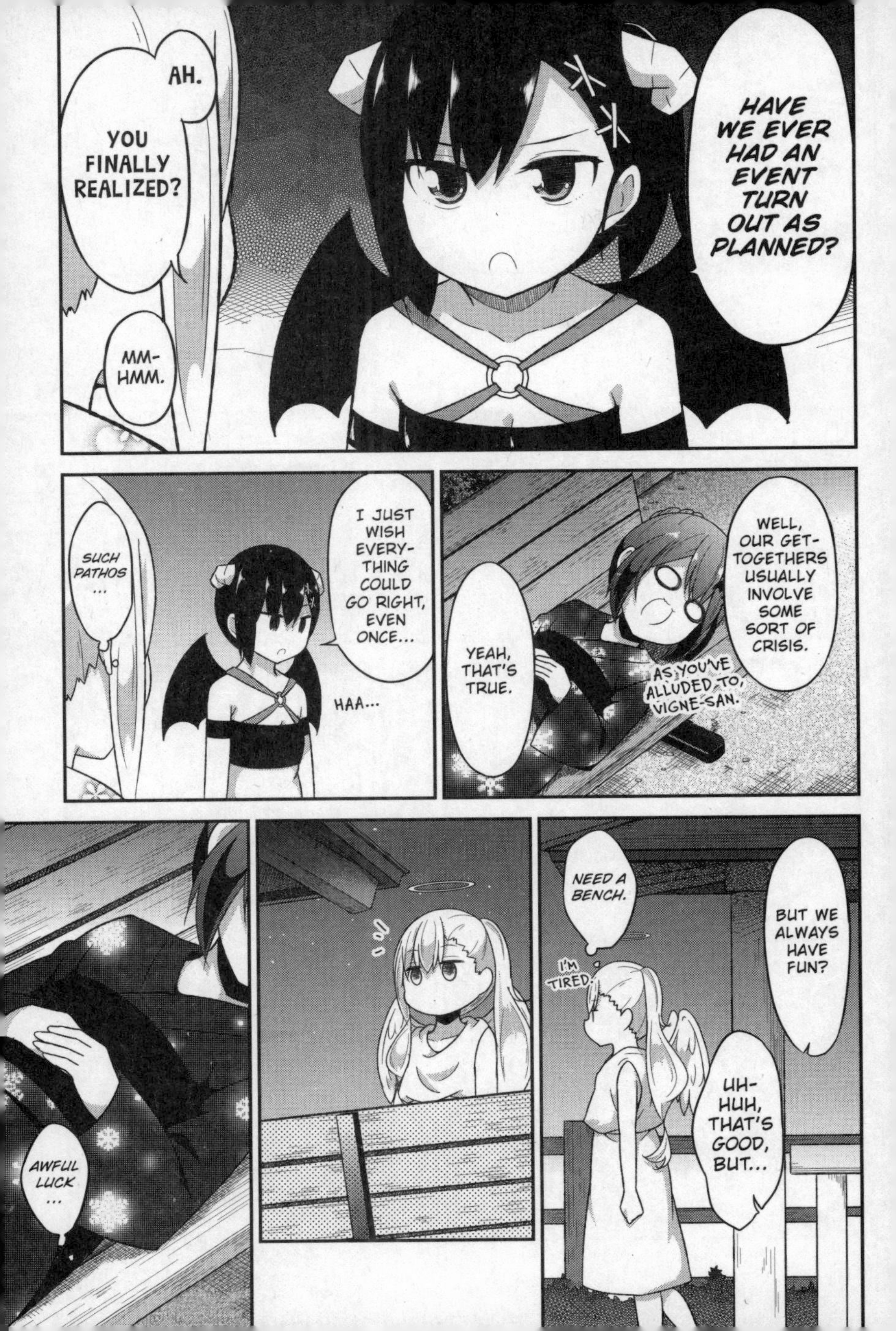
HAVE WE EVER HAD AN EVENT TURN OUT AS PLANNED?
AH.
YOU FINALLY REALIZED?
MM-HMM.
WELL, OUR GET-TOGETHERS USUALLY INVOLVE SOME SORT OF CRISIS.
AS YOU'VE ALLUDED TO, VIGNE-SAN.
YEAH, THAT'S TRUE.
I JUST WISH EVERYTHING COULD GO RIGHT, EVEN ONCE...
HAA...
SUCH PATHOS...
BUT WE ALWAYS HAVE FUN?
UH-HUH, THAT'S GOOD, BUT...
NEED A BENCH.
I'M TIRED.
AWFUL LUCK...

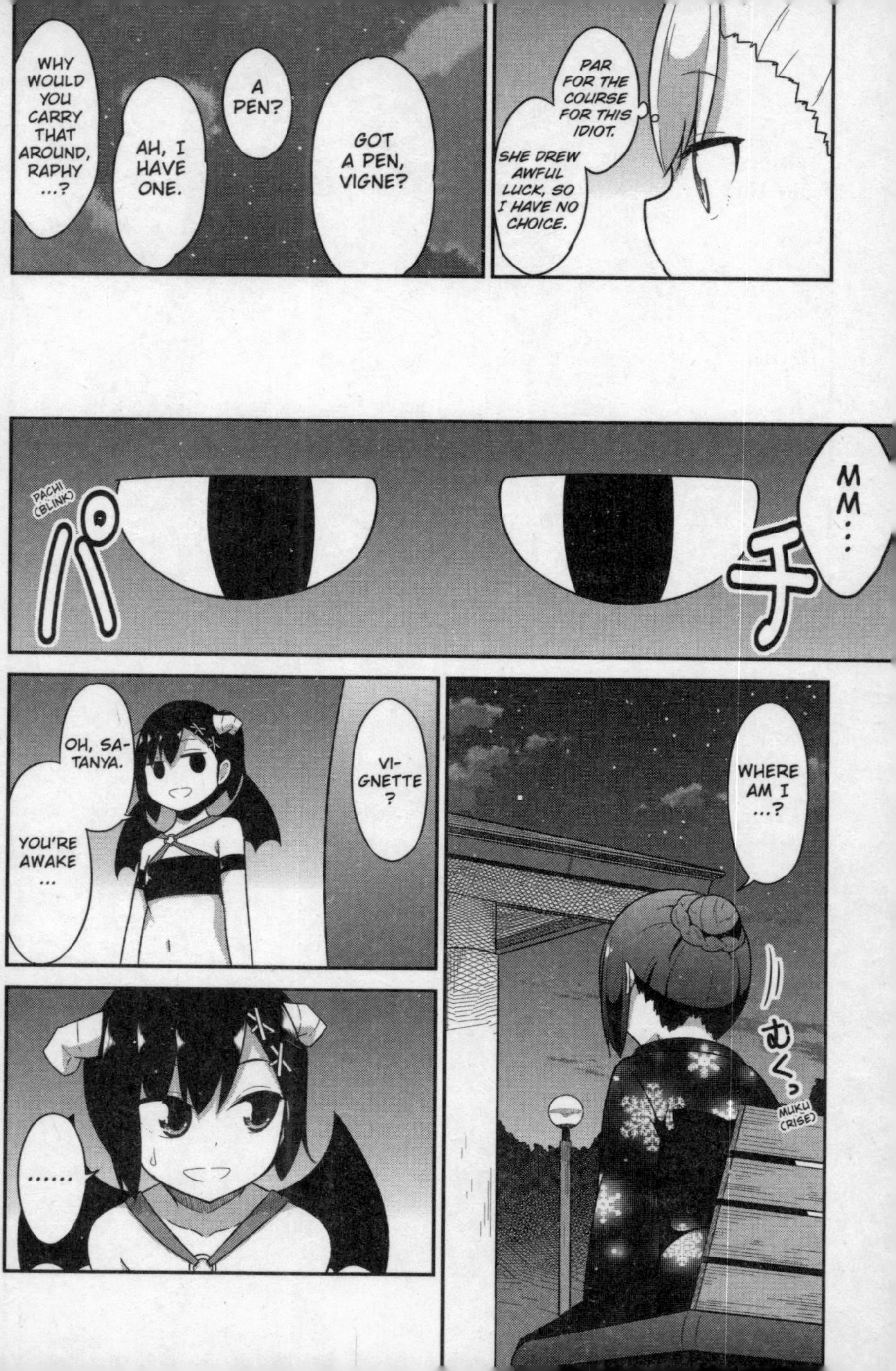
PAR FOR THE COURSE FOR THIS IDIOT.
SHE DREW AWFUL LUCK, SO I HAVE NO CHOICE.
GOT A PEN, VIGNE?
A PEN?
AH, I HAVE ONE.
WHY WOULD YOU CARRY THAT AROUND, RAPHY ...?
MM...
パチ
PACHI (BLINK)
WHERE AM I ...?
むくっ
MUKU (RISE)
VI-GNETTE ?
OH, SA-TANYA.
YOU'RE AWAKE ...
......

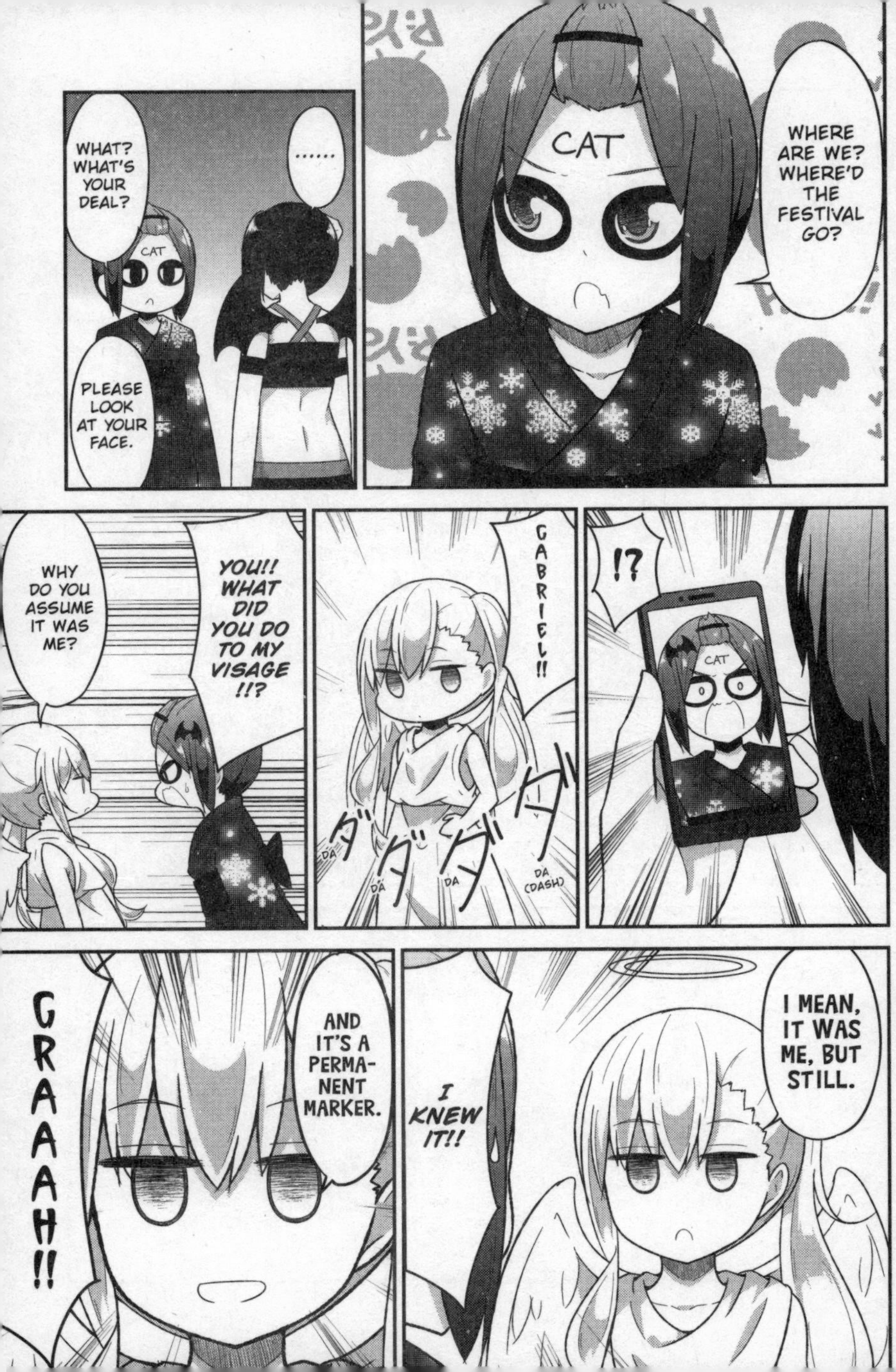
CAT
WHERE ARE WE? WHERE'D THE FESTIVAL GO?
....
WHAT? WHAT'S YOUR DEAL?
CAT
PLEASE LOOK AT YOUR FACE.
!?
CAT
GABRIEL!!
DA
DA
DA
DA (DASH)
YOU!! WHAT DID YOU DO TO MY VISAGE!!?
WHY DO YOU ASSUME IT WAS ME?
I MEAN, IT WAS ME, BUT STILL.
I KNEW IT!!
AND IT'S A PERMA-NENT MARKER.
GRAAAAH!!

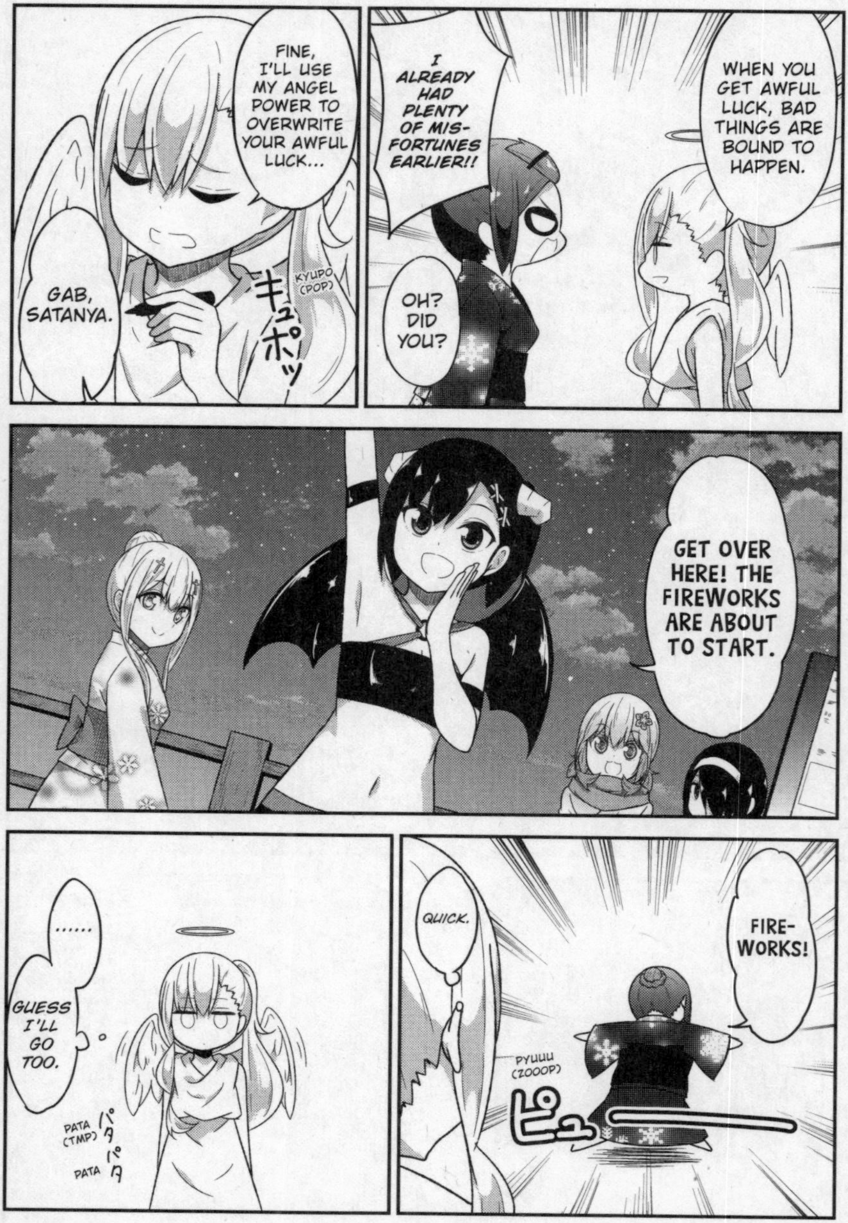
WHEN YOU GET AWFUL LUCK, BAD THINGS ARE BOUND TO HAPPEN.
I ALREADY HAD PLENTY OF MIS-FORTUNES EARLIER!!
OH? DID YOU?
FINE, I'LL USE MY ANGEL POWER TO OVERWRITE YOUR AWFUL LUCK...
KYUPO (POP)
キュポッ
GAB, SATANYA.
GET OVER HERE! THE FIREWORKS ARE ABOUT TO START.
FIRE-WORKS!
PYUUU (ZOOOP)
ピュー
QUICK.
......
GUESS I'LL GO TOO.
PATA (TMP)
パタ
PATA
パタ

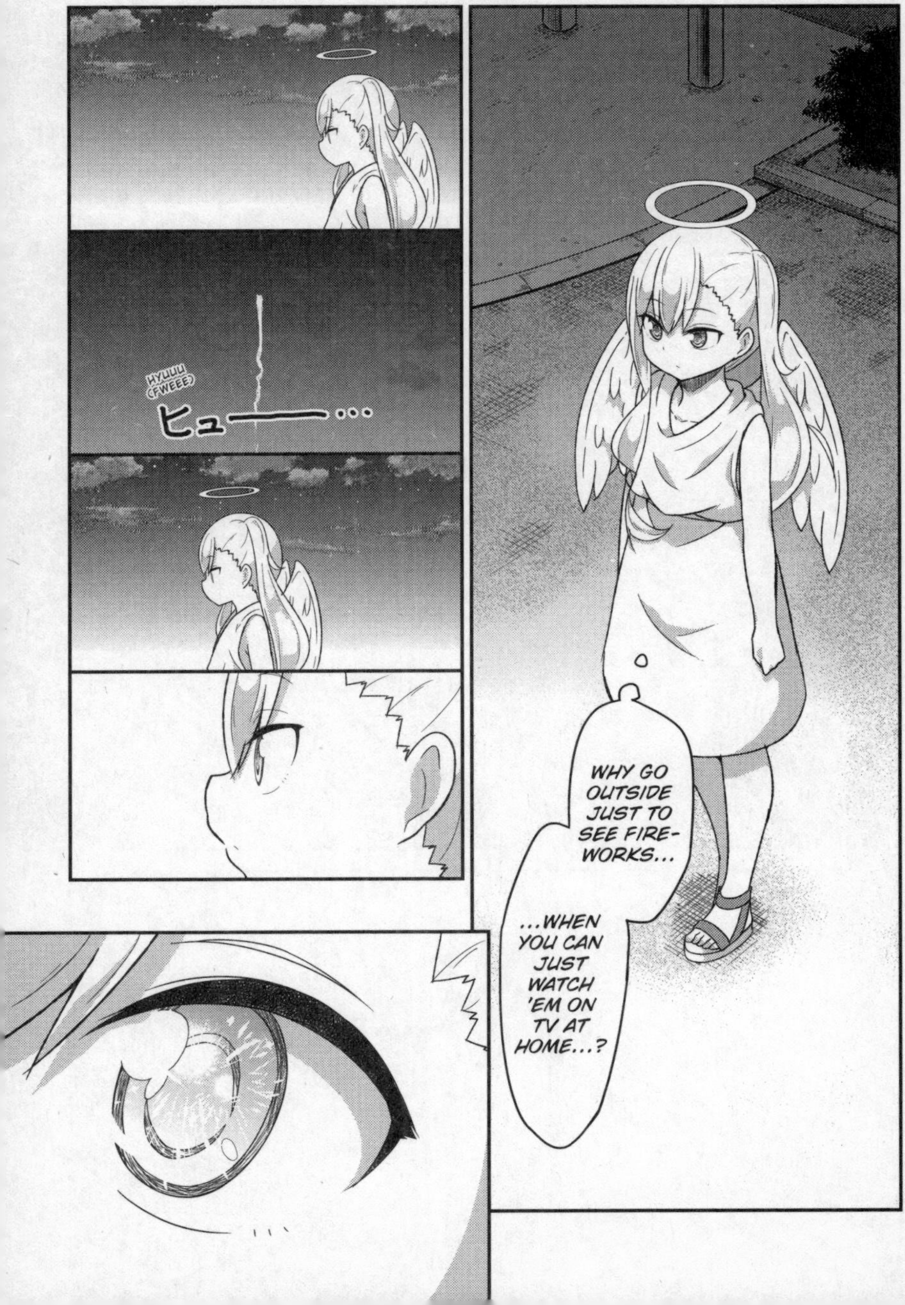
WHY GO OUTSIDE JUST TO SEE FIRE-WORKS...
...WHEN YOU CAN JUST WATCH 'EM ON TV AT HOME...?
HYUUU (FWEEE)
ヒュー…

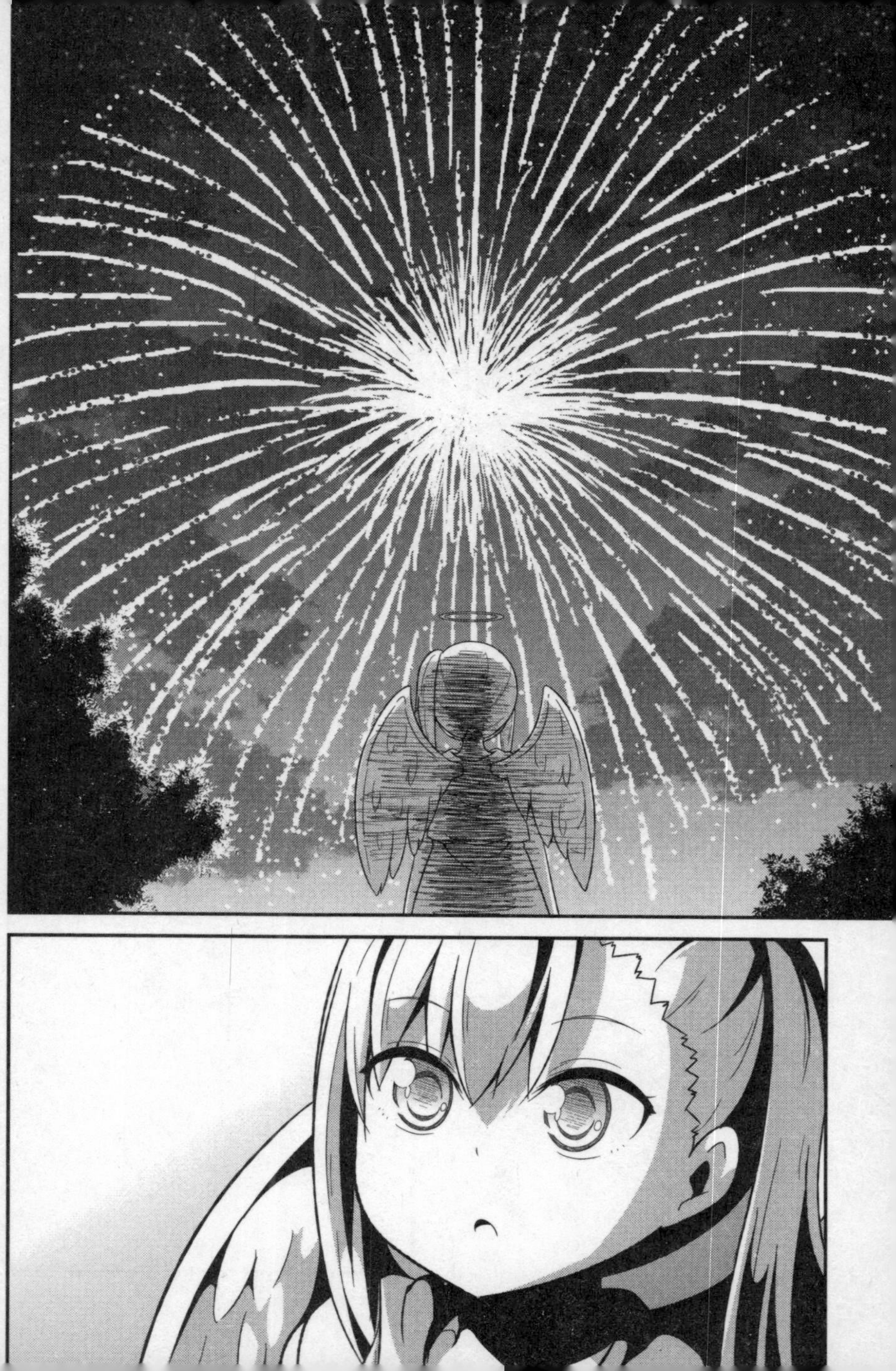

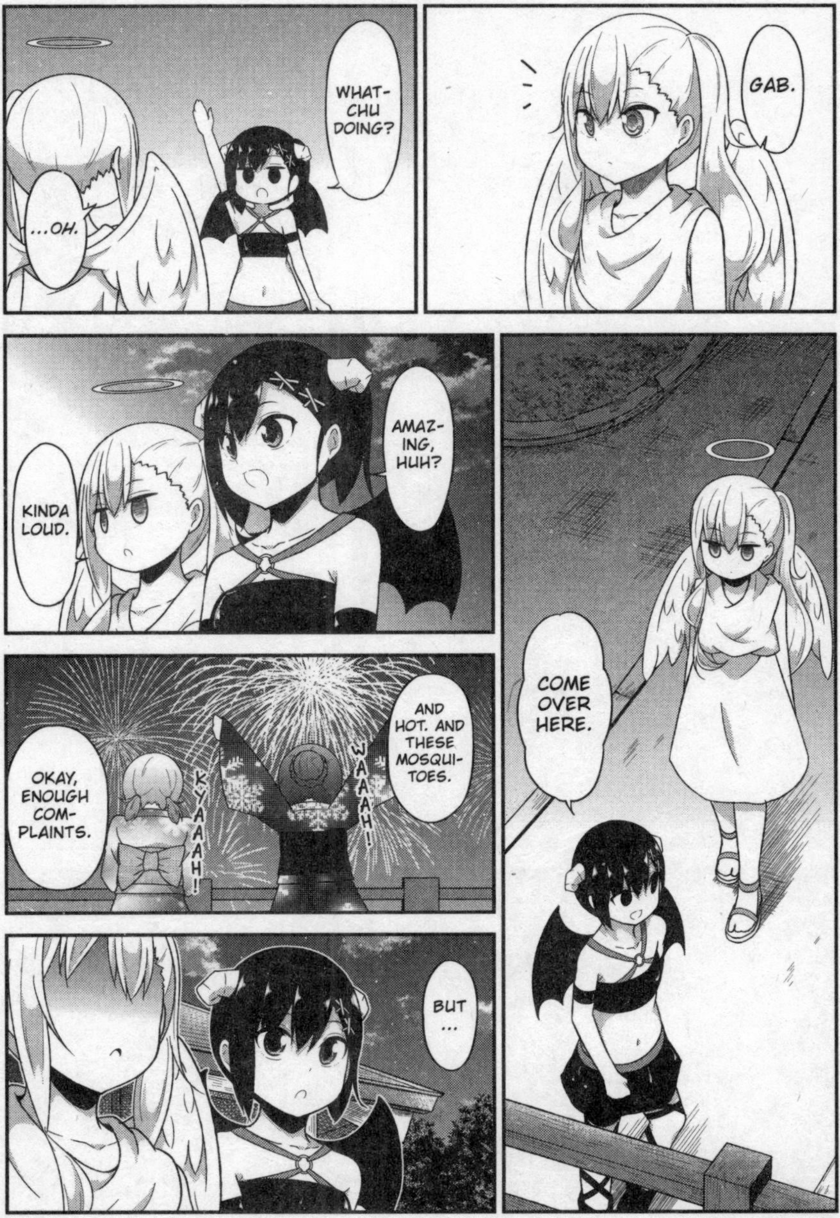
GAB.
WHAT-CHU DOING?
...OH.
COME OVER HERE.
AMAZ-ING, HUH?
KINDA LOUD.
AND HOT. AND THESE MOSQUI-TOES.
WAAAAH!
KYAAAAH!
OKAY, ENOUGH COM-PLAINTS.
BUT ...

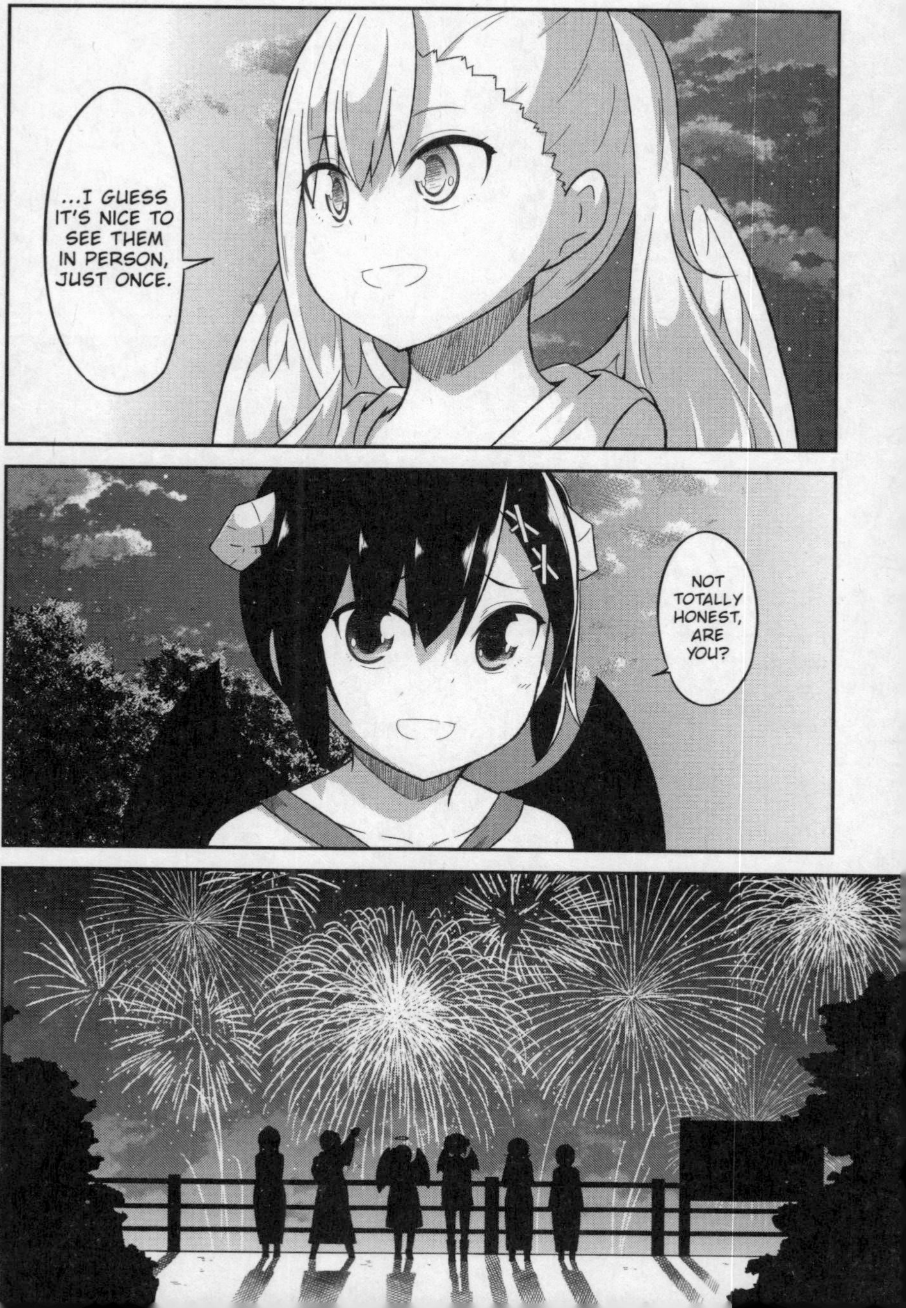
...I GUESS IT'S NICE TO SEE THEM IN PERSON, JUST ONCE.
NOT TOTALLY HONEST, ARE YOU?

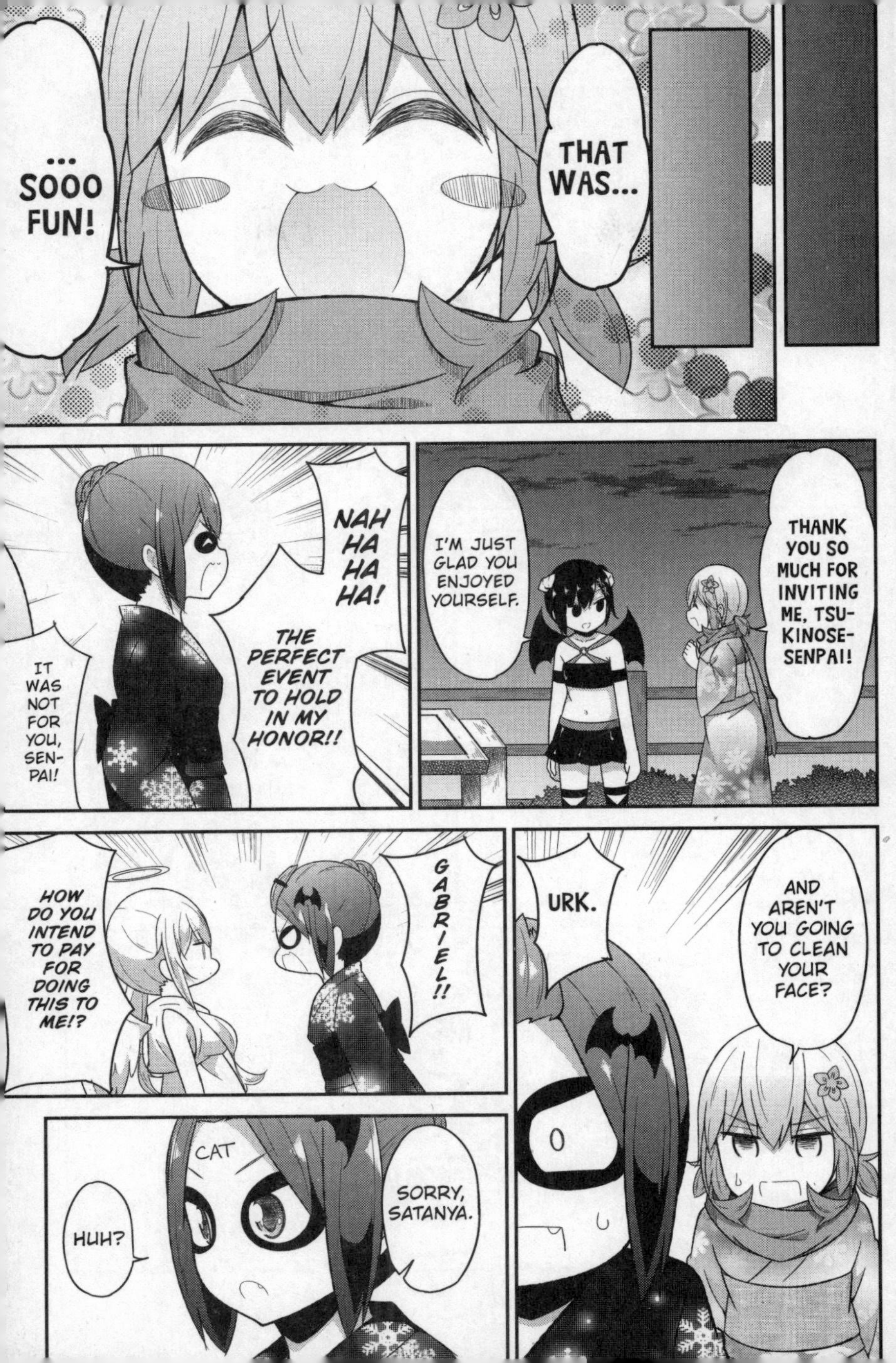
THAT WAS...
... SOOO FUN!
THANK YOU SO MUCH FOR INVITING ME, TSU-KINOSE-SENPAI!
I'M JUST GLAD YOU ENJOYED YOURSELF.
NAH HA HA HA!
THE PERFECT EVENT TO HOLD IN MY HONOR!!
IT WAS NOT FOR YOU, SEN-PAI!
AND AREN'T YOU GOING TO CLEAN YOUR FACE?
URK.
GABRIEL!!
HOW DO YOU INTEND TO PAY FOR DOING THIS TO ME!?
SORRY, SATANYA.
CAT
HUH?

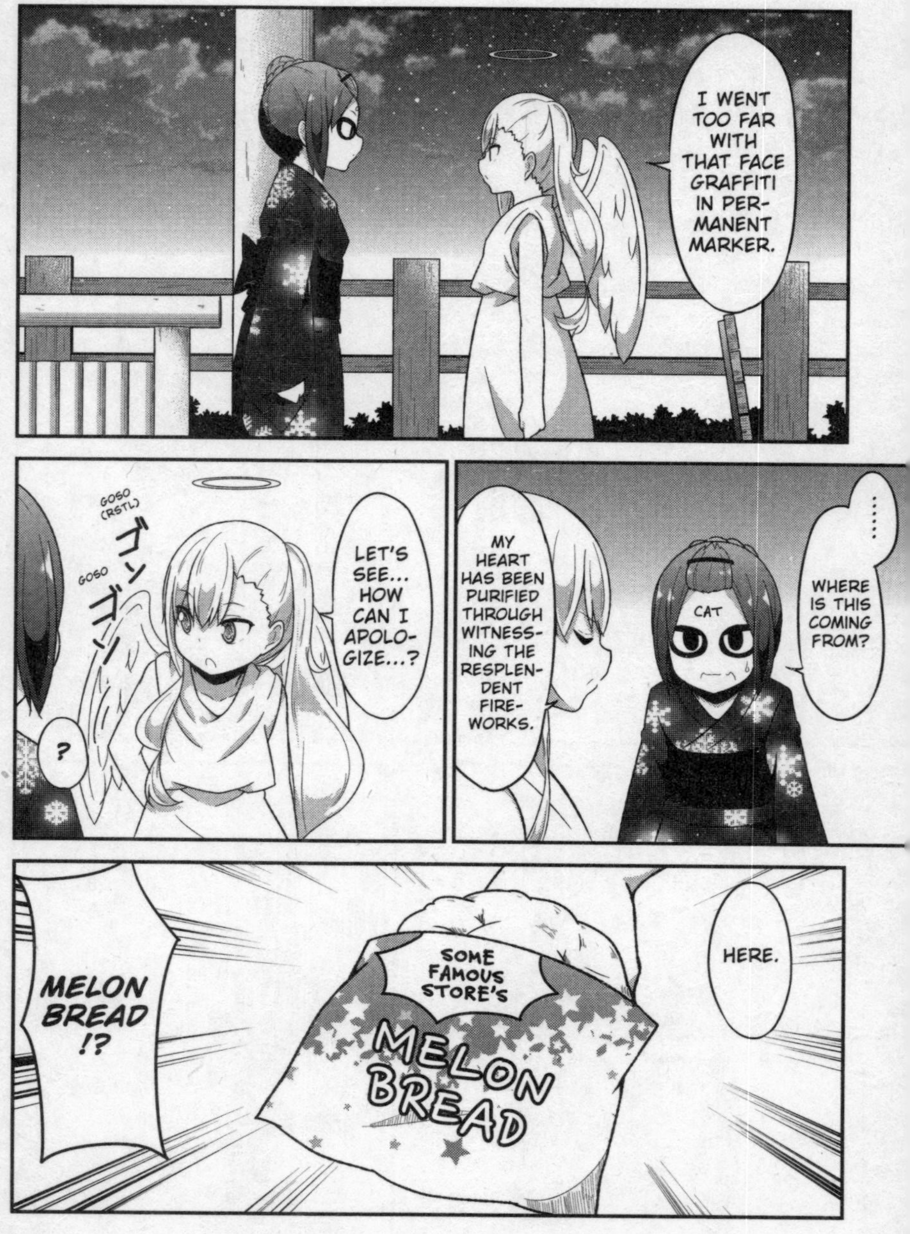
I WENT TOO FAR WITH THAT FACE GRAFFITI IN PER-MANENT MARKER.
......
WHERE IS THIS COMING FROM?
CAT
MY HEART HAS BEEN PURIFIED THROUGH WITNESS-ING THE RESPLEN-DENT FIRE-WORKS.
LET'S SEE... HOW CAN I APOLO-GIZE...?
ゴソ GOSO (RSTL)
ゴソ GOSO
?
HERE.
SOME FAMOUS STORE'S
MELON BREAD
MELON BREAD !?

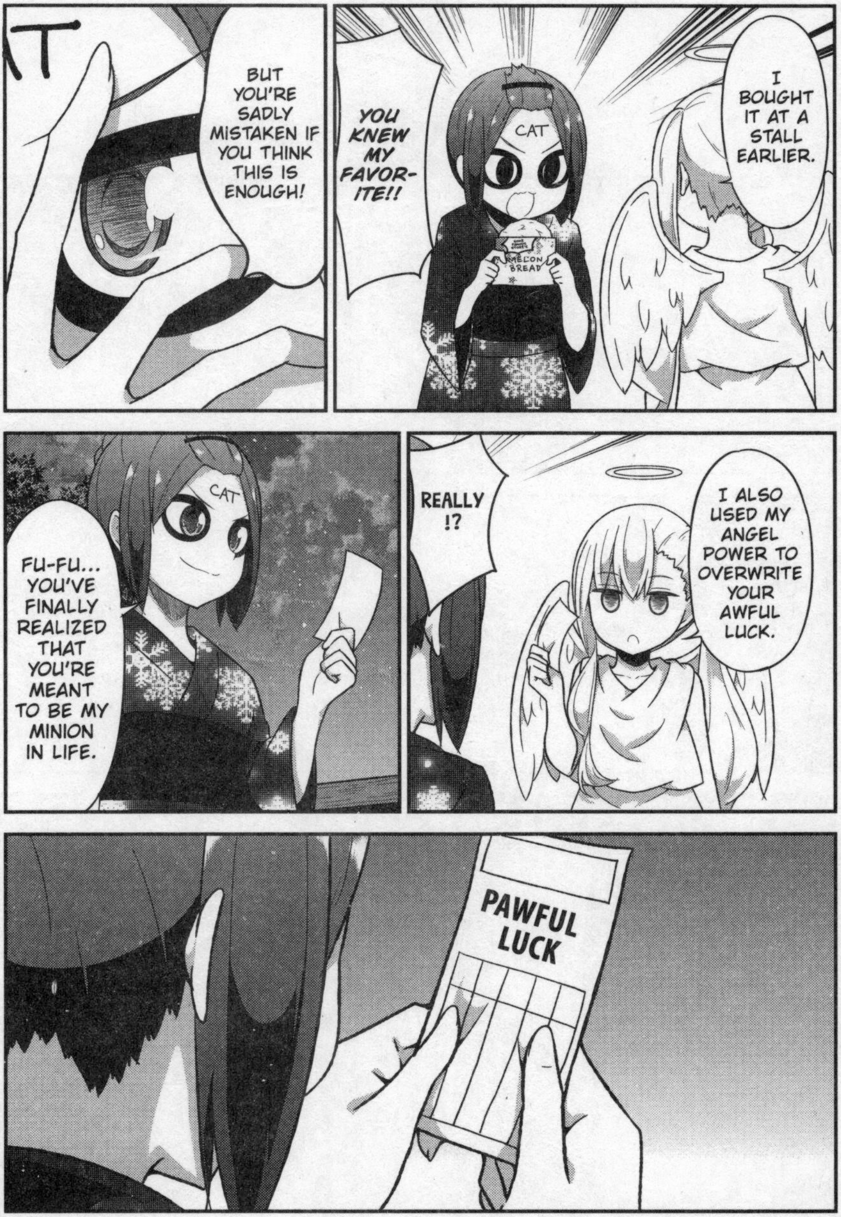
I BOUGHT IT AT A STALL EARLIER.
YOU KNEW MY FAVOR-ITE!!
CAT
MELON BREAD
BUT YOU'RE SADLY MISTAKEN IF YOU THINK THIS IS ENOUGH!
I ALSO USED MY ANGEL POWER TO OVERWRITE YOUR AWFUL LUCK.
REALLY !?
CAT
FU-FU... YOU'VE FINALLY REALIZED THAT YOU'RE MEANT TO BE MY MINION IN LIFE.
PAWFUL LUCK

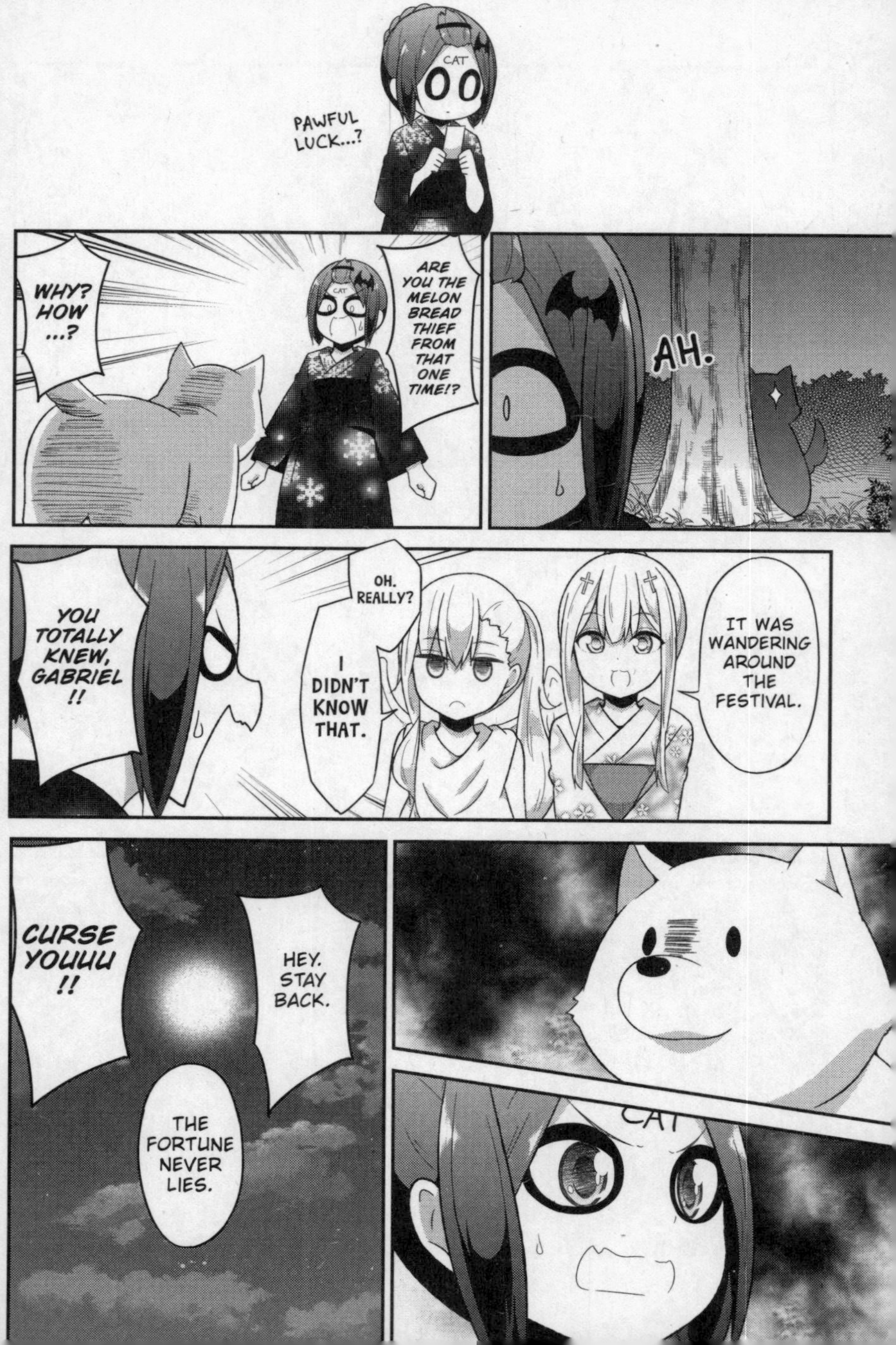
CAT
PAWFUL LUCK...?
AH.
CAT
ARE YOU THE MELON BREAD THIEF FROM THAT ONE TIME!?
WHY? HOW ...?
IT WAS WANDERING AROUND THE FESTIVAL.
OH. REALLY?
I DIDN'T KNOW THAT.
YOU TOTALLY KNEW, GABRIEL!!
CAT
HEY. STAY BACK.
CURSE YOUUU!!
THE FORTUNE NEVER LIES.

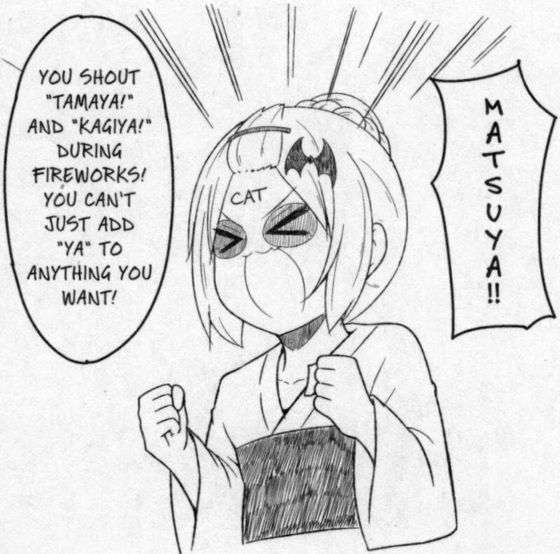
MATSUYA!!
CAT
YOU SHOUT "TAMAYA!" AND "KAGIYA!" DURING FIREWORKS! YOU CAN'T JUST ADD "YA" TO ANYTHING YOU WANT!

Gabriel DropOut

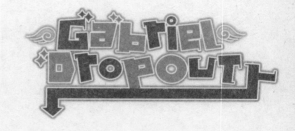

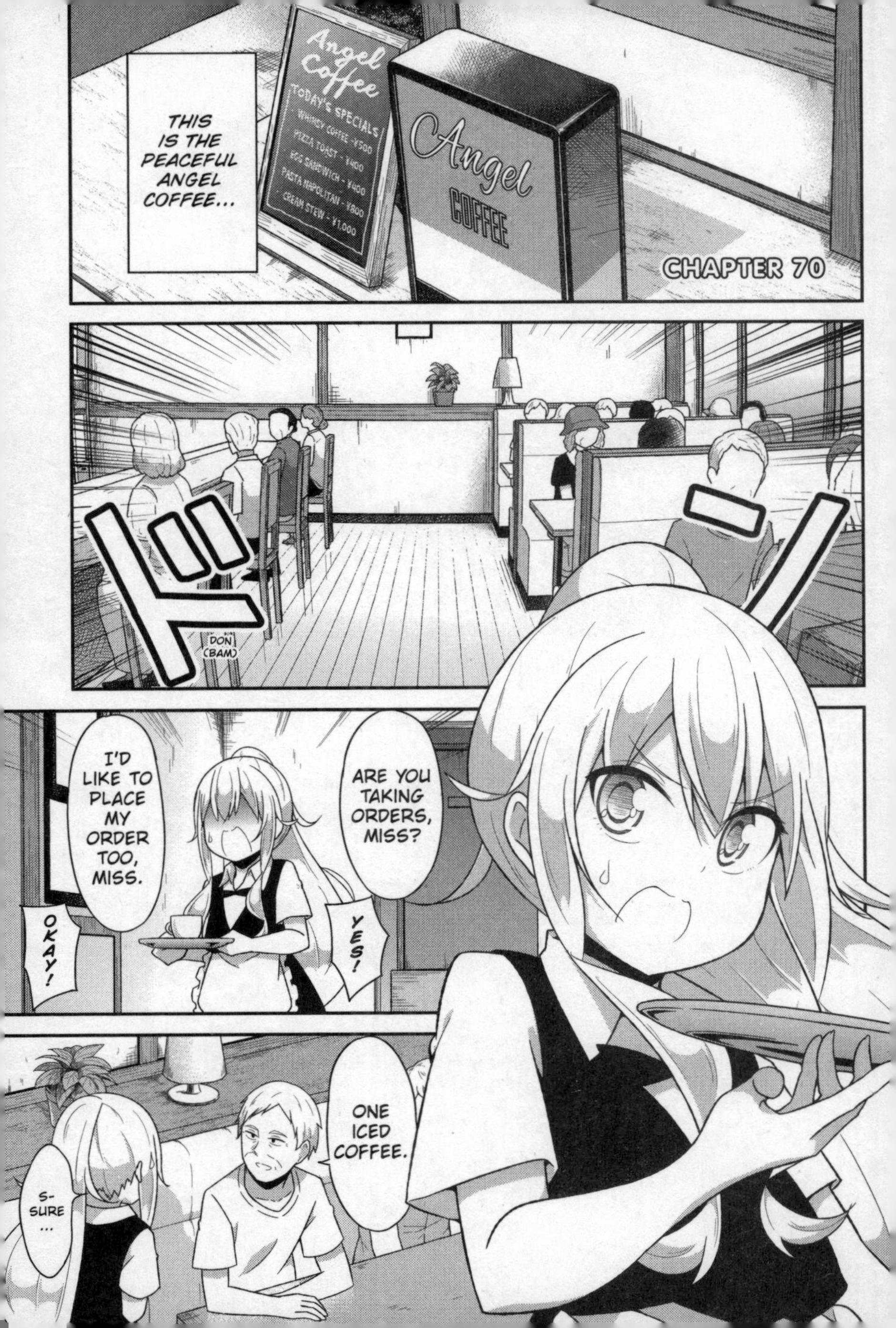
CHAPTER 70
Angel COFFEE
Angel Coffee
TODAY's SPECIALS
PIZZA TOAST - ¥400
EGG SANDWICH - ¥400
PASTA NAPOLITAN - ¥800
CREAM STEW - ¥1,000
THIS IS THE PEACEFUL ANGEL COFFEE...
ドーン
DON (BAM)
ARE YOU TAKING ORDERS, MISS?
YES!
I'D LIKE TO PLACE MY ORDER TOO, MISS.
OKAY!
ONE ICED COFFEE.
S-SURE...

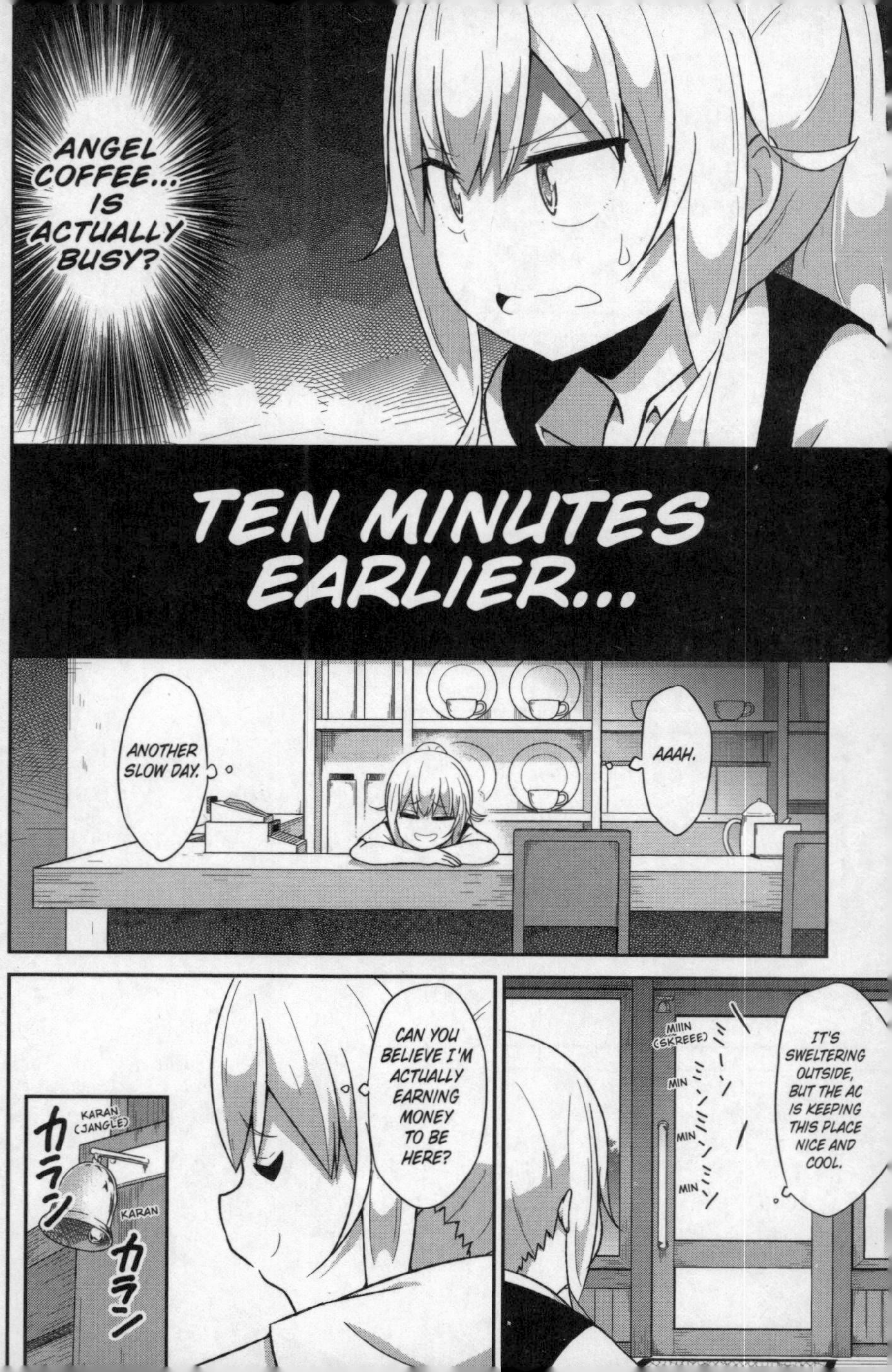
ANGEL COFFEE... IS ACTUALLY BUSY?
TEN MINUTES EARLIER...
AAAH.
ANOTHER SLOW DAY.
IT'S SWELTERING OUTSIDE, BUT THE AC IS KEEPING THIS PLACE NICE AND COOL.
MIIIN (SKREEE)
MIN
MIN
MIN
CAN YOU BELIEVE I'M ACTUALLY EARNING MONEY TO BE HERE?
KARAN (JANGLE)
カラン
KARAN
カラン

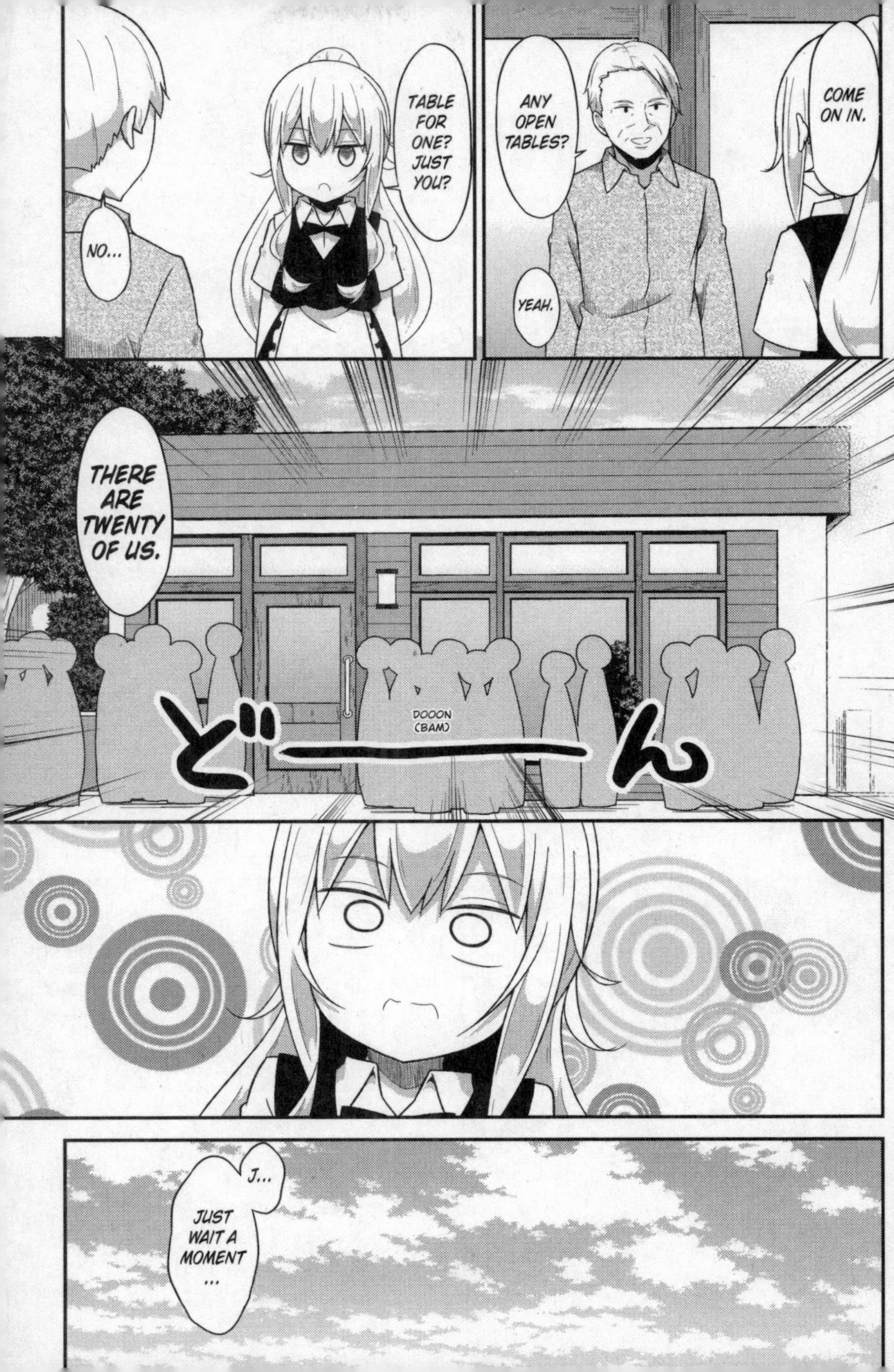
COME ON IN.
ANY OPEN TABLES?
YEAH.
TABLE FOR ONE? JUST YOU?
NO...
THERE ARE TWENTY OF US.
どーーーん
DOOON (BAM)
J...
JUST WAIT A MOMENT ...

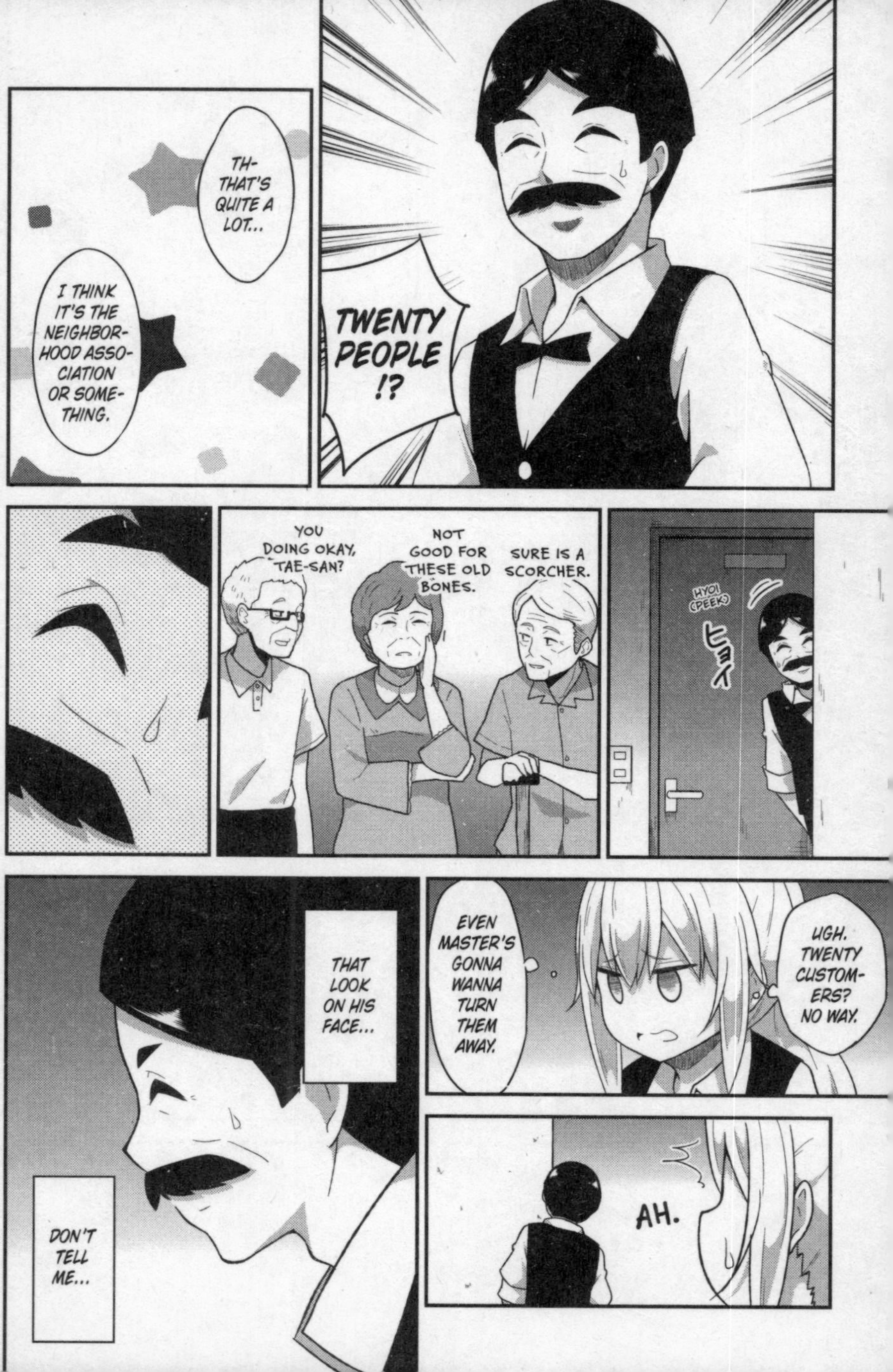
TWENTY PEOPLE!?
TH-THAT'S QUITE A LOT...
I THINK IT'S THE NEIGHBORHOOD ASSOCIATION OR SOMETHING.
HYOI (PEEK)
ヒョイ
SURE IS A SCORCHER.
NOT GOOD FOR THESE OLD BONES.
YOU DOING OKAY, TAE-SAN?
UGH. TWENTY CUSTOMERS? NO WAY.
EVEN MASTER'S GONNA WANNA TURN THEM AWAY.
AH.
THAT LOOK ON HIS FACE...
DON'T TELL ME...

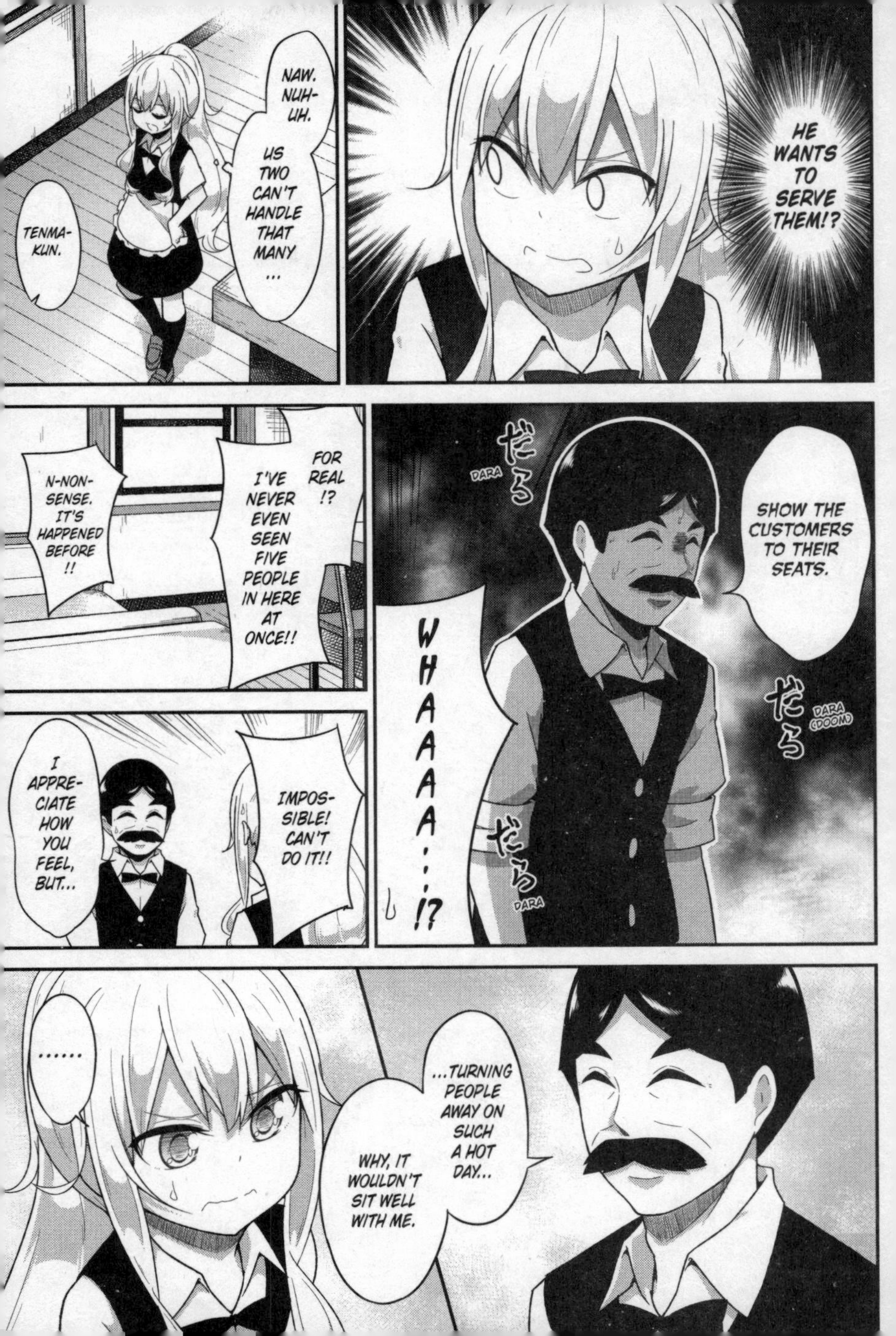

HE WANTS TO SERVE THEM!?
NAW. NUH-UH.
US TWO CAN'T HANDLE THAT MANY ...
TENMA-KUN.
だら
DARA
SHOW THE CUSTOMERS TO THEIR SEATS.
だら
DARA (DOOM)
だら
DARA
WHAAAAA...!?
FOR REAL!?
I'VE NEVER EVEN SEEN FIVE PEOPLE IN HERE AT ONCE!!
N-NON-SENSE. IT'S HAPPENED BEFORE!!
IMPOS-SIBLE! CAN'T DO IT!!
I APPRE-CIATE HOW YOU FEEL, BUT...
...TURNING PEOPLE AWAY ON SUCH A HOT DAY...
WHY, IT WOULDN'T SIT WELL WITH ME.
......

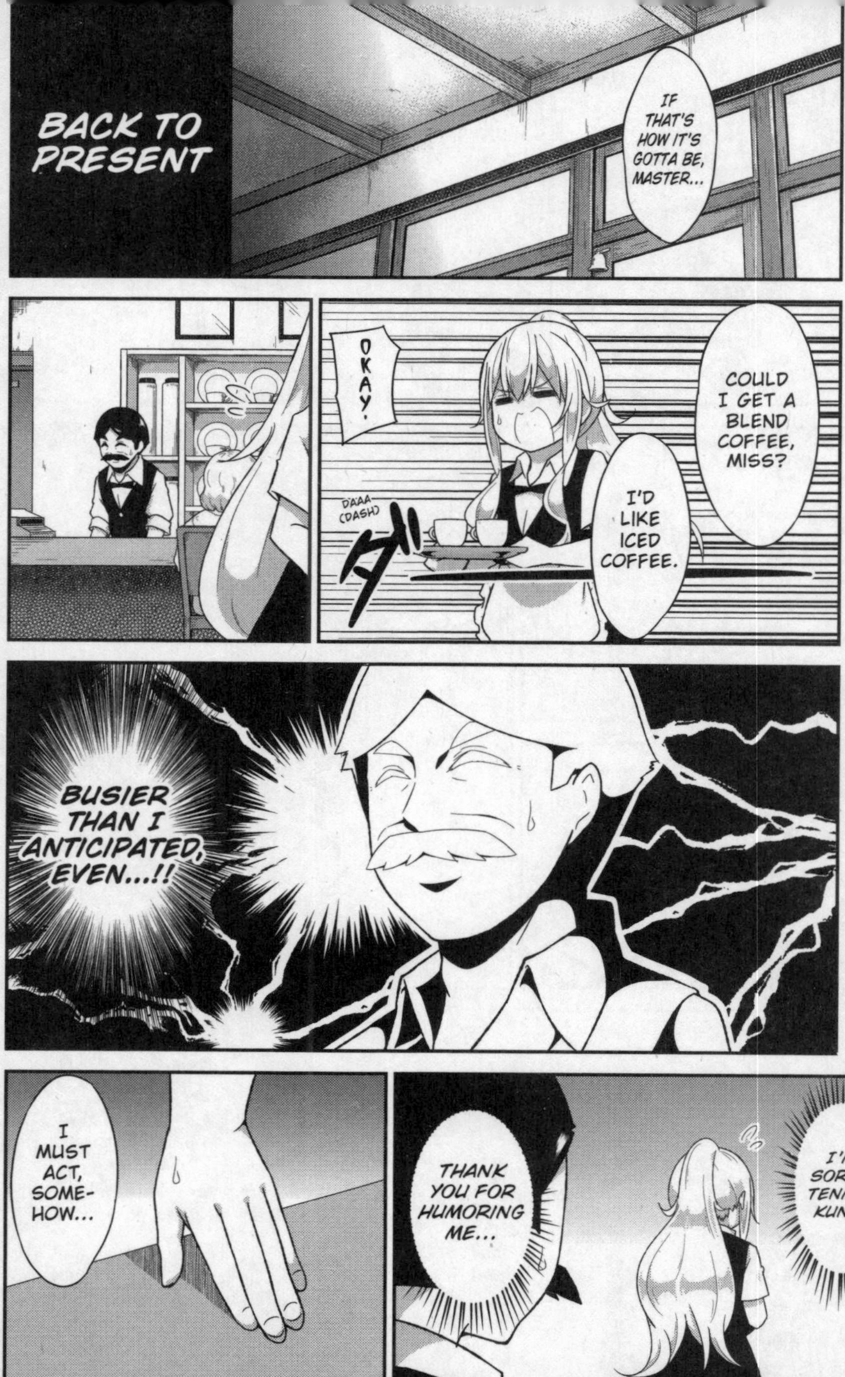
IF THAT'S HOW IT'S GOTTA BE, MASTER...
BACK TO PRESENT
COULD I GET A BLEND COFFEE, MISS?
OKAY.
I'D LIKE ICED COFFEE.
DÀAA (DASH)
BUSIER THAN I ANTICIPATED, EVEN...!!
I'M SORRY, TENMA-KUN...
THANK YOU FOR HUMORING ME...
I MUST ACT, SOMEHOW...

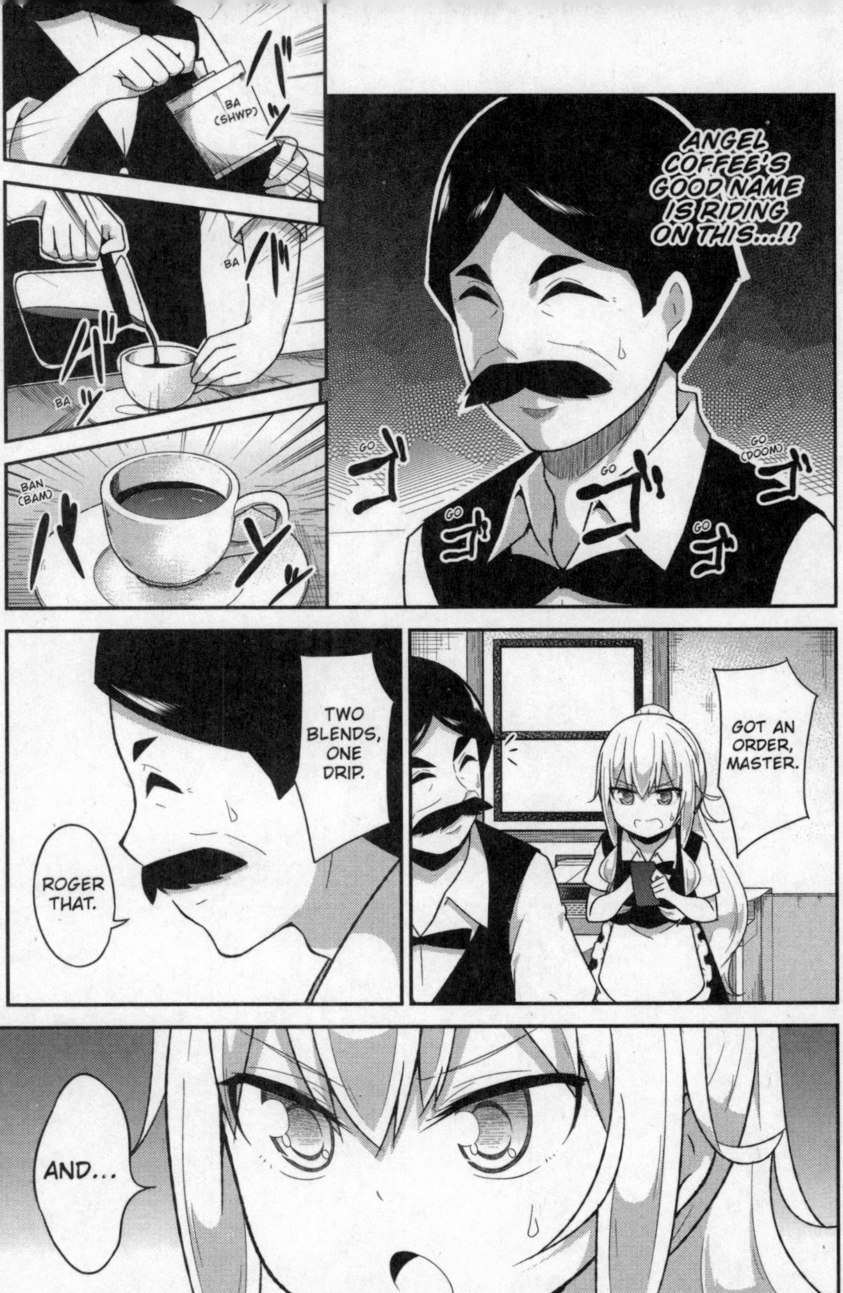
ANGEL COFFEE'S GOOD NAME IS RIDING ON THIS...!!
GO (DOOM)
GO
GO
GO
GO
BA (SHWP)
BA
BA
BAN (BAM)
GOT AN ORDER, MASTER.
TWO BLENDS, ONE DRIP.
ROGER THAT.
AND...

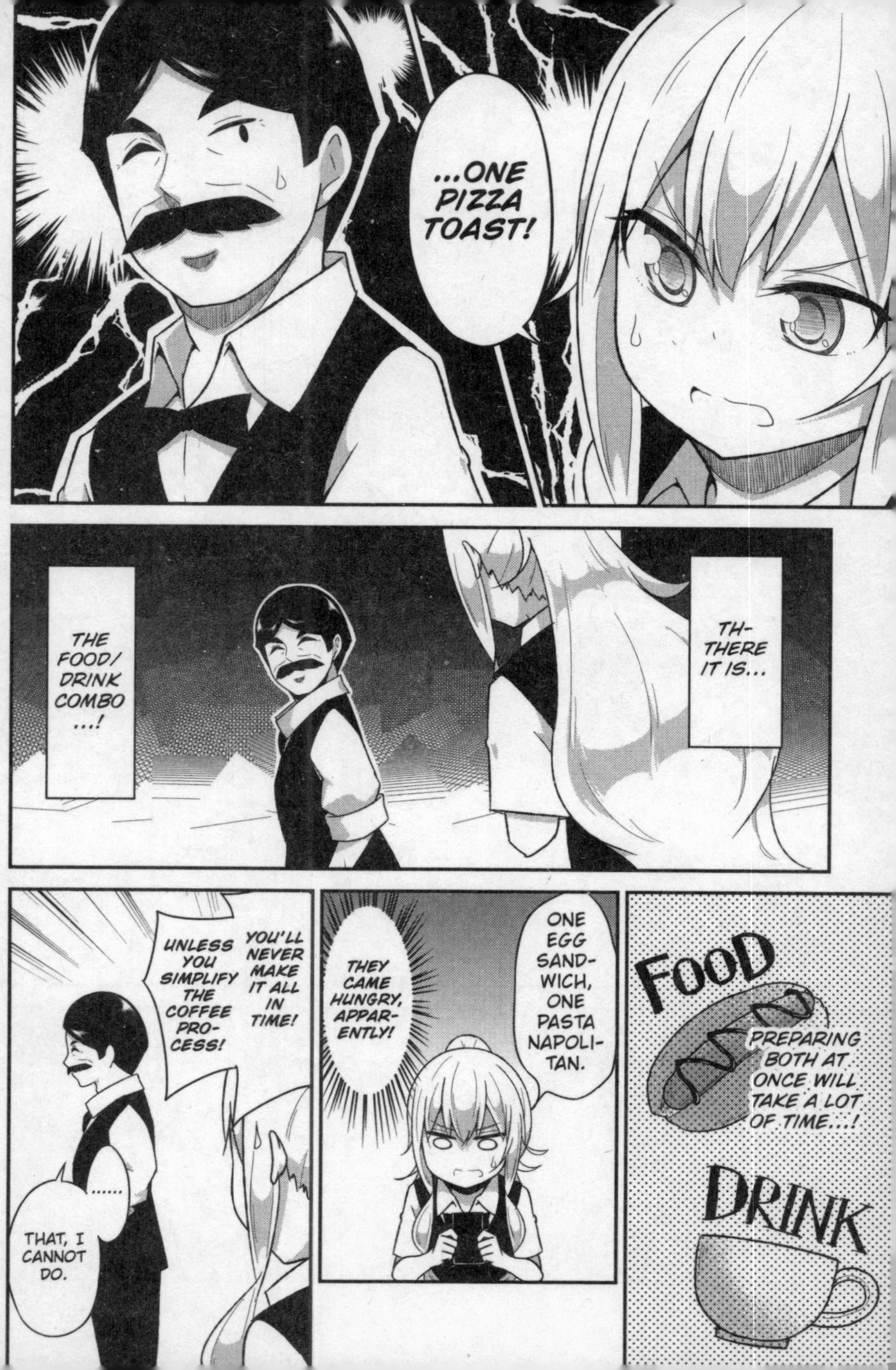
...ONE PIZZA TOAST!
TH- THERE IT IS...
THE FOOD/ DRINK COMBO ...!
FOOD
PREPARING BOTH AT ONCE WILL TAKE A LOT OF TIME...!
DRINK
ONE EGG SAND-WICH, ONE PASTA NAPOLI-TAN.
THEY CAME HUNGRY, APPAR-ENTLY!
YOU'LL NEVER MAKE IT ALL IN TIME!
UNLESS YOU SIMPLIFY THE COFFEE PRO-CESS!
......
THAT, I CANNOT DO.

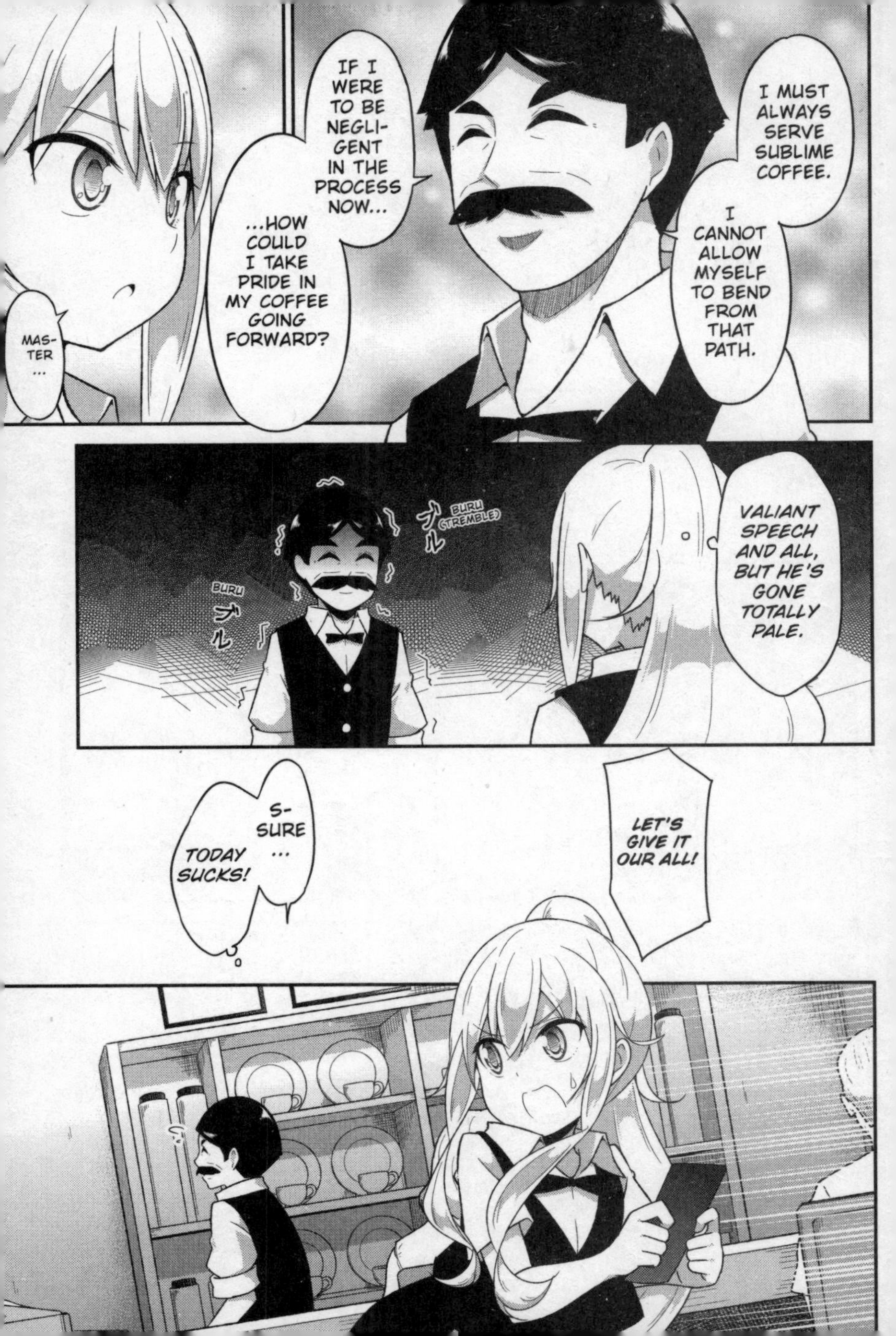
I MUST ALWAYS SERVE SUBLIME COFFEE.
I CANNOT ALLOW MYSELF TO BEND FROM THAT PATH.
IF I WERE TO BE NEGLIGENT IN THE PROCESS NOW...
...HOW COULD I TAKE PRIDE IN MY COFFEE GOING FORWARD?
MASTER...
VALIANT SPEECH AND ALL, BUT HE'S GONE TOTALLY PALE.
BURU (TREMBLE)
BURU
LET'S GIVE IT OUR ALL!
S-SURE...
TODAY SUCKS!

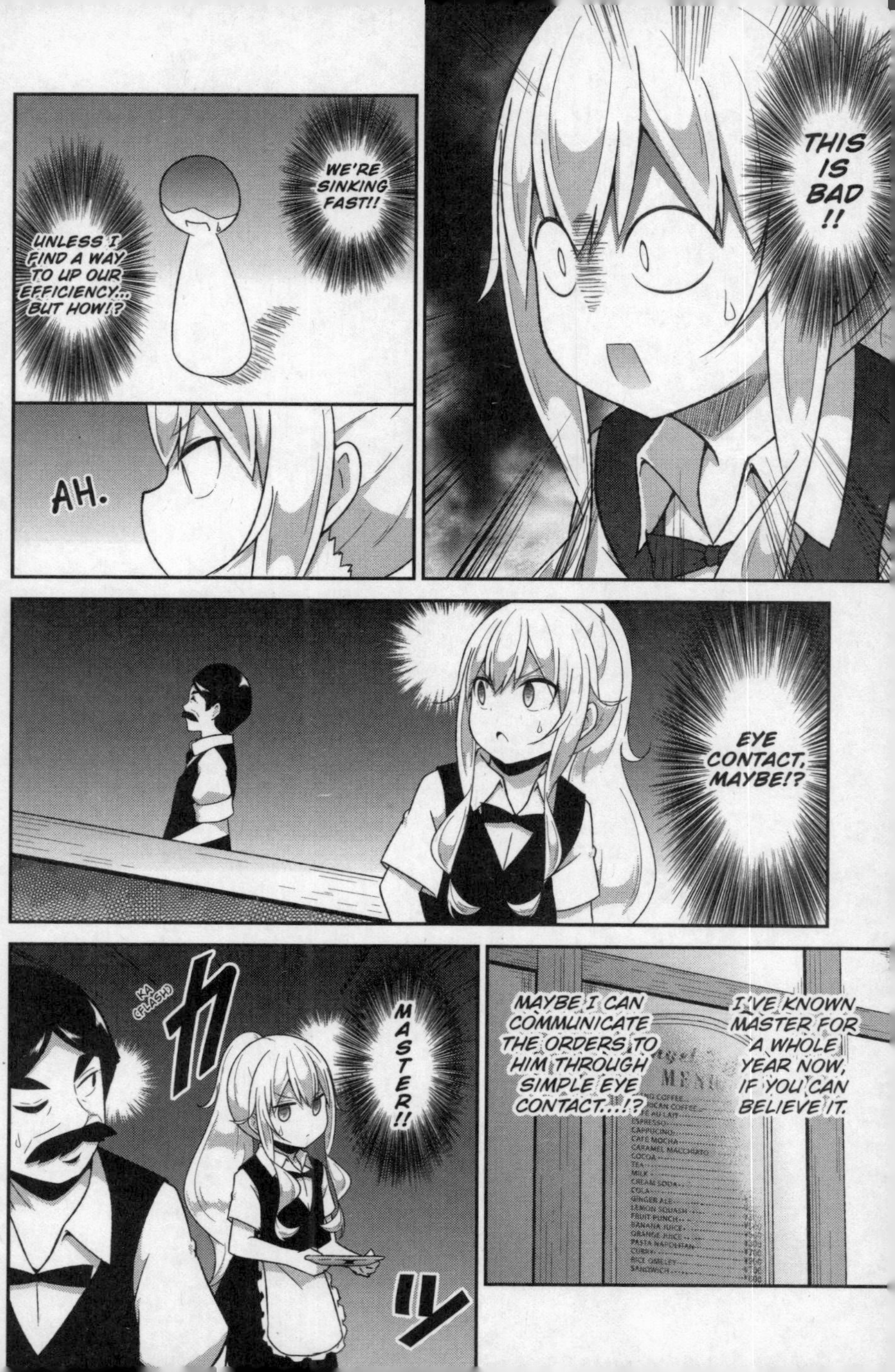
THIS IS BAD!!
WE'RE SINKING FAST!!
UNLESS I FIND A WAY TO UP OUR EFFICIENCY... BUT HOW!?
AH.
EYE CONTACT, MAYBE!?
I'VE KNOWN MASTER FOR A WHOLE YEAR NOW, IF YOU CAN BELIEVE IT.
MAYBE I CAN COMMUNICATE THE ORDERS TO HIM THROUGH SIMPLE EYE CONTACT...!?
MASTER!!
KA (FLASH)

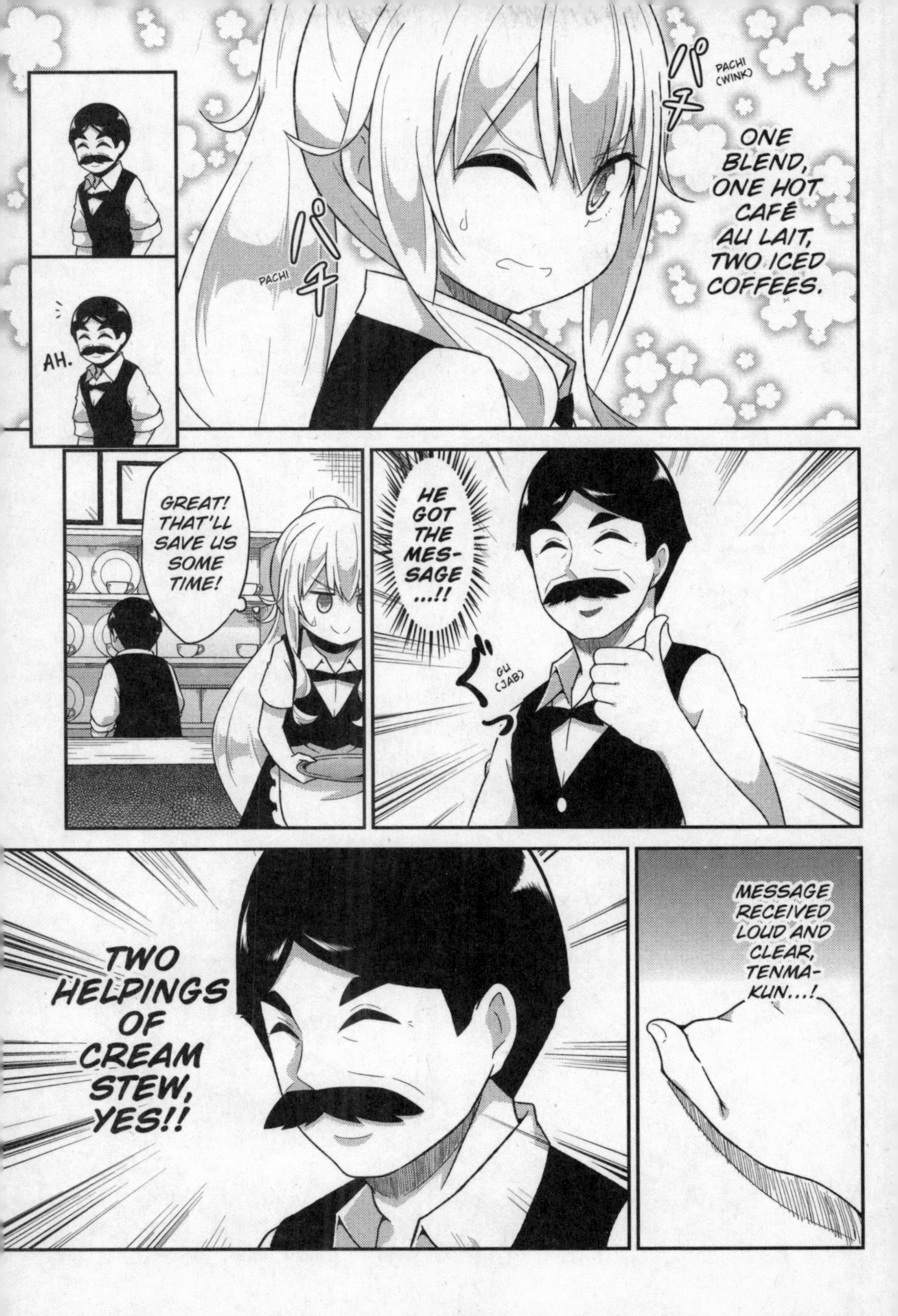
PACHI (WINK)
ONE BLEND, ONE HOT CAFÉ AU LAIT, TWO ICED COFFEES.
PACHI
AH.
HE GOT THE MES-SAGE...!!
GU (JAB)
GREAT! THAT'LL SAVE US SOME TIME!
MESSAGE RECEIVED LOUD AND CLEAR, TENMA-KUN...!
TWO HELPINGS OF CREAM STEW, YES!!

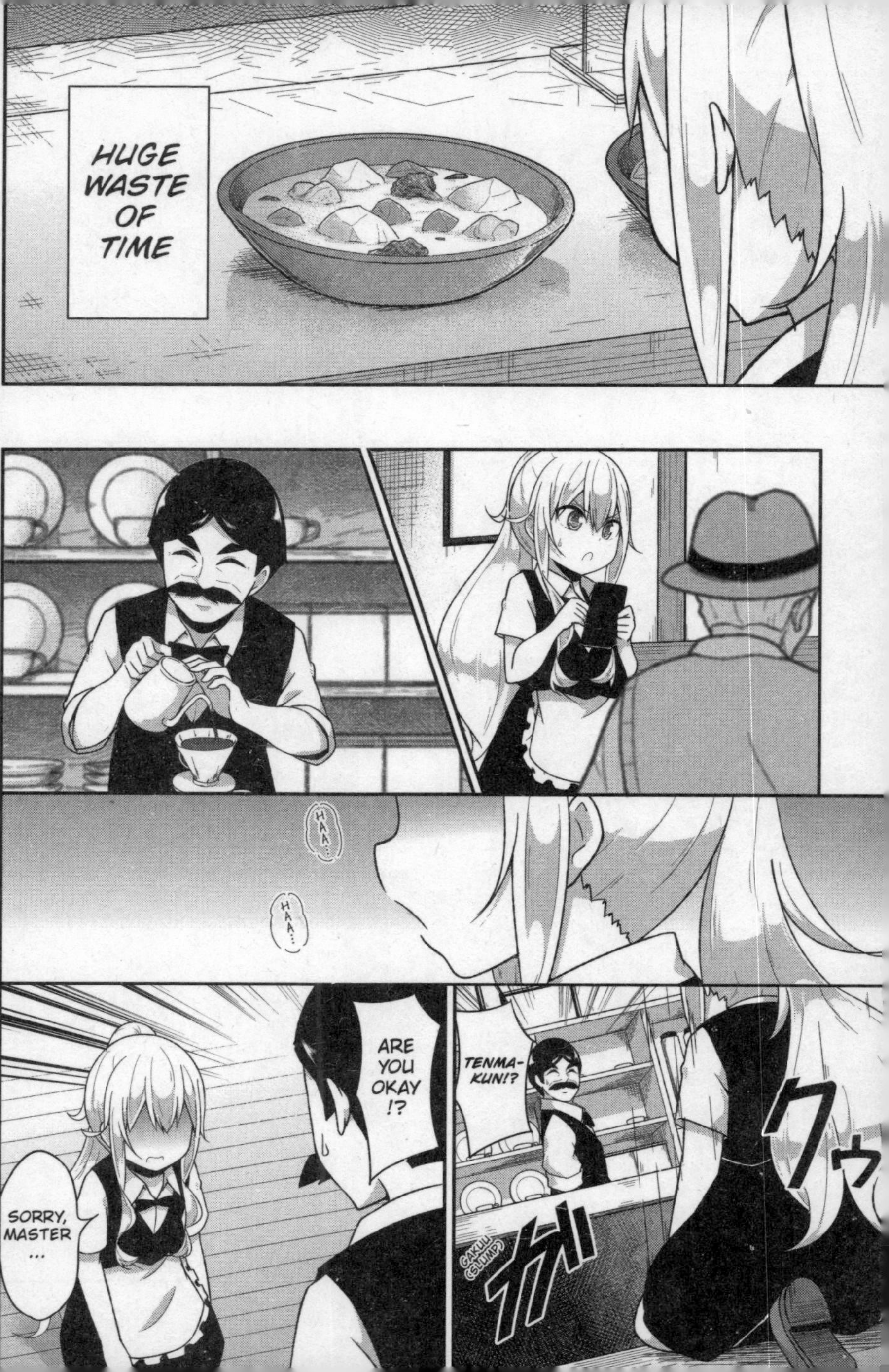
HUGE WASTE OF TIME
HAA...
HAA...
TENMA-KUN!?
GAKUU (SLUMP)
ARE YOU OKAY !?
SORRY, MASTER ...

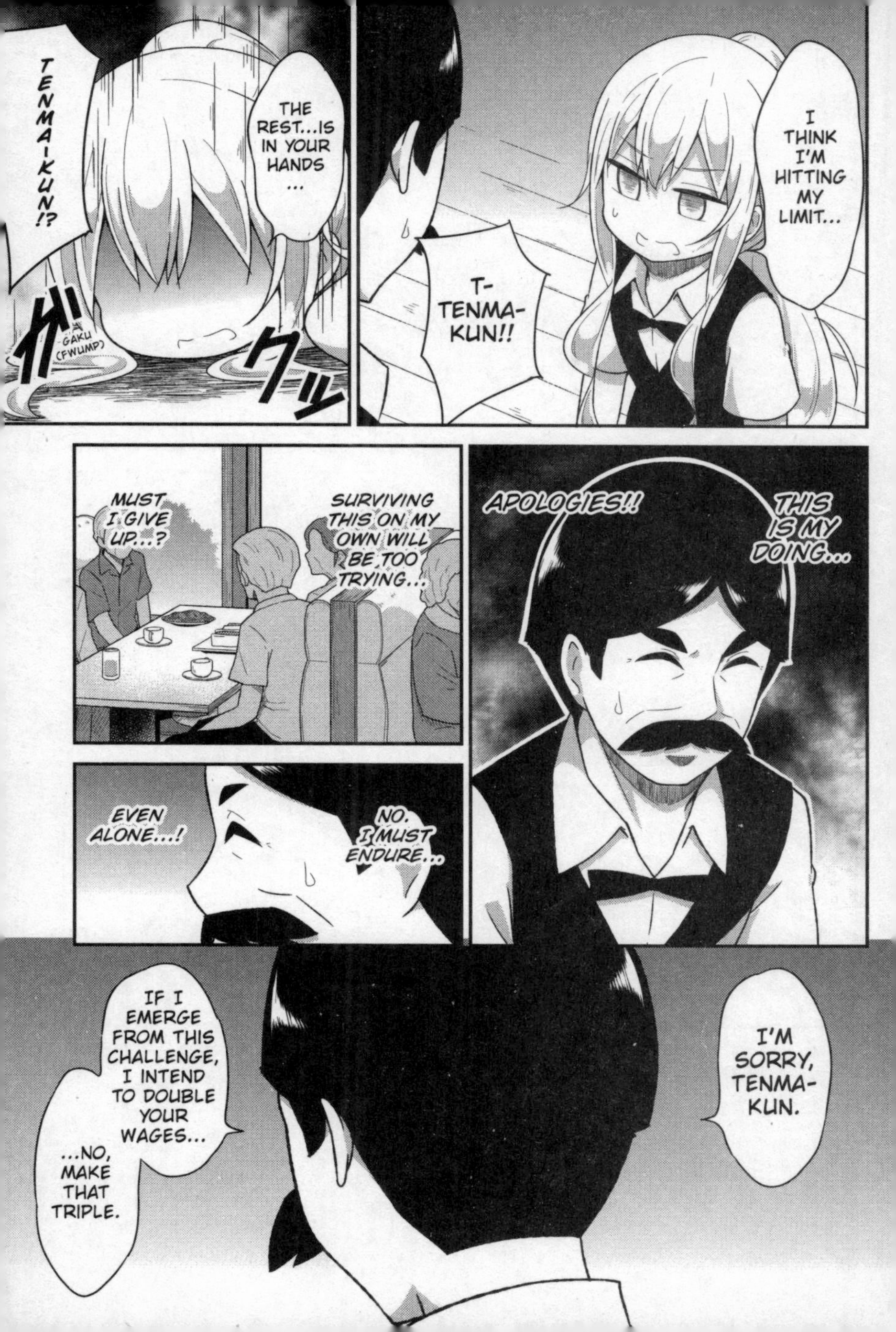
I THINK I'M HITTING MY LIMIT...
T-TENMA-KUN!!
THE REST...IS IN YOUR HANDS ...
TENMAIKUN!?
GAKU (FWUMP)
THIS IS MY DOING...
APOLOGIES!!
SURVIVING THIS ON MY OWN WILL BE TOO TRYING...
MUST I GIVE UP...?
NO. I MUST ENDURE...
EVEN ALONE...!
I'M SORRY, TENMA-KUN.
IF I EMERGE FROM THIS CHALLENGE, I INTEND TO DOUBLE YOUR WAGES...
...NO, MAKE THAT TRIPLE.

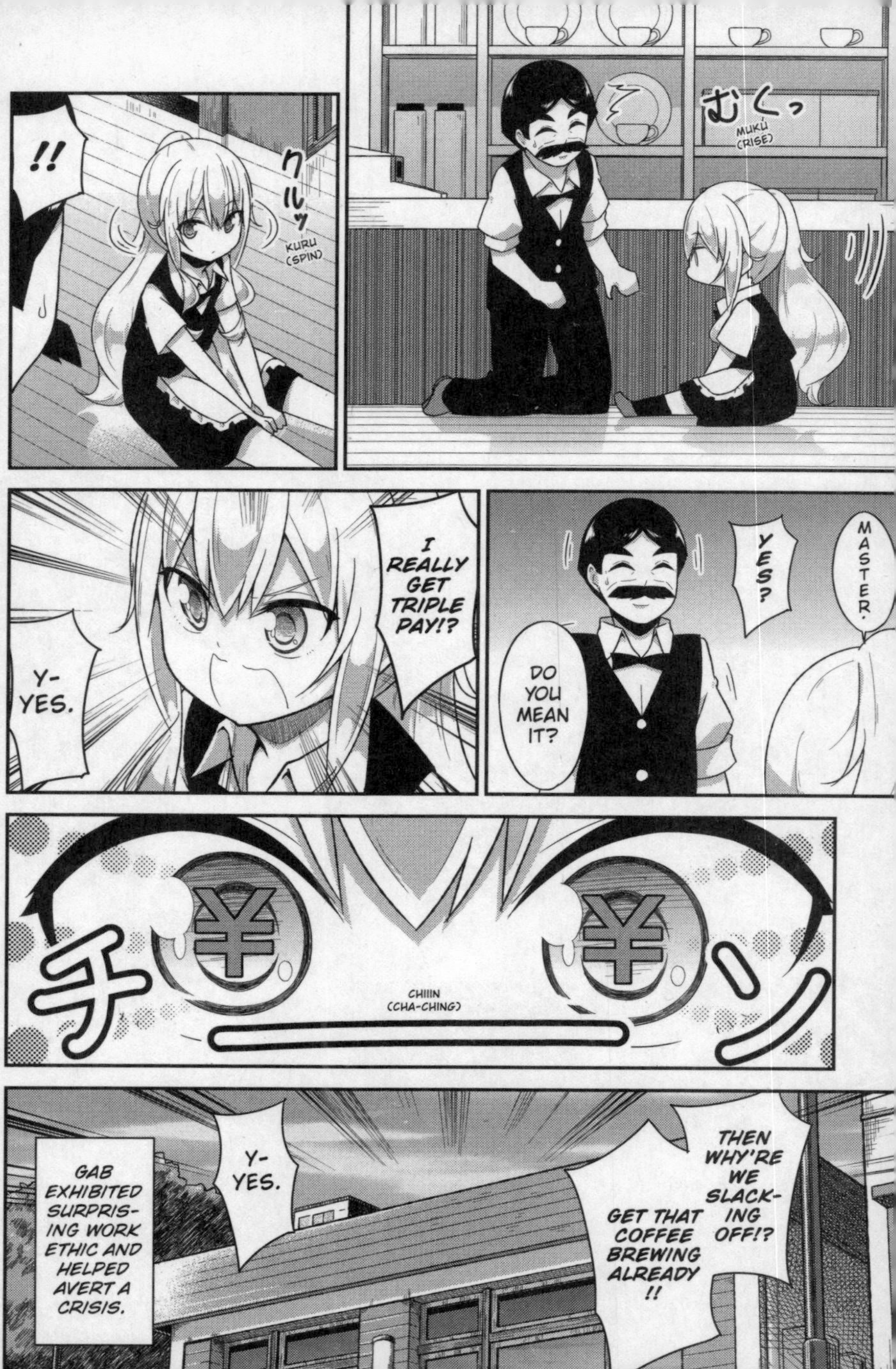
むくっ
MUKU (RISE)
!!
クルッ
KURU (SPIN)
MASTER.
YES?
DO YOU MEAN IT?
I REALLY GET TRIPLE PAY!?
Y-YES.
チーーーン
CHIIIN (CHA-CHING)
THEN WHY'RE WE SLACKING OFF!?
GET THAT COFFEE BREWING ALREADY!!
Y-YES.
GAB EXHIBITED SURPRISING WORK ETHIC AND HELPED AVERT A CRISIS.

GABRIEL WORKS TO GET PAID
SOME ANGEL YOU ARE.

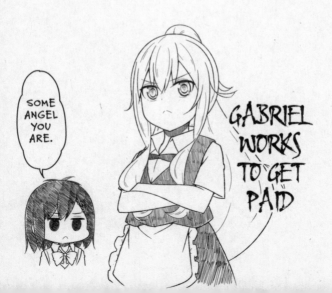

Gabriel Dropout

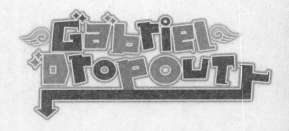

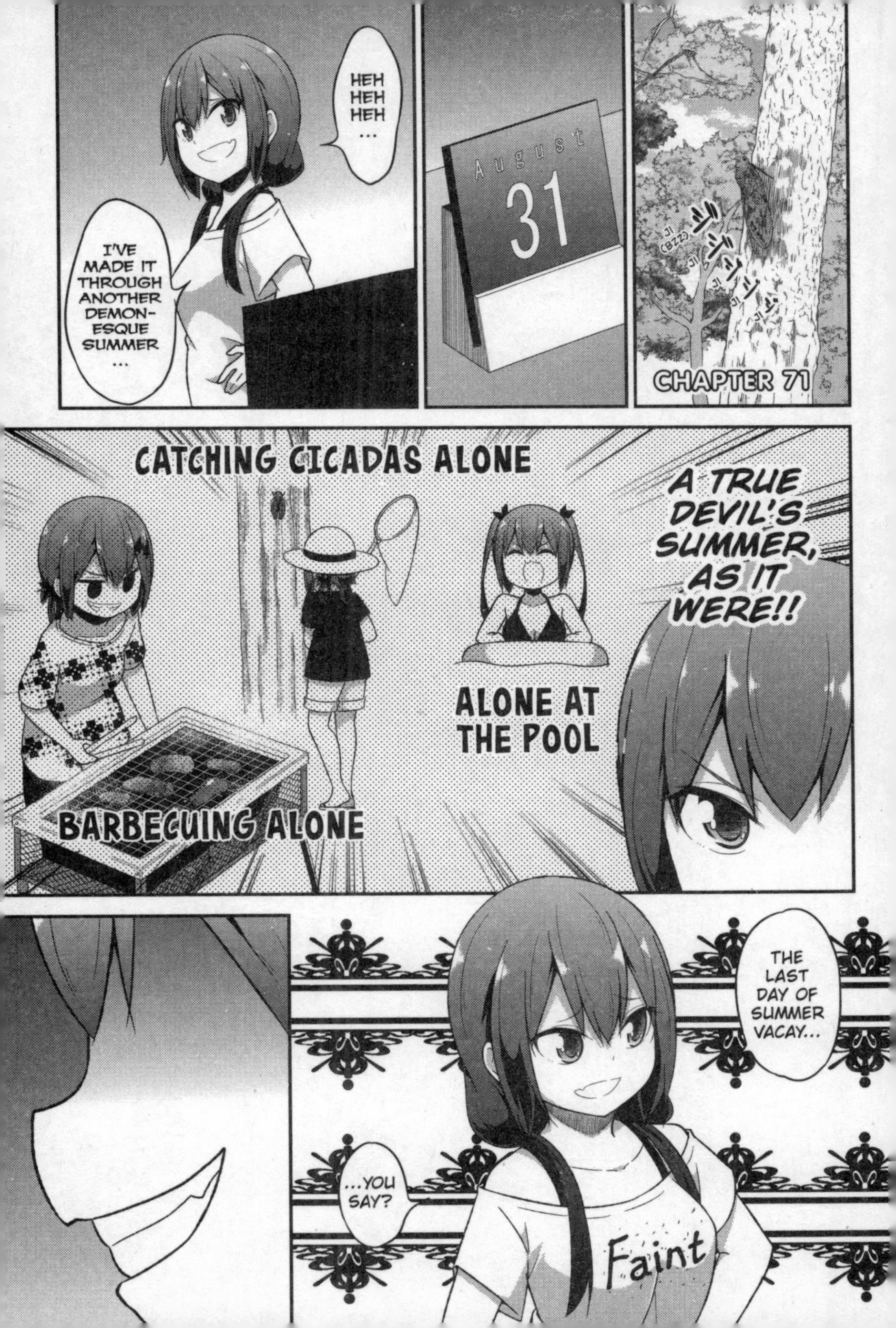
JI (BZZ)
JI
JI
JI
CHAPTER 71
August
31
HEH HEH HEH ...
I'VE MADE IT THROUGH ANOTHER DEMON-ESQUE SUMMER ...
A TRUE DEVIL'S SUMMER, AS IT WERE!!
ALONE AT THE POOL
CATCHING CICADAS ALONE
BARBECUING ALONE
THE LAST DAY OF SUMMER VACAY...
Faint
...YOU SAY?

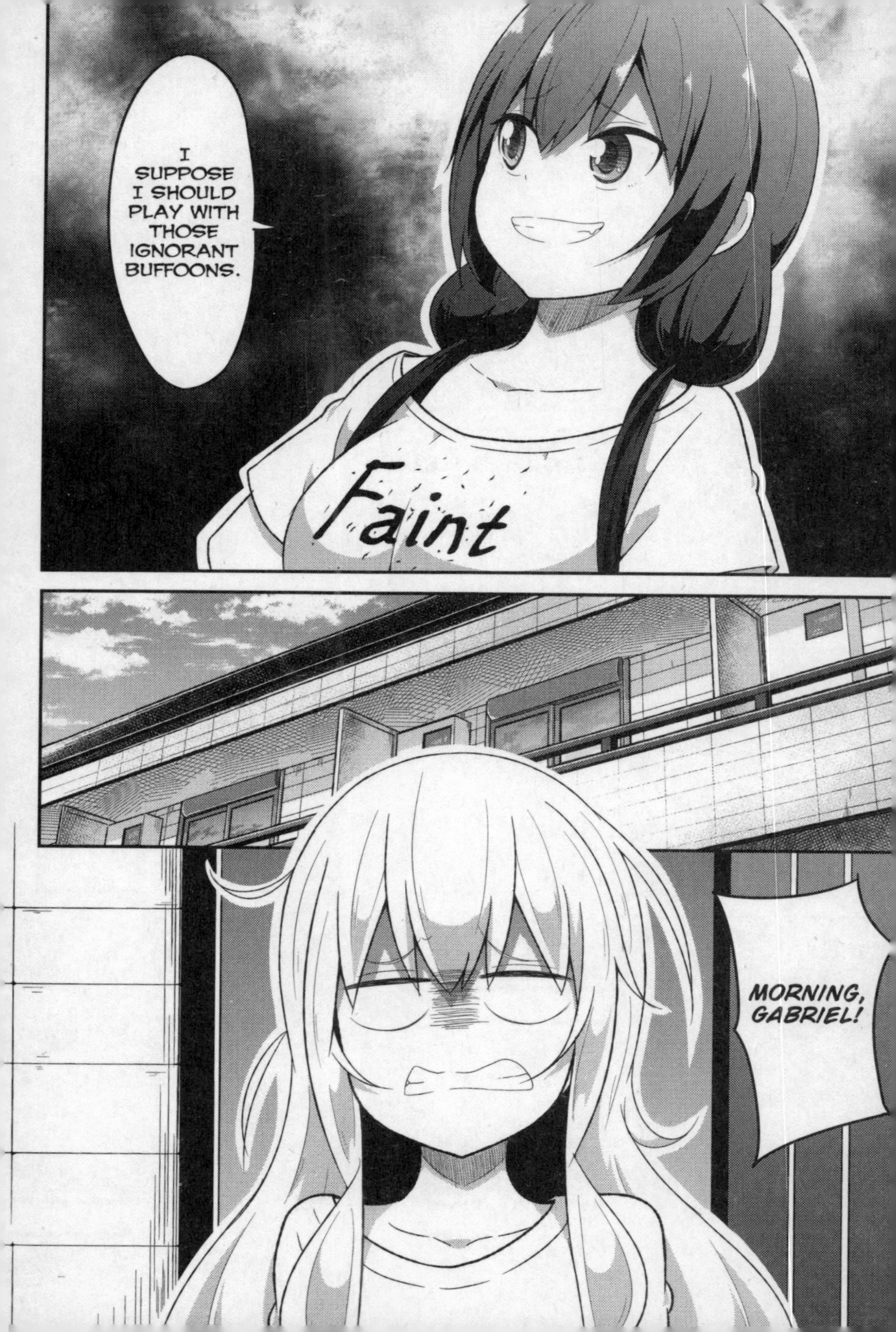
I SUPPOSE I SHOULD PLAY WITH THOSE IGNORANT BUFFOONS.
Faint
MORNING, GABRIEL!

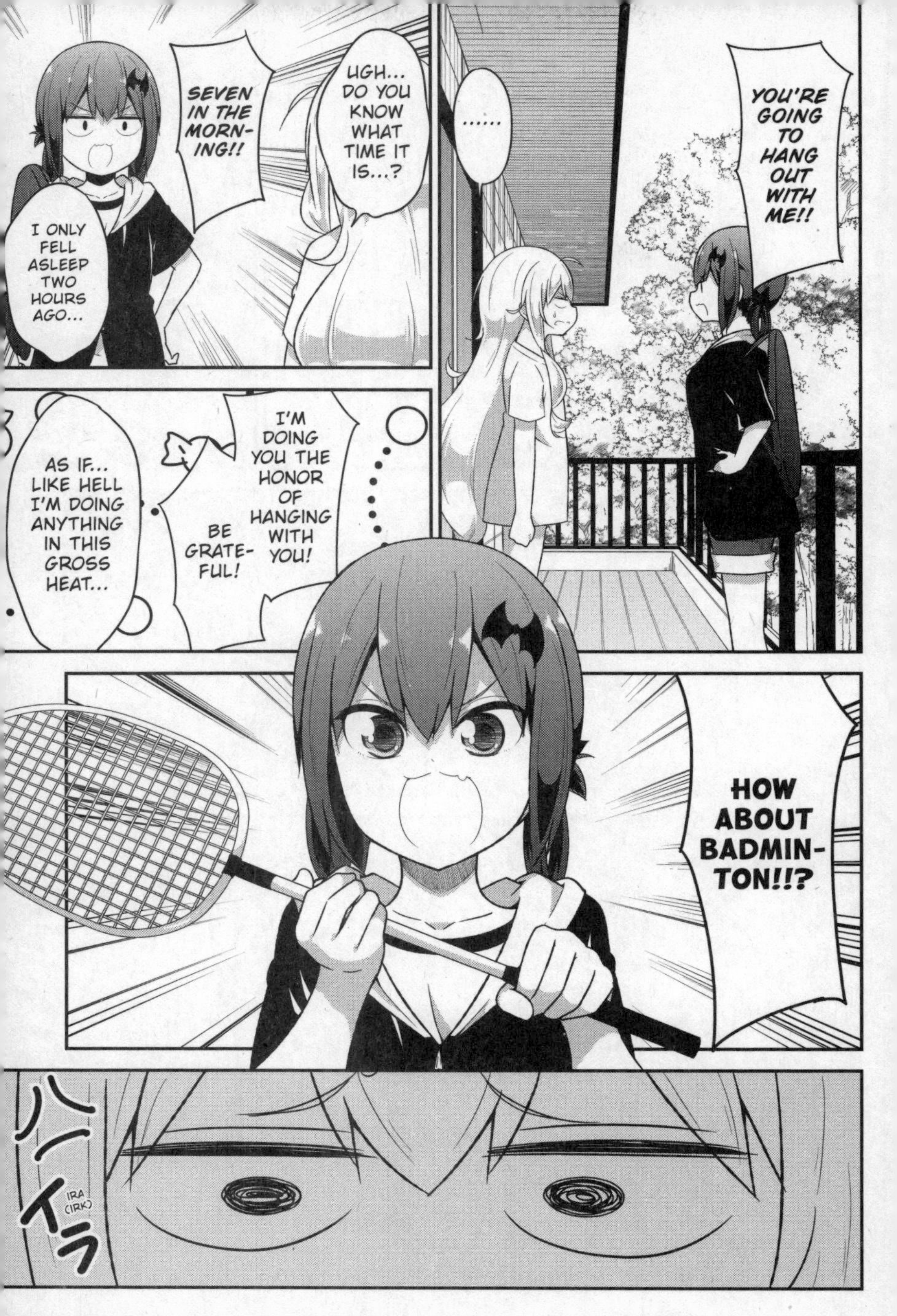
YOU'RE GOING TO HANG OUT WITH ME!!
......
UGH... DO YOU KNOW WHAT TIME IT IS...?
SEVEN IN THE MORNING!!
I ONLY FELL ASLEEP TWO HOURS AGO...
I'M DOING YOU THE HONOR OF HANGING WITH YOU!
BE GRATEFUL!
AS IF... LIKE HELL I'M DOING ANYTHING IN THIS GROSS HEAT...
HOW ABOUT BADMINTON!!?
IRA (IRK)

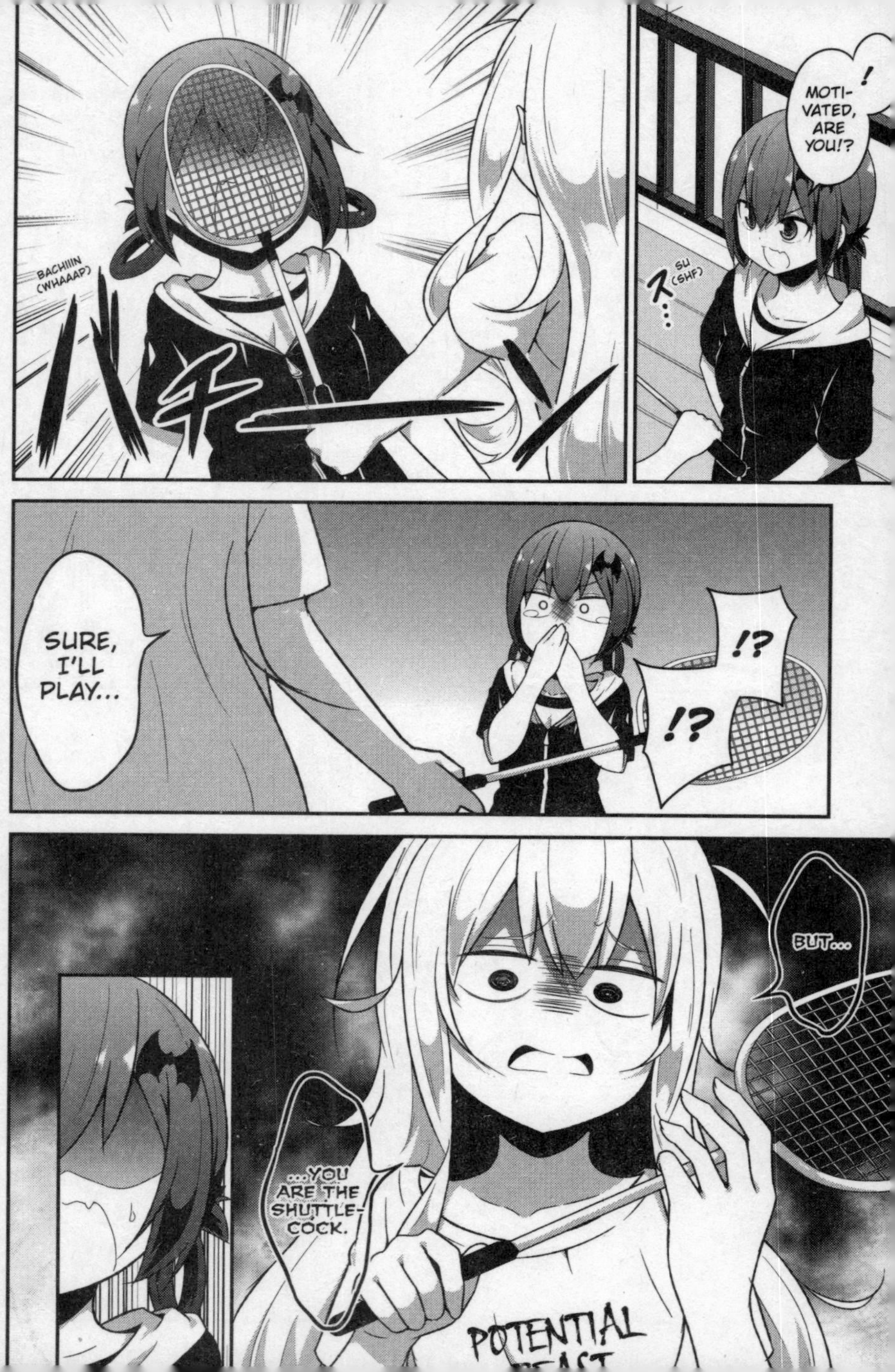
!
MOTI-VATED, ARE YOU!?
SU (SHF)
BACHIIN (WHAAAP)
!?
!?
SURE, I'LL PLAY...
BUT...
...YOU ARE THE SHUTTLE-COCK.
POTENTIAL

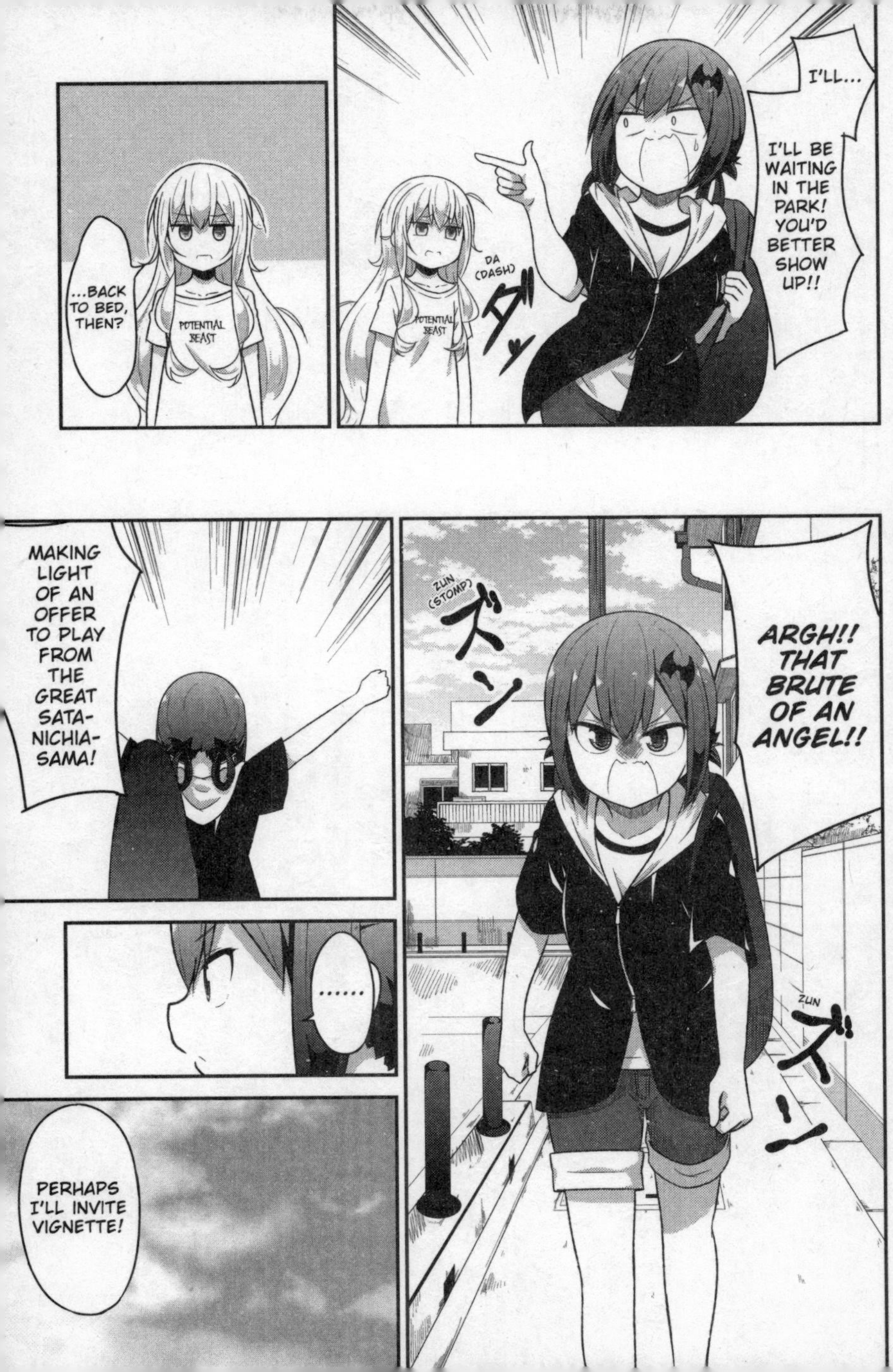
I'LL...
I'LL BE WAITING IN THE PARK! YOU'D BETTER SHOW UP!!
DA (DASH)
POTENTIAL BEAST
...BACK TO BED, THEN?
POTENTIAL BEAST
ARGH!! THAT BRUTE OF AN ANGEL!!
ZUN (STOMP)
ZUN
MAKING LIGHT OF AN OFFER TO PLAY FROM THE GREAT SATANICHIA-SAMA!
......
PERHAPS I'LL INVITE VIGNETTE!

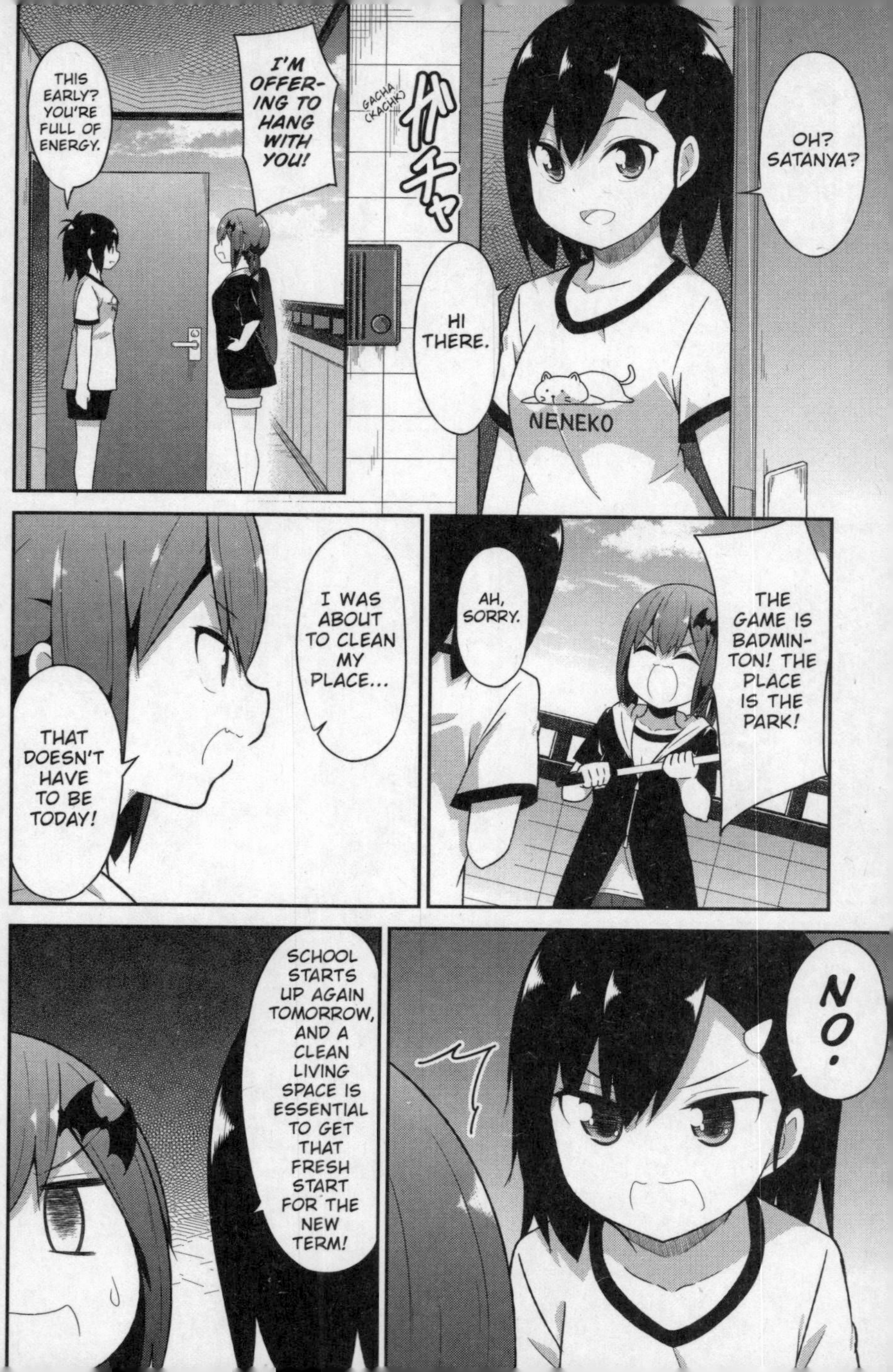

OH? SATANYA?
GACHA (KACHK)
ガチャ
HI THERE.
NENEKO
I'M OFFERING TO HANG WITH YOU!
THIS EARLY? YOU'RE FULL OF ENERGY.
THE GAME IS BADMINTON! THE PLACE IS THE PARK!
AH, SORRY.
I WAS ABOUT TO CLEAN MY PLACE...
THAT DOESN'T HAVE TO BE TODAY!
NO.
SCHOOL STARTS UP AGAIN TOMORROW, AND A CLEAN LIVING SPACE IS ESSENTIAL TO GET THAT FRESH START FOR THE NEW TERM!

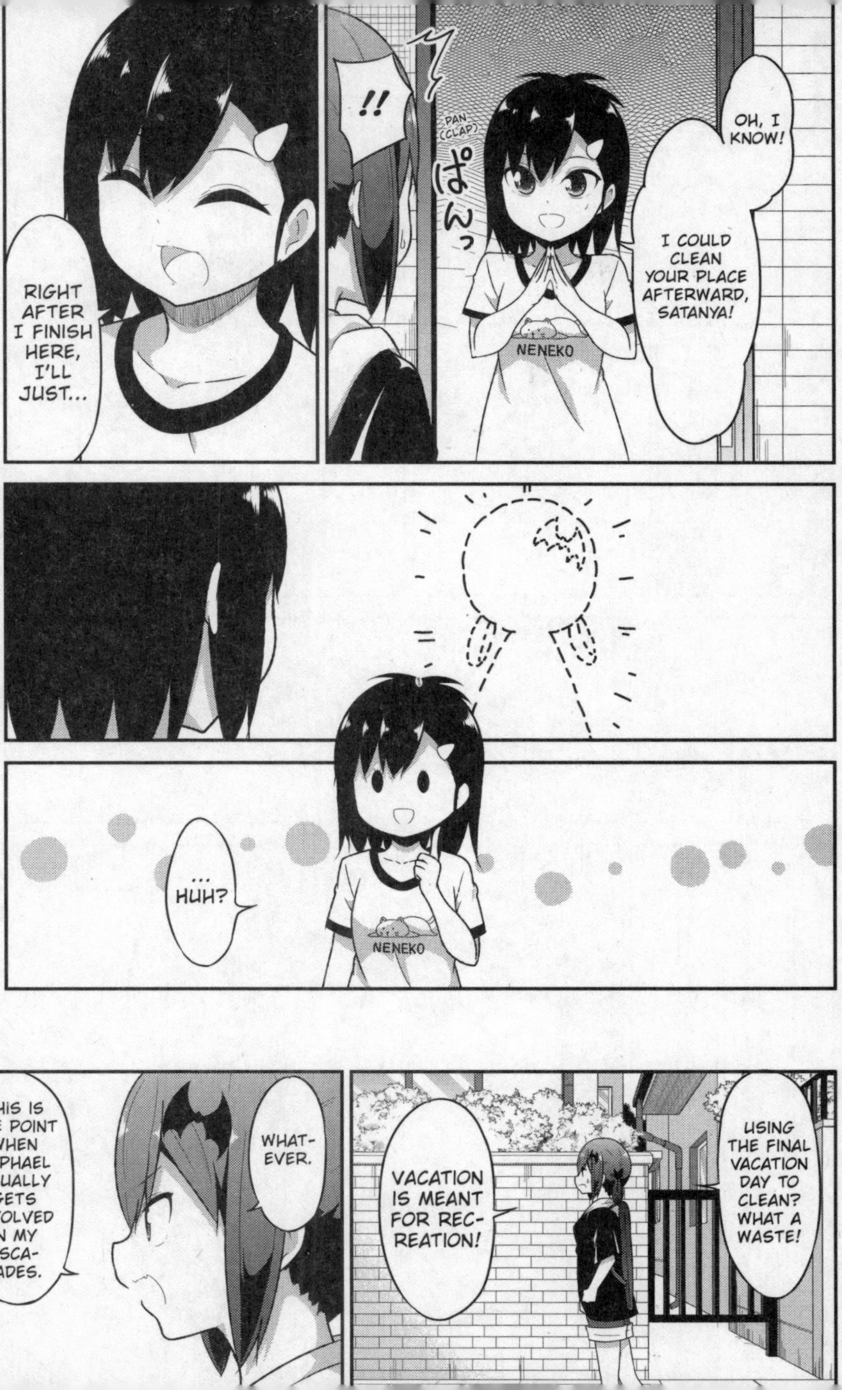
OH, I KNOW!
PAN (CLAP)
ぱんっ
I COULD CLEAN YOUR PLACE AFTERWARD, SATANYA!
NENEKO
!!
RIGHT AFTER I FINISH HERE, I'LL JUST...
... HUH?
NENEKO
USING THE FINAL VACATION DAY TO CLEAN? WHAT A WASTE!
VACATION IS MEANT FOR RECREATION!
WHATEVER.
THIS IS THE POINT WHEN RAPHAEL USUALLY GETS INVOLVED IN MY ESCAPADES.

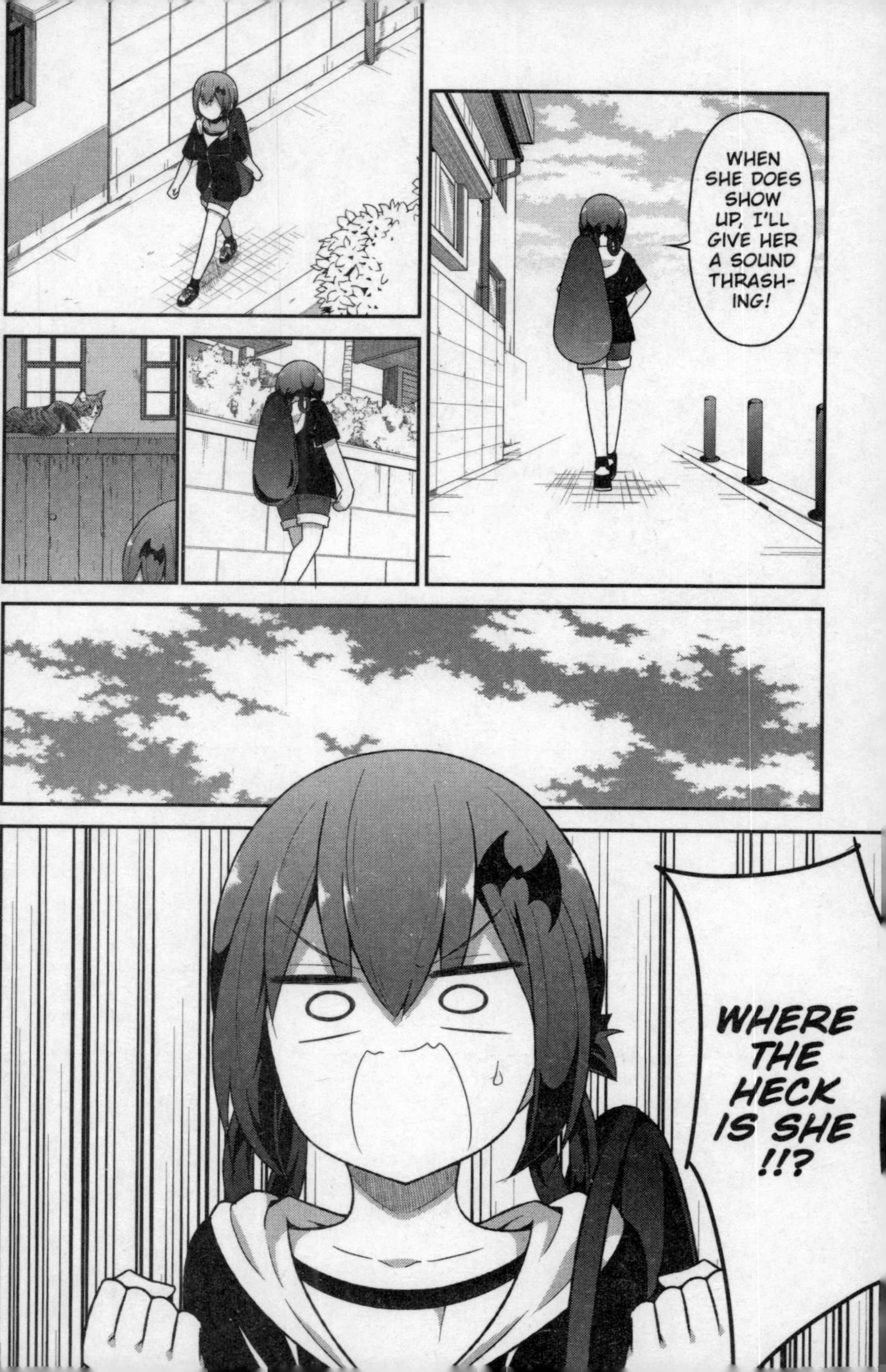
WHEN SHE DOES SHOW UP, I'LL GIVE HER A SOUND THRASH-ING!
WHERE THE HECK IS SHE !!?

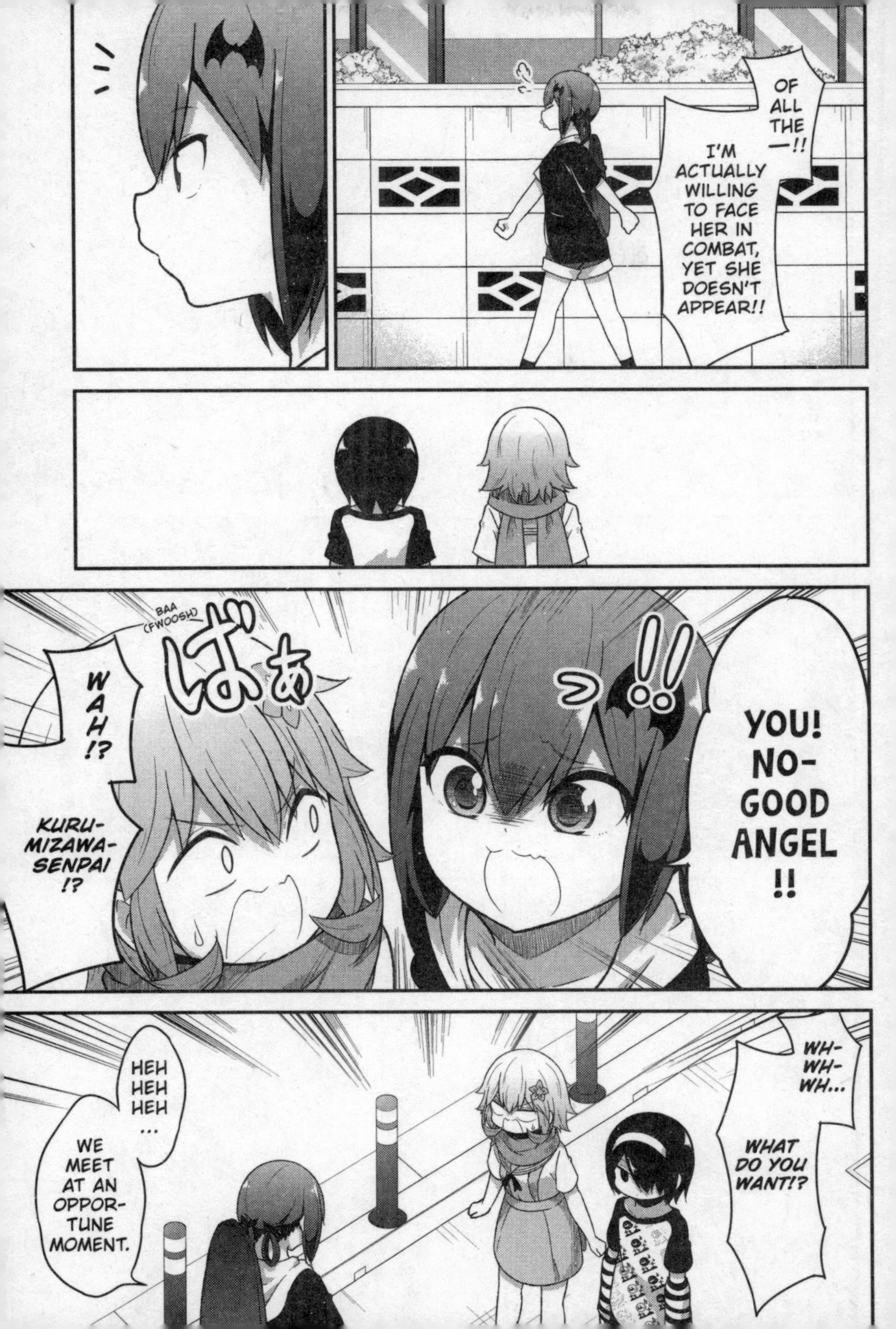

OF ALL THE—!!
I'M ACTUALLY WILLING TO FACE HER IN COMBAT, YET SHE DOESN'T APPEAR!!
YOU! NO-GOOD ANGEL!!
っ!!
ばぁ
BAA (FWOOSH)
WAH!?
KURUMIZAWA-SENPAI!?
WH-WH-WH...
WHAT DO YOU WANT!?
HEH HEH HEH...
WE MEET AT AN OPPORTUNE MOMENT.

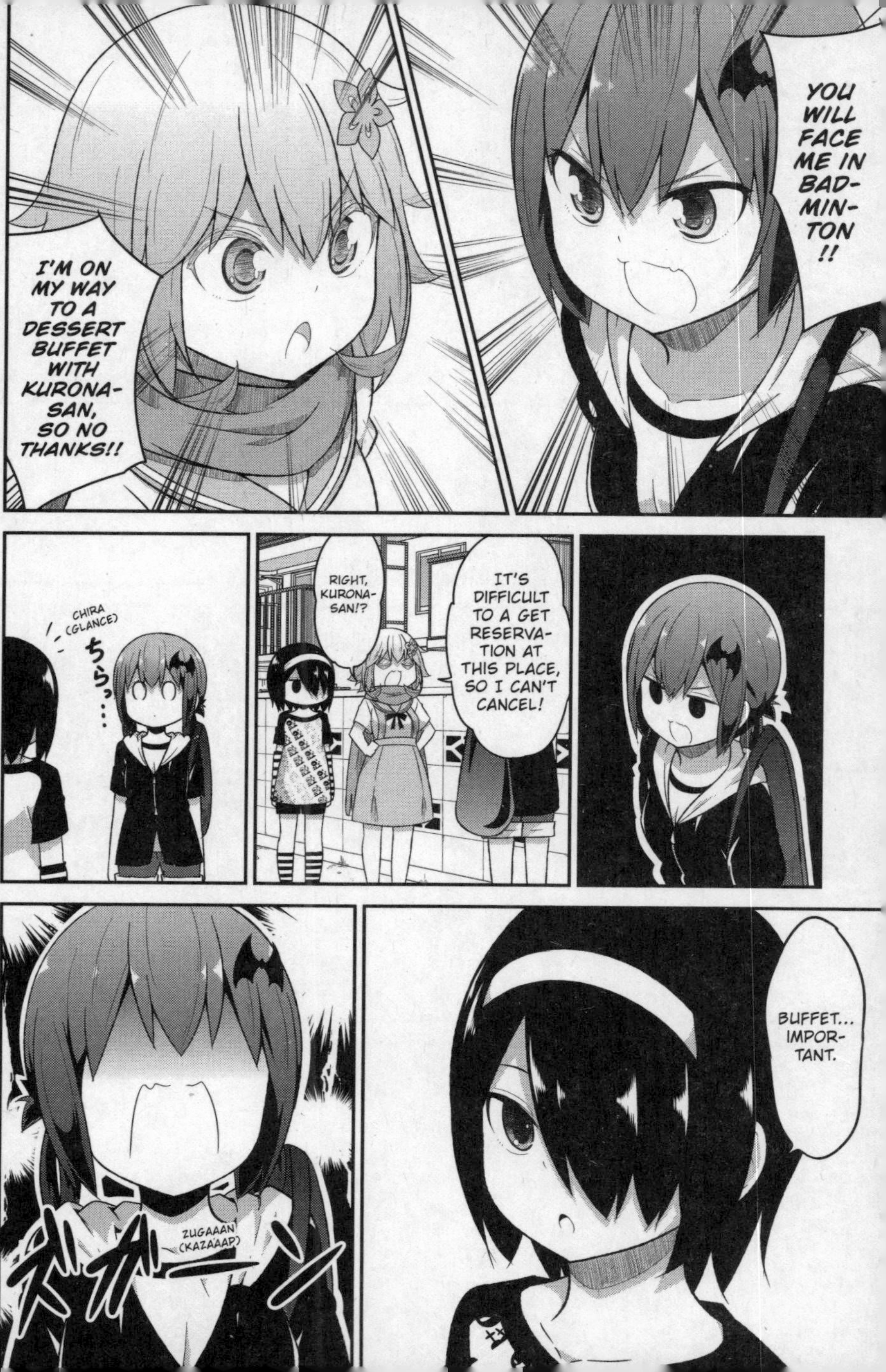
YOU WILL FACE ME IN BAD-MIN-TON!!
I'M ON MY WAY TO A DESSERT BUFFET WITH KURONA-SAN, SO NO THANKS!!
IT'S DIFFICULT TO A GET RESERVA-TION AT THIS PLACE, SO I CAN'T CANCEL!
RIGHT, KURONA-SAN!?
CHIRA (GLANCE)
ちらっ…
BUFFET... IMPOR-TANT.
ZUGAAAN (KAZAAAP)

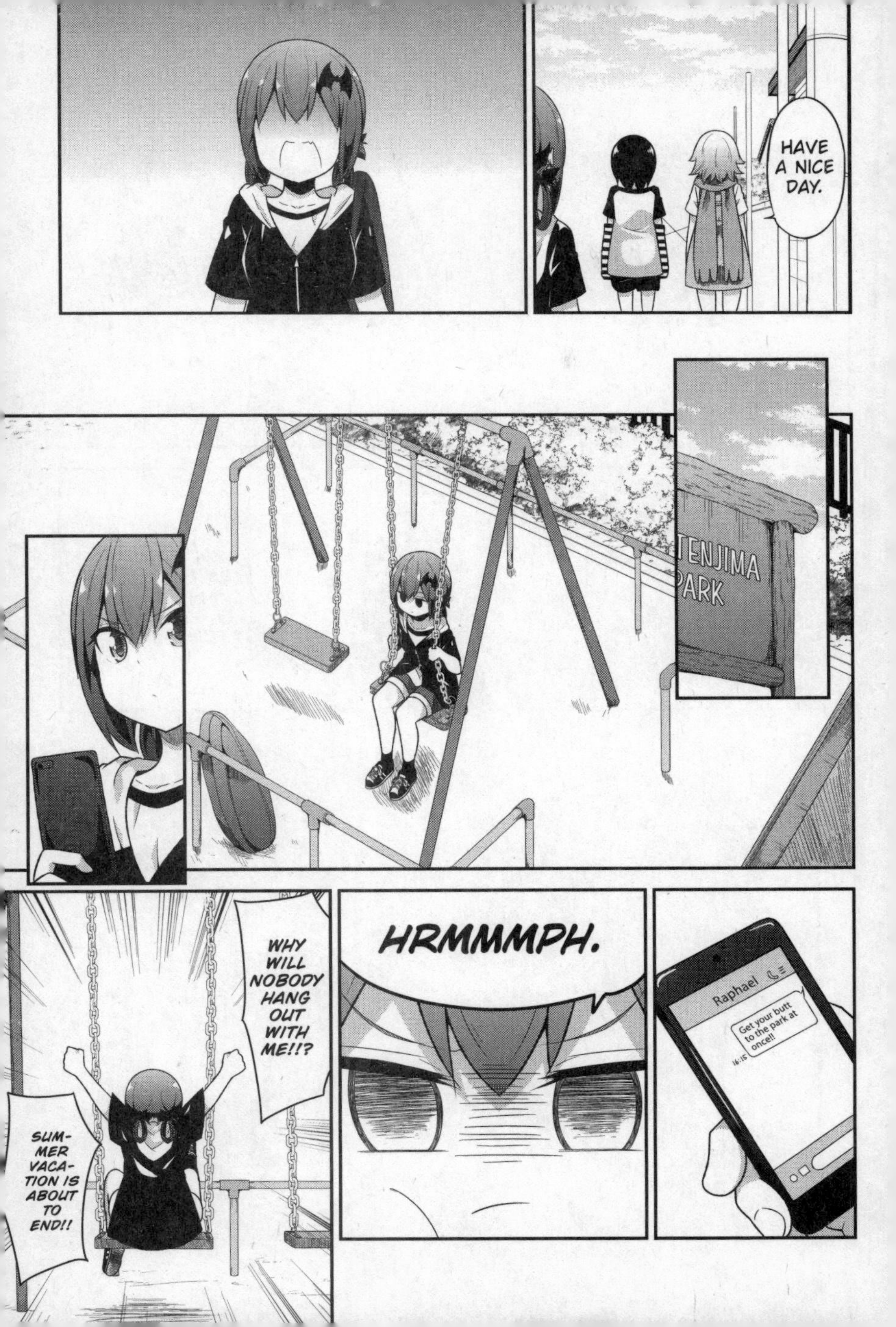
HAVE A NICE DAY.
TENJIMA PARK
Raphael
Get your butt to the park at once!!
16:15
HRMMMPH.
WHY WILL NOBODY HANG OUT WITH ME!!?
SUMMER VACATION IS ABOUT TO END!!

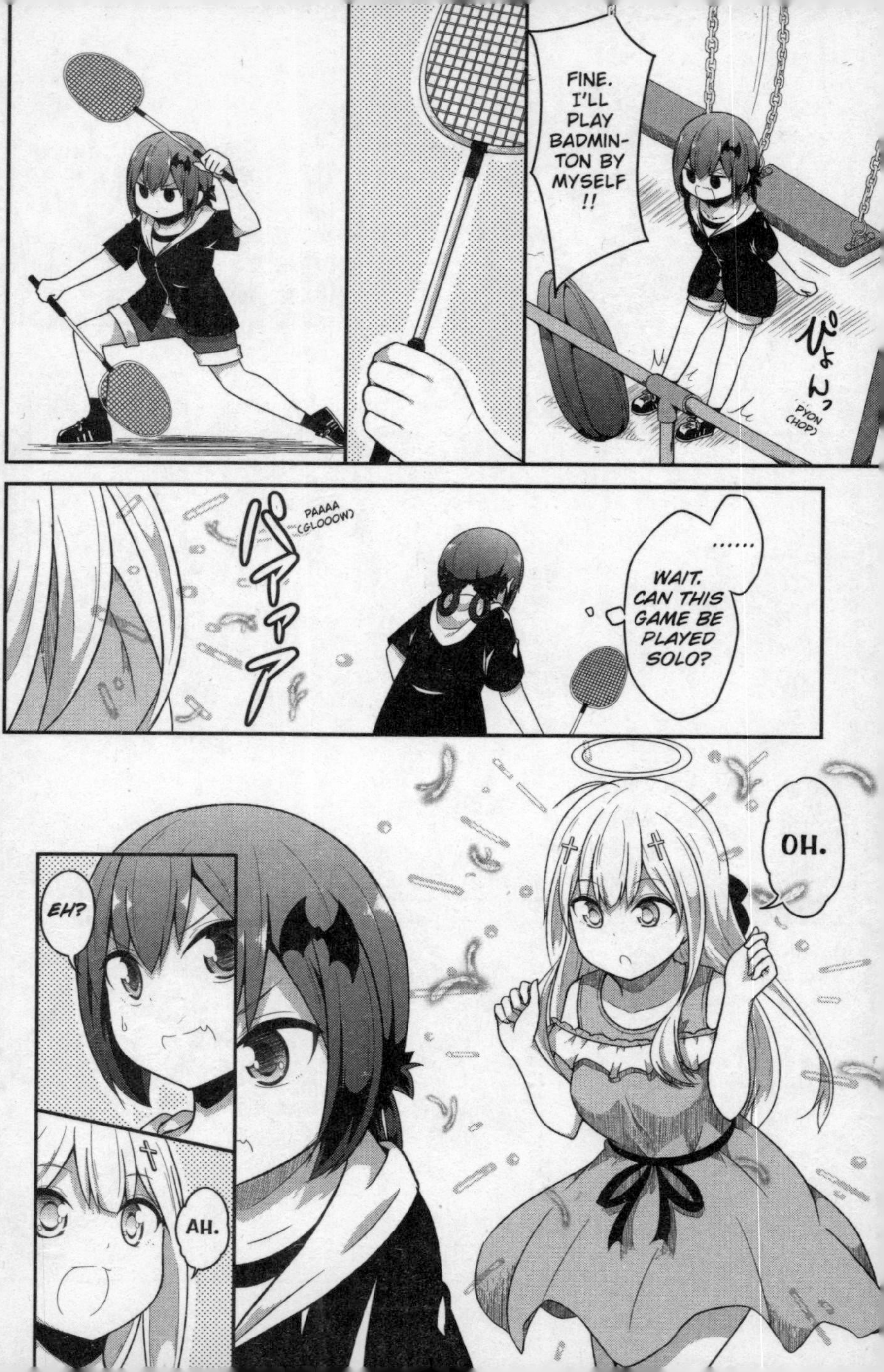
FINE. I'LL PLAY BADMINTON BY MYSELF !!
ぴょんっ
PYON (HOP)
......
WAIT. CAN THIS GAME BE PLAYED SOLO?
パァァア
PAAAA (GLOOOW)
OH.
EH?
AH.

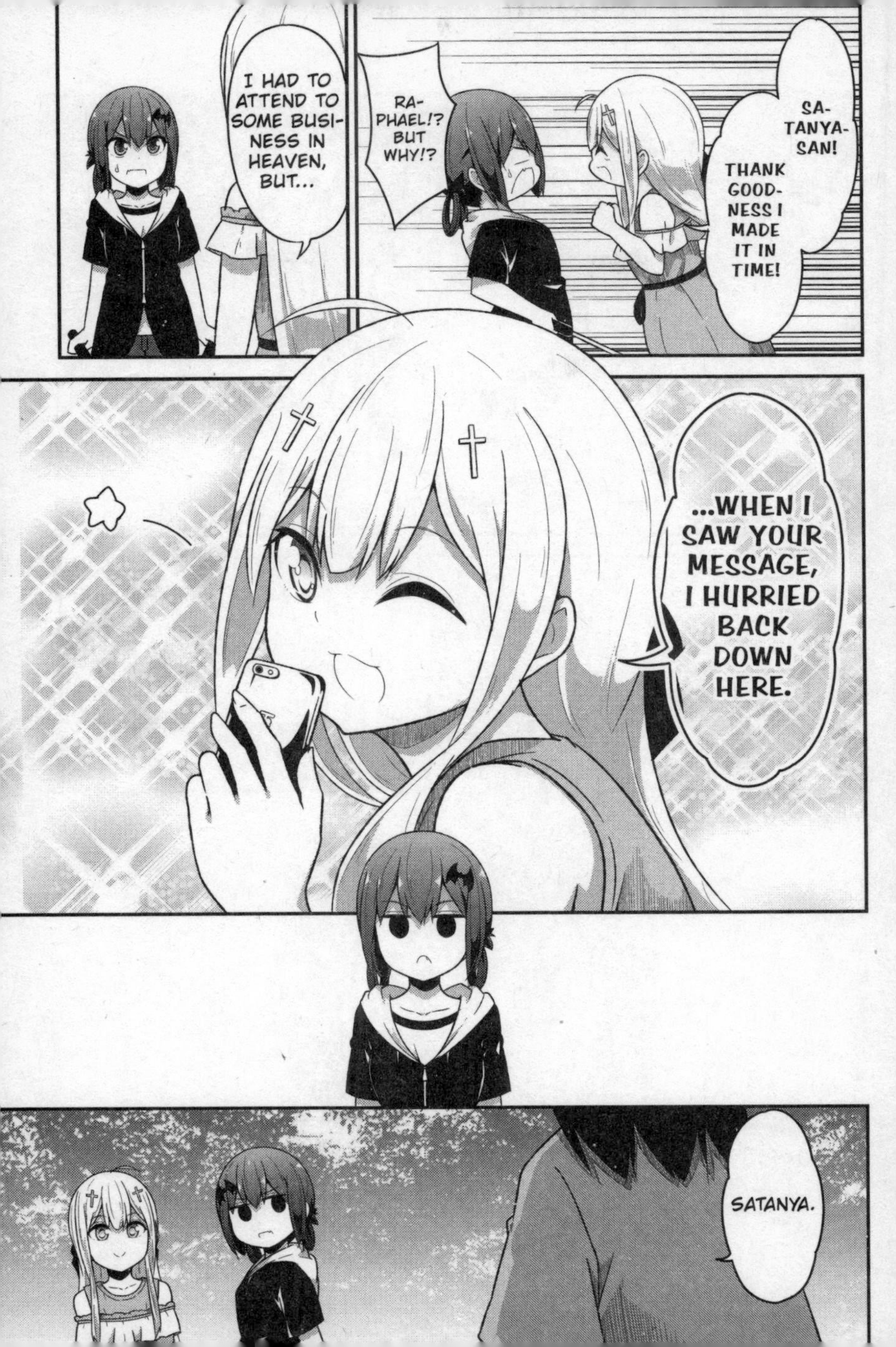
SA-TANYA-SAN!
THANK GOODNESS I MADE IT IN TIME!
RA-PHAEL!? BUT WHY!?
I HAD TO ATTEND TO SOME BUSINESS IN HEAVEN, BUT...
...WHEN I SAW YOUR MESSAGE, I HURRIED BACK DOWN HERE.
SATANYA.

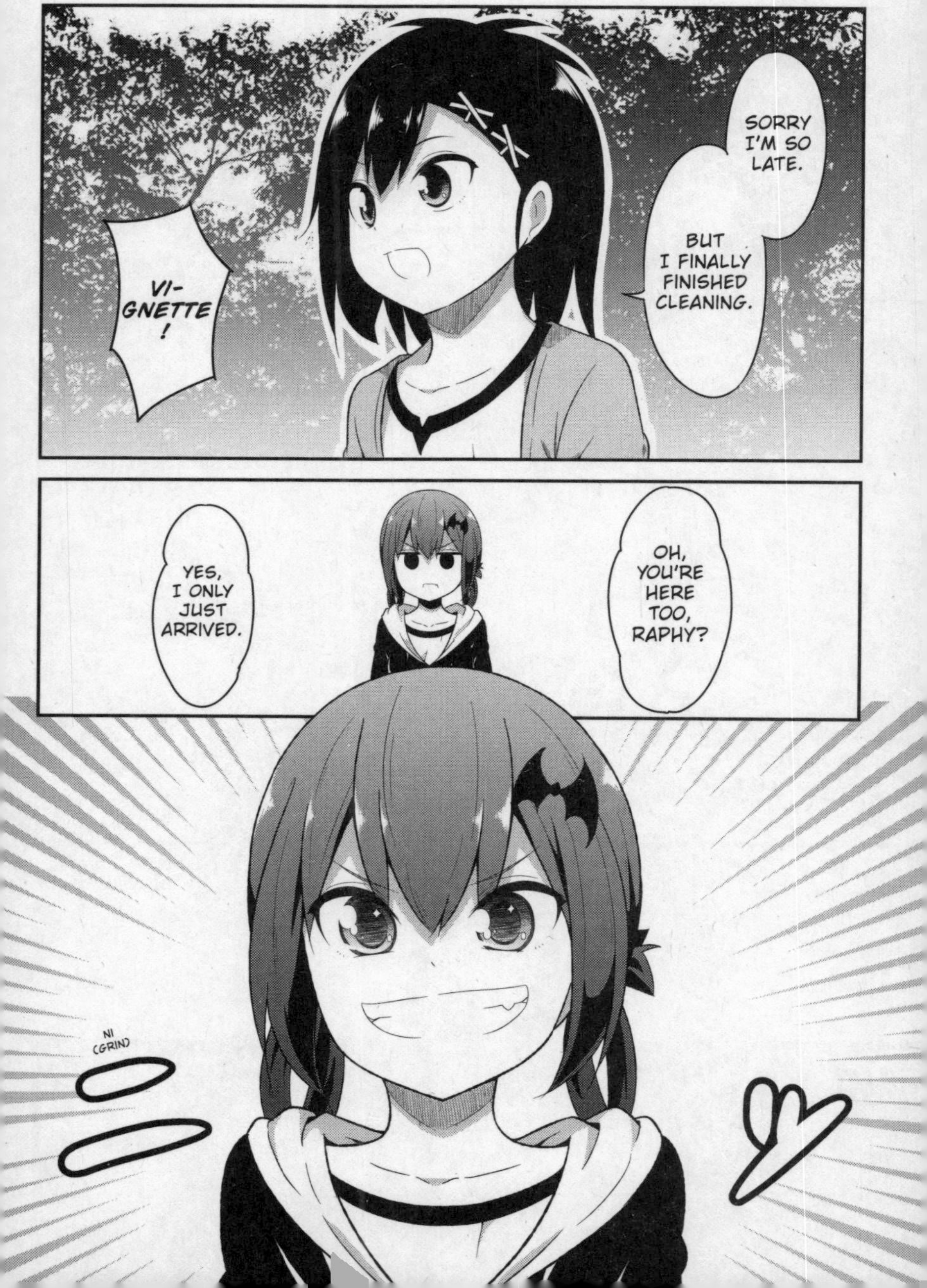
SORRY I'M SO LATE.
BUT I FINALLY FINISHED CLEANING.
VI-GNETTE!
OH, YOU'RE HERE TOO, RAPHY?
YES, I ONLY JUST ARRIVED.
NI (GRIN)

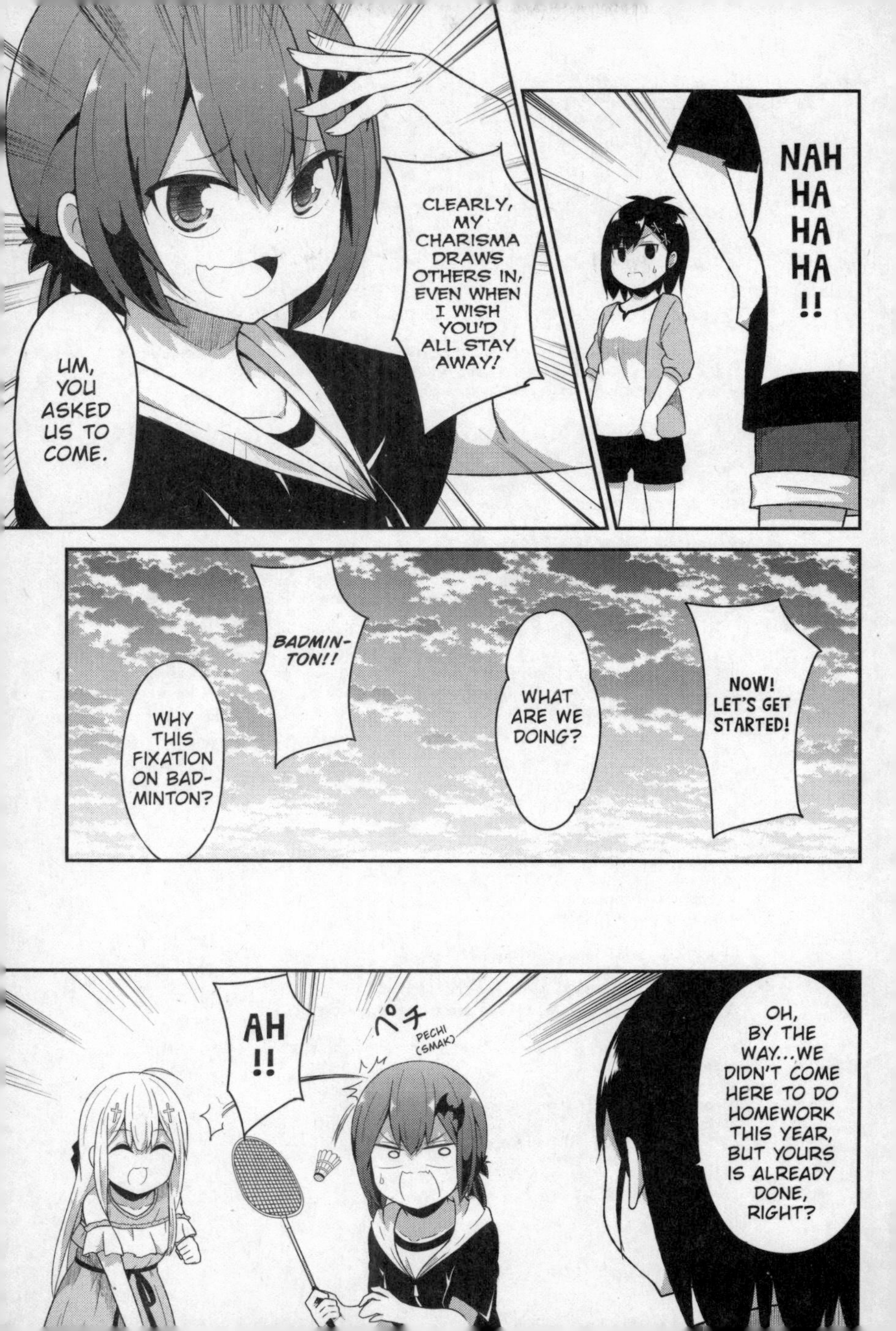
NAH HA HA HA!!
CLEARLY, MY CHARISMA DRAWS OTHERS IN, EVEN WHEN I WISH YOU'D ALL STAY AWAY!
UM, YOU ASKED US TO COME.
NOW! LET'S GET STARTED!
WHAT ARE WE DOING?
BADMINTON!!
WHY THIS FIXATION ON BADMINTON?
OH, BY THE WAY...WE DIDN'T COME HERE TO DO HOMEWORK THIS YEAR, BUT YOURS IS ALREADY DONE, RIGHT?
ペチ
PECHI (SMAK)
AH!!

UKAMI

Translation: Caleb D. Cook ⁄ Lettering: Rochelle Gancio

Gabriel Dropout Vol. 9
©UKAMI 2020
First published in Japan in 2020 by KADOKAWA CORPORATION, Tokyo.
English translation rights arranged with KADOKAWA CORPORATION, Tokyo through TUTTLE-MORI AGENCY, INC., Tokyo.

English translation © 2020 by Yen Press, LLC

Yen Press
150 West 30th Street, 19th Floor
New York, NY 10001

Visit us!
⁄ yenpress.com
⁄ facebook.com/yenpress
⁄ twitter.com/yenpress
⁄ yenpress.tumblr.com
⁄ instagram.com/yenpress

First Yen Press Edition: December 2020

Yen Press is an imprint of Yen Press, LLC.
The Yen Press name and logo are trademarks of Yen Press, LLC.

The publisher is not responsible for websites (or their content) that are not owned by the publisher.

Library of Congress Control Number: 2017945425

ISBNs: 978-1-9753-1673-0 (paperback)
       978-1-9753-1674-7 (ebook)

10 9 8 7 6 5 4 3 2 1

WOR

Printed in the United States of America